Studies on the Chinese Market Economy Series

Theory and Reality of Transition to a Market Economy

Chief Editors:
Gao Shangquan *and* Chi Fulin
Written by:
Sun Xiuping, Zhu Huayou *and* Yao Tiejun

FOREIGN LANGUAGES PRESS   BEIJING

First Edition 1995

ISBN 7-119-01816-7

© Foreign Languages Press, Beijing, China, 1995

Published by Foreign Languages Press
24 Baiwanzhuang Road, Beijing 100037, China

Distributed by China International Book Trading Corporation
35 Chegongzhuang Xilu, Beijing 100044, China
P.O. Box 399, Beijing, China

Printed in the People's Republic of China

Editors' Note

The 14th National Congress of the Communist Party of China (CPC) determined that the objective of China's economic restructuring was to establish a socialist market economy. The decision marked a historical breakthrough, symbolizing that China's economic system has entered a new stage. The main goal of China's reform prior to the end of this century is to realize the transition from a highly-centralized planned economy to a socialist market economy, establishing preliminarily a socialist market economic structure. Accomplishing this goal will be an arduous task of historical significance, and both the theory and reality of our reform efforts are encountering new opportunities, as well as challenges. We must explore and find answers to key theoretical issues, while at the same time researching and resolving contradictions and difficulties surfacing during reform. We must analyze crucial points, hot spots of contention and difficult problems related to actual development, all the while adopting corresponding measures.

In July 1993, as part of an effort to add impetus to China's transition to a market economy, the China (Hainan) Reform and Development Research Institute, together with the China Economic Society of Chinese Students Studying in the United States and the China Economic Society of Great Britain, sponsored an international seminar on theoretical and practical issues concerning China's transition to a market economy. The seminar attracted more than 100 people, including economists and scholars from mainland of China, Hong Kong, Taiwan, the United States and Great Britain, as well as representatives from the World Bank, the International Monetary Fund and the Asian Development Bank, and Chinese students studying in the United States, Great Britain and Australia. The attendees participated in lively discussions on essential theoretical and practical problems facing China during the transition to a market economy. The conferees proposed various viewpoints with high academic value, and realistic opinions. This book was written on the basis of documents related to the seminar, speeches presented by experts in attendance and studies carried out by the China (Hainan) Reform and Development Research Institute, as well as numerous other materials.

Throughout the six special topics, the book approaches key theoretical and practical problems China has encountered in its transition to a market economy. Its editors and writers focused on practical explorations, strove to include in-depth discussions of the hot spots of contention and focal points emerging during the practice of reform, and advanced concrete ideas and programmes in order to promote China's successful and rapid transition to a market economy. The book makes no attempt to offer the sole solution, nor ultimate conclusion to various issues, but instead presents readers with diversified ideologies, viewpoints and opinions of Chinese and foreign experts, as well as related heated debates. Therefore, readers are provided the opportunity to gain enlightenment by making their own comparisons and differentiations.

Editors
October 1993

Contents

Chapter I
Essential Issues Concerning China's Transition to a Market Economy

1. Evaluation and Analysis of China's Economic System Reform

(1) Assessment by Chinese experts: Economic reform in China has scored monumental achievements, and a system featuring the coexistence of diversified economic sectors which enjoy common development has gradually taken shape.

Since the end of 1978, economic reform in China has roughly gone through four stages. The first stage (the end of 1978—October 1984): The reform achieved success and featured initial breakthroughs in rural areas, while main efforts in urban areas were devoted to carrying out comprehensive and special reform experiments centering on expanding the decision-making power of enterprises. The second stage (October 1984—September 1988): Economic restructuring was marked by a shift in the focus of reform from the countryside to cities, and overall reform endeavors unfolded in all fields. The third stage (September 1988 —the end of 1991): This stage was characterized by improvement of economic environment, rectification of economic order and the deepening of reform. The fourth stage (unfolded in early 1992): Early that year, Deng Xiaoping made a series of important remarks during an inspection tour of south China. Somewhat later, the Party's 14th National Congress determined that the objective of China's economic system reform was to establish a socialist market economy. Since then, the pace of reform and opening up has been accelerated, and the effort has entered a new historical period.

The deepening and expansion of the reform and opening policies have led to profound changes in China's economic structure and operational mechanisms.

The structure has gradually been shaped, in which the public ownership plays the dominant role, with the state-owned economy, or the economy owned by the people as a whole, and the collective, private, individual and foreign-funded economies coexisting and attaining common development. The unitary pattern of ownership in the former economic system, which was divorced from the level of productive forces, has been abandoned. Township enterprises, firms with foreign funds, and private and individual businesses have experienced rapid development. In terms of the present industrial output value, the share of the sector owned by the whole people accounts for 53 percent of the total, while collective firms hold 35 percent, the private and individual enterprises and enterprises with foreign funds contribute 12 percent. From the standpoint of the total volume of retail sales of social commodities, sales of marketing concerns owned by the whole people constitute 40 percent of the total, with collectives accounting for 30 percent, and jointly managed, individual and private ventures sharing the remaining 30 percent. The rapid development of the non-state and non-public economic sectors has injected vitality and vigor into the Chinese economy.

In line with the principle of separating the functions of government from those of enterprises, and separating ownership from management, the managerial mechanisms of state-owned enterprises are being gradually transformed towards a market orientation. Various enterprise reform measures, which focus on granting autonomy for production and management to enterprises, have started with straightening out the relationship between the government and enterprises. Some 93 percent of industrial and commercial enterprises owned by the whole people have introduced various forms of responsibility system of operation on contracting basis. In addition, a group of innovative conglomerates have been established to add impetus to the rational alignment of essential productive factors. Some small and medium-sized state-owned enterprises have either been leased or sold outright, while others have reoriented their production line. In recent years, while exploring effective forms of public ownership and establishing new enterprise systems, a large number of enterprises have introduced diverse forms of shareholding system. By the end of 1992, the country had over 3,700 shareholding enterprises, and to date, 120-odd enterprises have been listed on stock exchanges in Shenzhen and Shanghai.

The commodity market system has initially taken shape, market mechanisms have been brought into full play, and the market is serving as the major factor determining prices. At the same time, price controls on a number of commodities have been lifted. At present, in terms of the total purchase volume of farm produce, the share of products subject to prices fixed by the state has dropped below 15 percent. In addition, of the gross sales, only 10 percent of industrial consumer goods and 30 percent of the means of production are subject to state-set prices. Meanwhile, factors markets, including the stock, foreign exchange, labor, technology and land markets, have experienced rapid development.

The macroeconomic regulation and control system is being changed from direct administrative control to indirect regulation and control by comprehensively employing economic and legal means. State planning has been changed from the former direct management mode under which the state assumed sole responsibility to the determination of production targets, allocations of investments and materials, and the approval of projects. The level of mandatory planning has been dramatically reduced. For example, prior to 1979, in industrial production, quotas subject to mandatory plans accounted for 95 percent of the total industrial output value, a figure which now stands at only 7 percent. The list of capital goods subject to unified state allocation and Category One commodities under planned state purchases has also been cut appropriately. At the same time, financial policies are playing an increasingly important role.

A social distribution structure based on the principle of remuneration according to work and allowing the coexistence of diversified forms of distribution is in place, and a new social security system is taking shape. The policy which encourages certain people to be the first to get rich through honest labour to appropriately widen the income gap has greatly aroused the initiatives of labourers.

The opening effort has served as a tremendous driving force to promote domestic reform and development. A new structure of opening to the outside world has taken shape, with diverse multi-level opening endeavors being carried out in all areas, including special economic zones, coastal and border open cities and regions, and the hinterland. By the end of 1992, China had approved over 84,000 enterprises with foreign funds, with negotiated investments approaching US$100 billion and actual inputs of US$33 billion. In the realm of foreign trade, China will administer its import and export affairs in accordance with international conventions and the General Agreement on Tariffs and Trade (GATT) so as to meet the needs to expand the foreign economic and technological cooperation and participate in market competition. The goal of opening to the outside world is not only to attract foreign capital, but also to boldly learn from and draw on the advanced experience and successful practices of other countries in order to accelerate the effort to adapt the Chinese market to the international market.

Profound changes in the economic system and operational mechanisms have in turn resulted in tremendous changes in Chinese society and the national economy. Over the past 15-odd years of reform, China's gross national product (GNP) has maintained an average annual increase of 9 percent. The 1990 gross value of social products hit 3,800 billion yuan, with per-capita GNP standing at 1,547 yuan.

In conjunction with sustained economic growth and the overall improvement of national economic strength, the characteristics of China's economic progress have witnessed remarkable and diversified changes. Economic growth in the 1980s featured the rapid expansion of the industry manufacturing consumer goods, with the production of various mainstay manufacturers outstripping demand. As a result, a shortage of consumer goods which had long plagued the Chinese economy has basically been made up. Thanks to the introduction of foreign funds and technology over the past decade, the level of China's industrial technology and capabilities in scientific research and development have scored marked progress. The improved production capacity and rising level of industrial technology have greatly promoted the export of finished industrial products, ushering in a new trend of the internationalization of the Chinese economy. Even though a number of problems have surfaced and will still exist in the process of economic progress, the fact that should not be neglected is that the aforementioned major changes truly indicate that the Chinese economy has accomplished phased development after experiencing the process of sustained rapid growth in the 1980s. In a word, the Chinese economy has basically passed through the stage of economic revival and entered a historical period of transition to a mature economy.

Rapid economic growth has also led to distinct improvements in the people's living standards, with long-standing shackles on their thinking and concepts having been removed. The emancipation of the thinking of the people and the pursuit of a practical and realistic spirit have in turn propelled reform to a higher level.

To sum up, although reform of the economic system has experienced certain setbacks and mishaps, the achievements themselves in economic development fully demonstrate that the reform orientation, tactics and methods China employed during the 1980s were basically correct.

(2) Comments by foreign experts: China's economic reform has been miraculous, and the country's rate of economic development leads the world.

A great many foreign experts and scholars hold that China's economic reform proved successful. The objective conclusion was reached after comparing conditions in China prior to and after reform, as well as considering the reality in other countries which have simultaneously attempted to carry out reform.

Firstly, the rate of China's economic development over the past 15-odd years of reform has far surpassed the record pace prior to the implementation of reform effort, elevating China to a top position in the world in terms of development during the corresponding period. This fact presents a striking contrast to the situation in the former Soviet Union and East European nations which have not only been unable to improve the long-standing depressions, but have also suffered from new rounds of economic recession, since they implemented radical reform programs. Over past years, their citizens have lived in a virtual state of destitution. Secondly, reform has brought about various changes in China's economic system. In fact, the Chinese economy has stridden across the watershed between the traditional planned and market economies. The main operational modes of the Chinese economic system, from income distribution to investment decisions, determination of prices, selection of new economic policies, and employment of the work force, have to a great extent been divorced from the former Soviet-style planned economic mode. The economy has been subject to the increasing domination of market forces.

Over the past 15-odd years, the Chinese economy has simultaneously accomplished the structural reform of the system and the rapid growth in national income. Foreign experts noted that a situation of this magnitude has rarely occurred in the history of worldwide economic development. Following the fall of the regime of Salvador Allende, the military government of Chile forcefully introduced a market orientation, rapidly transforming the country's economic system. Nonetheless, the country suffered serious economic setbacks over the ensuing five years. Although Chile experienced economic recovery, the common people have not as yet enjoyed the benefits resulting from economic growth. Since they were forced to introduce liberalized reform in the 1970s, many Latin American and African nations have suffered from political chaos and economic stagnation, with most facing difficulties in carrying out their reform policies. Although the former Soviet Union and East European countries initiated reform earlier than China, actual returns have been unsatisfactory, and radical economic reform has created serious difficulties for most of them. It is thus quite obvious, when compared with the aforementioned situations, China's achievements in both reform and economic growth over the past 15-odd years have indeed been a miracle.

(3) Carrying out reform progressively is a successful experience of China, and the practice is in line with actual conditions of the country.

Why is China the only socialist country which has achieved great success in economic reform? What are China's successful experiences in carrying out reform?

A typical viewpoint says, China's success is attributed to the fact that it adopted progressive, rather than radical economic reform.

The economic reform of socialist countries requires transforming traditional planned economies and centralized planning to a system based on market economic operation. There have long been two different opinions concerning the correct method to be employed. The first approach calls for radical method under which the government first formulates a set of laws and regulations, then transform the entire system of the country or the system of a major sector into a new structure at the same time, or use strict macro-controls, and decontrol the market in an all-round way in one step. This is the so-called "shock therapy," or the method of "maintaining strict control over the currency, while decontrolling prices." This method is advocated by numerous Western economists. The second approach favors a progressive way under which rough ideas and principles are determined in advance, and reform is carried out in certain fields with high prospects for success. Thereafter, in line with the given conditions and possibilities, reforms are gradually expanded by making the best use of the situation, over a broader area and from grassroot units to the superstructure. This is actually the method China has taken in its economic reform.

Looking back at the reform practices of various socialist countries, there were no successful examples of implementation of the first method prior to the disintegration of the former Soviet Union and East European nations in 1991. In other words, their reforms remained simply idle words or wordy documents which were not truly put into practice, and thus were merely a waste of time. However, in the wake of 1991, due to the change of political positions, some countries have attempted to implement the "shock therapy" method. Judging from the current situation, some are gaining favorable returns. However, they had undergone a considerable period of sharp declines in production and price hikes, with the living standards of the people falling dramatically and various sectors suffering from difficulties. Even today, some countries have not as yet seen the light at the end of the tunnel in terms of improvement of their economies. Therefore, had they had any other choice at the time, many might have refrained from adopting the radical method. Precisely because of this phenomenon, many Western economists have shown an appreciation for or even highly praised China's progressive approach to reform. This indicates not only that the Chinese reform efforts over the past 15-odd years have proved successful, but also that the method China selected to carry out reform serves as an important experience. China's progressive approach has manifested itself through the initial implementation of structural reform on a trial basis, followed by the gradual popularization throughout the country. In other words, new reform measures are first carried out in selected enterprises and are promoted nationwide after the accumulation of adequate experience. For this reason alone, the state has designated a number of reform and development experimental zones, as well as pilot cities, counties and enterprises to undertake either comprehensive or individual reform experiments. For example, reform focused on rural areas in the initial period and was then gradually introduced to urban areas. The popularization effort began with the establishment of special economic zones and was spread first to coastal areas and then to inland regions. The initial reform effort focused on developing the township, individual, private and foreign-funded economies and strengthening the role of market mechanisms in these sectors. The role market mechanisms was later introduced to the state-owned economic sector. Reform in the microeconomic domains and the expansion of autonomy of enterprises over production and operations have added impetus to the reform endeavors in the macroeconomic fields, including the planning, financial and banking sectors. This progressive type of reform was developed by the Chinese people and is in fact the outcome of their unremitting exploration carried out in actual practice.

Price reform, a typical example, has long been a headache for some countries as they attempted to carry out reforms. It was also a dilemma China encountered at the very beginning of its reform. However, both the Chinese Government and economists were well aware of the importance of price reform and realized that the market orientation of pricing is a prerequisite for giving full play to market mechanisms, encouraging fair competition amongst enterprises and guiding the optimum allocation of resources. However, they also contended that price reform should be combined with the cultivation of the market. Since price reform can be accomplished in a shorter period than the actual cultivation of the market, it is unrealistic to require the latter to keep pace with the former. Moreover, price reform must be backed up by a solid financial basis to meet the requirements for rationalizing various price parities and ensuring that the interests of the broad masses are free of infringements during the process of reform. In addition, price reform also has a bearing on different industries and products. Industries with a higher price elasticity coefficient are able to achieve a market balance soon after decontrolling of prices. However, some products, requiring huge inputs to production, longer processing periods and higher technological requirements, are unable reach a market balance for quite a long time after the lifting of price controls. Therefore, price changes might in some cases lead to serious inflation. In view of the aforementioned factors, China has adopted active and safe measures, instead of decontrolling prices in one gigantic move. In accordance with the characteristics of different industries and products, appropriate reform measures were implemented at different times. Although China still faces a tough challenge in price reform, the country has nonetheless passed the critical stage.

China based its decisions to employ the progressive approach on numerous factors. Generally speaking, the goal of reform, which is considered as China's second revolution, is to fundamentally change the economic system and operational mechanisms. The unprecedented cause represents a creative effort with no ready mode to follow. Therefore, China has been forced to grope forward through practice and make steady progress. There are also reasons of profound significance.

First of all, the progressive approach is based on public awareness. Reform is bound to exert influence on all aspects of society, involving every member of the social community. Reform will fundamentally benefit the people, while to some extent readjusting the interests and power of various economic entities. Therefore, reform must win the understanding and support of people from all walks of life. Reform measures, especially those focusing on readjusting patterns of interest, must have the understanding of the public. Therefore, experiments are a must before putting reform measures into practice in an all-round way. Only when understood by the people, can the implementation represent an act by the masses on their own initiatives. Otherwise, reform would likely be beset with difficulties, or even intensify contradictions, thereby wasting all previous efforts.

Secondly, the progressive approach conforms with the logic of the economic system. All links within the system are closely related. When carrying out reform, relations between various sectors should be properly coordinated, selecting the appropriate point to introduce reform. Problems should be solved one at a time, thereby leading to the final disentanglement of the knot itself. In view of China's experiences over the past 15-odd years, initial reforms normally got underway not in the most essential and difficult sectors, but in areas with the greatest possibility for success and those subject to easy transformation. In enterprise reform, for example, the reform of large and medium-sized state-owned enterprises was of vital importance, as well as extremely difficult. Therefore, reforms began by vigorously developing the non-state economies to form a competitive group outside the state-owned economy. This in turn pressured the state-owned economy, making it possible to bring about the fundamental transformation of the state-owned economy. Now it is hard to imagine, without such a progressive process could there have been a feasible way for the reform of the state-owned economic sector.

Thirdly, the adoption of the progressive approach has been determined by the complicated conditions in China. The basic situation in China features a huge population, a vast territory and imbalance in economic development between various sectors and regions. Therefore, conditions and the basis for carrying out reform vary greatly between different localities. This in turn has made it impossible for all regions to simultaneously march forward with the implementation of the reform. While some have been able to maintain a fast pace, others have been allowed to proceed at a slower pace. Imbalances in reform endeavors are actually a part of the process of progressive development which conforms to natural tendencies.

Fourthly, the progressive approach is also in keeping with political requirements. In order to carry on the reform, China needs to have a stable political and social environment. The radical reform method would undoubtedly exceed public endurance, thereby causing social disturbances and in the end doing harm to the reform effort. Maintaining social stability is a necessity for China, a large country with a population of over 1.1 billion, and hence the selection of any reform method must be based on promoting social stability.

Some were of the opinion that while progressive reform has scored achievements, it has also brought about problems of varying degrees. Those holding this opinion contend that reform endeavors with mature conditions should be accelerated.

A point well worth noting is that China has recorded monumental achievements in carrying out progressive reform, albeit with the emergence of a number of unexpected problems. Severe conflicts have emerged during the transition from the mandatory economy to the market economy, which have in some cases resulted in serious economic chaos and a massive loss of resources. China has passed through four periods of economic fluctuations since the implementation of reform, fluctuations considered inevitable during periods of economic transformation. The country is currently experiencing the fourth period of fluctuation.

Various problems may emerge during the transition from the mandatory planned economy to the market economy, with one being deformation of the reform effort. Under circumstances in which the old system continues to play a substantive role, with the new system not as yet completely in place, many beneficial or correct reform measures may possibly be reshaped, thereby gradually gaining compatibility with the old system. Situations such as this have occurred frequently. For instance, while the original goal of implementing the bonus system was to establish an interest mechanism, it nonetheless reverted to egalitarianism. Many other reform measures have also met similar fates, with many being reformed and intertwined with the old system. Hence, progressive reform may also encounter contradictory dilemmas. Due to the fact that it is progressive, reform may not in fact be equipped with complete and appropriate measures, which without other necessary conditions will make it extremely difficult to carry out correct reform measures.

Another problem emerging during the process of transformation centers on the fact that the old mandatory planned economy is being dismantled and is thus incomplete and unable to play its previous role. In the meantime, however, the market economic structure has not as yet been established, and the reform being carried out has been unable to play its true role in regulating the economy, thereby creating a vacuum. A good example is investment. In 1991, investment in the state-owned sector accounted for 65 percent of total inputs to social fixed assets. In this regard, most investments were normally determined by the government which bore no investment risk. In addition, the government to some extent interfered in the investment plans of state-owned enterprises. Since government performance is not subject to restraints, market regulations, or original mandatory plans, investments have expanded on a regular basis, which has in some cases resulted in chaos. Therefore the government has been faced with a dilemma during this particular stage. Macro-regulation by using administrative methods would have run counter to the direction of market reform. Just as in the period of economic retrenchment, the use of administrative interference would likely lead to the retrogression of reform. These factors are precisely the reason why this stage is considered as a rather difficult period for progressive reform. On the other hand, however, the length of the period can be shortened through reform. In other words, reform endeavors with mature conditions should be accelerated, and appropriate methods should be used to accelerate the transformation of the old system and reduce risks and losses resulting from clashes between the old and new systems.

An opposite opinion holds that the progressive reform is a contributive factor, rather than the fundamental reason for the success of China's reform.

Although many Chinese and foreign experts and scholars agree that implementing progressive reform has been one of the successful experiences in China's economic reform effort, some have raised queries, while others have offered different viewpoints.

They hold that China has adopted a progressive reform strategy on the whole, but they question the validity of the opinion that such a strategy can be accounted as the reason for the success of China's reform.

One basis for this reasoning is that prior to 1989 the former Soviet Union and most East European nations employed progressive reform, but recorded little success. For example, in 1968, Hungary introduced the so-called method of overall design (nonprogressivism), scoring obvious progress in the initial period. However, due to subsequent encroachments on the overall design by bureaucrats and monopolistic enterprises, various scheduled reform endeavors were abandoned, and the original comparatively systematic reform program became incomplete. The progressive approach Hungary employed later on was the outcome of the resistance of opposing factions, with the end result being a standstill in reform.

The Soviet Union carried out progressive economic reform over the 30-odd years from the death of Stalin to the time

Gorbachov left office. Just as scholars engaged in the study of the Soviet economic reform once pointed out, progressivism in the Soviet economic reform in fact demonstrated the limitations of the Soviet Government in relation to the reform issue, as well as the powerful influence of Soviet bureaucrats who opposed reform. In view of the historical fact that the former Soviet Union and East European countries achieved nothing from the practice of progressivism, scholars have systematically expounded the dangers of implementing progressive reform. Many scholars contend that the greatest danger is that the progressive reform may cause contradictions within an economic system and lead to disorder in economic performance, thereby providing opposing factions with opportunities and a tool to destroy reform. Based on this acknowledgement, the "shock therapy" approach has received wide-spread acclaim.

Another opinion calls for a concrete analysis of progressive reform carried out in China. In other words, China has implemented progressive reform only in the most essential sectors within the planned economy. For instance, reform of the state-owned enterprises has been carried out in a progressive manner. However, it has been difficult for such reform to progress, and the majority of state-owned economic sectors continue to operate with low efficiency. At the same time, China has adopted radical reform measures in the weak links inherent to the planned economy. For example, the country has made great strides in reform of various sectors such as the rural economy, township enterprises, special economic zones and the export-oriented economy. As a result, market mechanisms have rapidly assumed a leading role, and the economy has witnessed rapid development. In fact, shortly after China implemented reform, the double-track economic system embodying both the planned and unplanned sectors was in place, and sectors operating outside the framework of state planning recorded sustained rapid economic growth. Economic reform of sectors under state planning has been carried out progressively, while radical and open reform endeavors have been implemented for sectors outside the state planning. In addition, the range of economies outside state planning has been significantly expanded, and the framework of planned economies has gradually been reduced. Therefore, progressive reform cannot indiscriminately be considered as a successful experience of economic development. Hence, the requirement for a concrete analysis.

If there is in fact disagreement as to whether or not progressive reform is a successful experience of China's reform, what then is the reason for the success of the country's economic reform effort? In other words, why have other countries failed to achieve success in carrying out progressive reform, while China's efforts have proved fruitful?

One viewpoint centers on the fact that the fundamental reason for the success of China's economic reform stems from the dynamic structure formed due to the decentralization of powers during the process of reform. Those who hold this viewpoint note that one of the main characteristics of China's reform has been the sustained rapid growth of non-state economies, while such growth has benefited from the special organizational structure of the Chinese Government. If authorities in the former Soviet Union and East European countries are deemed to have introduced a vertical centralized organizational structure, the organizational structure of the Chinese Government has been characterized by the separation of administrative powers by various localities. Under such circumstances, non-state economies have numerous advantages and opportunities for expansion. At the same time, decentralization of authority has presented the possibility to weaken the strength of actions within the traditional planned economy which are opposed to reform.

Another viewpoint, which is in agreement with the statement concerning the separation of power, holds that the opinion attributing the success of reform to the decentralization of leadership has in fact grasped the crux of the matter. However, in terms of the success of reform, those who hold this viewpoint do not agree with giving credit solely to the decentralization of administrative powers. How does reform benefit from granting local governments greater power? Why are localities in favor of reform in case the central and local governments are both under the leadership of national authority? The former viewpoint fails to provide a clear explanation with regard to these issues. In fact, prior to 1990, scholars engaged in the study of China's economic reform paid a great deal of attention to the negative results of the separation of power. During the period, criticism of the so-called "separate economies" was quite prevalent amongst domestic research circles.

Those who hold this opinion say that the success of China's economic reform rests with fundamental changes in the interest structure involving decentralized decision-making power. They say that such changes have added great impetus to the advancement of reform. This opinion has raised its bases for reasoning. Firstly, the government is not simply a single entity of interests which can be divided into the central leadership, central departments and local governments. When proceeding from pure economic interests, the central leading body has a strong motive to carry out restructuring in order to improve economic efficiency, even though its intentions are often restricted by awareness and political considerations. Secondly, the decentralization of authority alone is not enough to enable the local governments to become reformers. A more important factor is that the Chinese Government has introduced a fiscal decentralization system which has altered the interest orientation of local governments when they draft policies. It has also allowed the pursuit of the efficient use of local resources to become the orientation of various localities for strengthening their interests. Thirdly, under the decentralized government structure, the central leadership, central departments and local governments jointly participate in the formulation and implementation of reform policies. The interrelated dynamic factors resulting from the individual interests of the three sides have brought progressive features to reform measures. The approach has also made it possible for the retention, rather than abandonment of reform, and further promotion of the reform effort in the period when progressive measures caused economic dislocation. This is the major differentiation between China and the former Soviet Union and East European countries. Prior to 1989, at times when progressive reform in the former Soviet

Union and East European countries led to economic dislocation, forces opposing reform were always able to reverse the direction of policies, thereby setting back the wheels of reform. However, in China, over the past 15-odd years in particular, economic chaos resulting from progressive measures have been the catalyst for people calling for the deepening of reform. The reason behind this situation rests in the fact that profound changes have taken place in the interest structure between policy-makers amongst the ranks of decentralized authorities.

Yet another viewpoint holds that the key to the success of China's economic reform and the rapid development of Chinese economy rests with the rapid and successful growth of the non-state economy. Alongside the rise of the non-state economy, the market prices have been introduced through the double-track system. The effort has not only led to the accelerated and rapid growth of the non-state economy, but has also spurred improvements in the operational efficiency of state-owned enterprises. In addition, signals from the market outside the realm of state planning have urged the government to react to problems arising during the process of reform, thereby avoiding the accumulation and general outbreak of problems which might in turn lead to the failure of reform. In summary, the success of China's reform has been the result of the introduction of the market economy which operates outside the realm of state planning.

2. Fundamental Issues Concerning China's Transition to a Market Economy

(1) The effective operation of the socialist market economy relies on an in-depth understanding of the market economy itself.

The first requirement for the effective operation of the socialist market economy is a complete comprehension of the theory and related connotations. Different viewpoints emerged during discussions of this issue.

One viewpoint centered on the fact that the socialist market economy is an operational system which integrates both planning and the market.

The term of socialist market economy does not necessarily imply a socialist character. The market economy and the planned economy are simply economic operational forms, and do not represent the innate attributes of the socialist system. The market economy, or the market-oriented economy, is regulated by market mechanisms and belongs to neither capitalism nor socialism. Such an economy exists not only under the capitalist system where it plays its due role in economic regulation, but also exists and plays the same role under the socialist system. Therefore, the socialist market economy is in fact a market economy operating under socialist conditions.

Some people have suggested the establishment of a socialist market economic structure which would "put an end to the decades-long history of the coexistence of the market economy and mandatory planning." Some expressed their disgust at the planned economy and held that China should abandon the system completely. They claimed that great effort must be extended to guard against cosmetically eliminating the planned economy, but allowing it to return through the back door in the form of macro-management. In fact, this particular viewpoint fails to conform with prevailing conditions in China's economic operation, the theory advanced by Deng Xiaoping, or the spirit of 14th National Congress of the Communist Party of China. The planned economy is the manifestation of functioning law of planned national economic development, which exist only when socialized mass production and gross national product (GNP) are concentrated by a social center (the state). Had these two economic conditions existed, the law would anyhow exist and mandatorily carry out its functions regardless of whether or not people like it subjectively, and the planned economy and its regulation on national economy would appear in this or that kind of forms within a certain scope. The Socialist economy, which represents the same highly socialized economy as the capitalist economy, is characterized by the public-owned economy and is better equipped than capitalism to amass quite a large proportion of

GNP under state control. The fact is that even capitalist countries, which are based on private ownership, sometimes intervene in their respective national economies under the objective requirements for the development of social productive forces. How then is it possible for China, a socialist country based on public ownership, to run counter to the objective requirements of planned national economic advancement, assume the risk involved in sabotaging the development of social productive forces and completely abandon the regulatory functions of the planned approach to its national economy?

It is thus quite obvious that China's socialist market economy is an operating system which integrates both planning and the market, with market mechanisms mainly playing a regulatory role in microeconomic sectors. The weak points and negative role of the market economy indicate that a socialist country must strengthen macroeconomic controls. In turn, planned regulation must continue to play its due role in the macroeconomic sphere. The socialist market economy is a system which must enable the market to play its fundamental role in distributing resources under state macroeconomic control. Indeed, the system combines the strongpoints of both planning and the market. The market economy under socialism must and does in fact perform better than under capitalist conditions.

Another viewpoint holds that the socialist market economy means combination of social fairness and market efficiency.

What then is the socialist market economy? Can socialism coexist with the market economy? The answers to these questions depend on a true understanding of socialism and the socialist economy. Viewed in a traditional way, socialism is incompatible with the market economy, and the socialist market economy is actually a combination of social fairness and market efficiency. Socialism can be regarded either as a social system, a policy, or a moral. Nevertheless, the final objective is to attain social fairness combined with market efficiency. What in fact is socialist economy? This question seems quite simple, but the reality is quite the opposite. The socialist economy is a combination of the public-owned economy, which constitutes the mainstay, and various other economic sectors.

Why should the publicly-owned economy constitute the mainstay of the socialist economy, albeit in no specific proportion? A publicly-owned economy is not our only objective. However, we preserve it in order to realize other goals such as providing the government with necessary material conditions required for economic readjustment; satisfying social common demands; enabling eocnomy to develop in an even and coordinative way; and solving problems related to fair social distribution.

Therefore, socialist economy is conducive to the combination of social fairness and market efficiency. The socialist economy could not have been established, nor could it operate effectively, if publicly-owned economy accounted for the major proportion. We must develop diversified economies under the premise that the publicly-owned economy plays a leading role, but not a too large proportion.

Another issue concerns the combination of fair distribution and market efficiency. To boost a market economy, we must admit the disparity between public property, and the income gap it caused. Otherwise there will be no competition and no market economy. However, disparities in property will lead to unfair social distribution and the expansion of income gaps, both of which are grievances already aired by the people. However, focusing only on fair distribution will result in a lack of efficiency. Otherwise if we emphasize efficiency, we will be unable to guarantee fair distribution. These aspects have emerged as problems hindering the establishment of the socialist market economy.

(2) The basic issue in deepening the reform of the economic structure lies in the transformation of government functions. The focus of the reform is to create an environment favorable to the development of large enterprises.

China's transition to a market economy requires further reform of the economic structure. Different views unfolded concerning just what fundamental problems should be tackled during the deepening of reform. Nonetheless, a basic consensus was reached concerning the following main problems:

The first problem centers on cultivating and improving a unified market system. At present, the most important task is to establish and develop production elements market. In particular, the financial market has emerged as the main factor hindering the establishment of a market system. State banks should be granted relative independence in line with the principles of the market economy in order to enable them to play their true role in administering and controlling the financial market, and in turn bring the overall market system into full play. Specialized banks will be transformed into full-scale commercial banks. In addition, affiliates under the People's Bank of China will be separated from the headquarters bank, and will be transformed into policy-lending banks. The switch will ensure that the bank structure is more adaptable to the requirements of market economic progress, and will in turn bring the promotional and guiding role of the financial market into full play. Moreover, the labour force and property rights markets require meticulous restructuring to ensure that the market system gain maturity and perfection. In addition, price reforms, including reforms of the prices on the commodity, financial, labour force and property rights markets, must be placed at the top of the agenda and carried out effectively. We must readjust the prices of these markets in accordance with actual conditions in China.

The level of market management must be improved to minimize the negative role and phenomenon of the market, while at the same time giving full play to its positive role in order to enable the market to advance in a healthy and orderly manner. Therefore, legislative efforts must be strengthened to ensure the rapid enactment of laws related to the market economy, including the market law, the securities law, the anti-monopoly law and the enterprise law. The qualities of those who execute the laws must be improved in order to have laws to go by, to strictly execute laws and to prosecute those who violate the law. The active role of the legal system must be brought to the forefront to standardize market economic development and strengthen links with the world.

Secondly, establishing and improving the macroeconomic

control system. Development of a modern market economy requires corresponding macroeconomic controls to allow it to perform its true functions and solve related problems it fails to address. Combining the regulatory functions of both macroeconomic control and the micro-market is the only way to ensure the organic integration of proportionate macroeconomic development and a vigorous microeconomy needed to promote the rapid development of the social economy as a whole. Traditional mandatory planning must first be abandoned in order to establish a macroeconomic control system, followed by the establishment of an indirect macroeconomic control system focusing on the establishment of a series of guiding principles and using market mechanisms. In the end, macroeconomic control at the central and local levels must be organically combined to guarantee the healthy development of a modern market economy.

Thirdly, establishing a modern enterprise system and transforming government functions. This is the fundamental issue involved in establishing a new market economic structure and developing the market economy. Establishing a modern enterprise system requires transforming existing state-owned enterprises into shareholding companies, with the effort focusing on defining proprietary rights relationships. The corporate system and the traditional factory system are in fact worlds apart. At present, state-owned enterprises still operates as subsidiaries of government organizations, and are far from the corporate system which is the mainstay of the market and conduct independent management and shoulder sole responsibility for profits and losses. Therefore, we must transform the operational mechanisms of such enterprises by undertaking system reform to safeguard the normal development of the socialist market economy. The key of reform is to transform state-owned enterprises into shareholding enterprises in which the state controls or shares stocks, thereby elevating them to a position as the mainstay of the market, removing the malpractice of sole dependence on the state and eliminating low efficiency. The management system for state-owned assets should be changed to transform the administrative system based on a unitary entity, regional and departmental separation and the administrative monopoly into a socialized management system featured by unified management, diversified operations and concentrated utilization; to distinguish the state ownership from the ownership of enterprises, and government functions from enterprise management. Enterprises should be turned into truly independent economic entities and legal entities which are the leading force of the socialist market economy and as such are able to bring the superiorities of public ownership to the forefront. The success in transforming state-owned enterprises into the shareholding enterprises depends on the change of the functions of the government. Multi-faceted reforms of the past revolved around the government delegating rights and relinquishing interests to enterprises which allowed them to expand their decision-making power, thus enabling them to shoulder sole responsibility for profits and losses. Nonetheless, practice has proved that it was impossible to attain reform objectives by this approach. The only way to realize the goals of reform was to clearly define property rights relationships and promote reforms based on a shareholding system. This in turn required that the government to separate its property ownership function from administrative functions. The simple way for the government was to delegate property rights to special organizations and shift threefold functions—property rights, administrative rights and macroeconomic control rights—to the latter two functions. The government, with its function changed from micro- to macromanagement, no longer intervenes in microeconomic activities. The change in government functions has thus reduced governmental organizations and streamlined the government personnel system. The reshuffling effort has in turn allowed "smaller government" to better serve society as a whole. On the other hand, enterprises have become true legal bodies as the mainstay of the market, independent in management and responsible for profits and losses, respectively.

Finally, establishing a social security system which mainly covers unemployment, old-age pensions and guaranteed medical care. The new social security system must combine social security mechanisms with incentive mechanisms. The current tasks are to establish nationally unified social security management organizations, formulate unified policies and strengthen management and supervision. In the social security system governmental departments should also be separated from social security institutions, establishing non-government social security organizations; and the collection and use of social security funds, as well as activities against inflation and for increment should be carried out according to law so as to reduce their losses and waste.

3. Difficulties and the Breakthrough in the Current Economic Structural Reform

What obstacles in the present system must be removed in order to establish a socialist market economic structure? What difficulties must be overcome? What are the breakthrough points in the reform? These particular questions have sparked differing opinions.

The representative view is that fiscal and taxation, financial, and enterprise reforms are the three most difficult aspects at the present stage of economic reform. However, price reform is no longer an obstacle and China will be proceed smoothly in terms of price reform within years near.

China's taxation system was in a state of disarray, and the urgent tasks centered on the prompt establishment of a scientific and authoritative national tax collection system, standardizing the tax system and tax collection, and comprehensively promoting the value-added tax (VAT). No stone was left unturned in the effort to present reform drafts related to the tax distribution system and the practice of separating profits from taxes.

Prior to this, reform of the financial system was in a state of stagnation, and while the reform objective was defined, no real action was taken. The reform program to separate central banks from specialized banks, a program implemented in 1984, merely outlined the framework for a new financial system, and hesitated in pressing forward for several years. The central bank lacked its own distinct features and commercial banks were still burdened with many administrative functions. Policy-lending and commercial credits were intertwined, thus creating loopholes in fund utilization and making macroeconomic control ineffective. Based on this situation, how then was it possible for the country to effectively control the issuance of currency?

Enterprise reform constitute the key link in China's effort to restructure its economic system. At present, however, some one-third of state-owned enterprises continue to record losses, in addition to another one-third indicating latent losses—these facts have fettered China's economic growth. Even though the central government and the State Council paid great heed to the problem, and in July 1992 formulated regulations granting enterprises 14 decision-making rights in their management, no real break-throughs have been scored in the reform of enterprises. What steps must be taken next?

Though large enterprises can adopt shareholding system, while small enterprises can be leased or sold, shareholding system in enterprises must be standardized.

Reforms of the fiscal system and taxation, finance and enter-prises must be carried out simultaneously, while organizational reform must closely follow up.

Others contended that the major barriers involved in deepen-ing reform center on the operational mechanisms of state-owned enterprises, the change of government functions, and reform of the distribution and social security systems. All contradictions, however, focus on the operational mechanisms of enterprises.

The present stage of reform has witnessed the relative futility of initiating reform in a certain sector; the urgent need instead is to standardize and legalize many measures. While continuing with major reforms in certain fields, we must also pay attention to the unbalanced progress in various sectors. Relatively speak-ing, three aspects, i.e. the structural readjustment of economic ownership, the cultivation and development of the commodity economy, and export-oriented economy, have basically followed a successful path and developed rapidly. Future success can be achieved by following this established road. However, little prog-ress has been made in three other aspects, i.e. the transformation of the operational mechanisms of state-owned enterprises; macroeconomic control systems and the change of government functions; and the reform in distribution and social security systems. Thus far, no correct path leading to rapid progress has yet been found. These are the major difficulties in deepening reform and accelerating the establishment of a socialist market economy.

Among these three difficult aspects, the one of operational mechanisms of state-owned enterprises stands out most conspicuously. Since the autumn of 1991, efforts have been focused on the transformation of the operational mechanisms of enterprises. However, judging from present situation, no substantive and rapid progress has been made. The root cause rests with macroeconomic controls, with government functions unchanged and the distribution relationship between various interests far from being straightened. If these problems remain unsolved, the expected results cannot be achieved and the reform of operational mechanisms of enterprises stays as a mere idle talk. To solve problems in macroeconomic control and distribution will encounter considerable difficulties due to the fact that the former involves important readjustments of the original power distribution, and the latter concerns a major change in the current distribution pattern of interests. These will touch on major issues concerning large numbers of people in their ideology, work, as well as their income and living standards. Such issues are likely to arouse reactions from all directions, create dissatisfactions and run risks. However, it is simply out of the question to let these problems remain unsolved.

Since the beginning of reform, we have repeatedly stated that the essence of economic structural reform consists of important readjustments of power and interests. During the first ten years of reform, we mainly engaged in micro-readjustments which had little real effect on the people. Readjustments during the period were basically undirectional, and enterprises, localities and individuals experienced more gains than losses. However, micro-readjustments can no longer solve problems today. Since the state is no longer able to introduce one-way readjustments of interests, the only way to reach planned objectives is to introduce profound readjustments. Therefore, it is necessary to fully explain to the people the true situation, the prospects and possible results of reforms, enabling them to be ideologically prepared. Based on careful planning, estimation, preventive measures against possible risks and other necessary preparations, reforms in these difficult aspects should be carried out decisively and carefully, so as to ensure significant breakthroughs in tackling the lingering difficulties.

Another viewpoint held that the future reform should focus on creating a institutional environment favorable for the development of large enterprises.

Reforms centering on the cultivation of the financial market, transformation of shareholding enterprises, amalgamation and conglomeration of enterprises in the late 80s and early 90s, represent the main orientation for the present self-initiated transformation. Local governments and enterprises have exhibited great enthusiasm for reforms in these particular aspects. This indicates that under the pressure of market competition, effectively expanding the scale of enterprises, and enhancing their capability in organizing funds, personnel and technology through market, will serve as the key for the successful development of enterprises and the economic growth in the 90s. Regarding large market-oriented companies with a much greater capability to amass and adjust economic resources in terms of technical inventions and organization, it is easier for them to engage in large-scale production, and promote the unification of small and medium-sized enterprises and the modernization of traditional state-owned enterprises through circulation of necessary funds with them. Therefore, the focus of the economic structural reform in the 1990s will be to create an institutional environment favorable to the development of these large enterprises. Reforms will include cultivating a financial market, deepening reform of the enterprise system, strengthening enterprises organizationally, nurturing an independent enterprise stratum, and establishing a social security system.

Compared with the 1980s, China's reform strategy, organization and mobilization, and the functions of the central government, and the measures and actions it takes during the reform today must all undergo major changes. Deeper reforms must rely on the inner stamina of micro-organizations as they confront the market. The delegation of administrative power from the central to local governments, and the creation of an institutional environment favorable to the development of large enterprises indicate an expanded effort to deepen reform and the central government's shift in its promotion effort from directly to indirectly. The central government will no longer be directly involved in the design of most of the reform measures, but instead will promote reform by enhancing the originality and capability of large market-oriented companies and local governments.

In terms of reforms in specific spheres, the central government will no longer need to initiate large-scale social mobilization.

On the other hand, as time passes, some reforms which involve many social sectors and must be carried out by governments at various levels, particularly the central government, can be introduced in such a way as to avoid taking measures which will have a major impact on the whole society. A case in point being price reform. Since market mechanisms have already held a dominant position in the distribution of resources, enterprises no longer regard the pricing right of their products and production planning right as key factors hindering their development. Therefore, price reform can now be carried out in a way without creating any major impact on the society. As industries gain maturity, the scope for mandatory planning and government fixed prices can be timely narrowed so that a market orientation can be achieved in a step by step manner. In principle this policy also applies to reforms in macro-control system, including material distribution, investment planning, finance and taxation, and state banking system. With regard to the reform of the labour system, though it has been carried out in a slower pace than price reform, the large-scale labour service market, consisting of an expanded labour force, retirees, and workers and staff of joint ventures, cooperative and solely foreign-funded enterprises, as well as non-governmental organizations, private firms, and a large number of former farmers, has already formed a market price of labour force which is playing an effective regulatory role. As the economic development leads to a substantial increase in the number of market-oriented enterprises, the labour service market will grow rapidly and the labour system will gradually change. At present it is unnecessary to compulsively promote the reforms of labour service market when the state-owned enterprises need to deepen their reforms and social security system is still imperfect.

To stress self-initiated transformation as the main tendency does not mean that the role of the central government is no longer important in the reform process. The fact is quite to the contrary, because the formation and development of self-organized reform forces depend on the institutional environment provided by the central government. Their enthusiasm for reform is mainly based on increased microeconomic returns, therefore they rely on the central government to maintain a balance between economic returns and fairness, and to coordinate the concerted macro-targets in terms of increments, reform and social stability. With regard to the self-initiated transformation of localities and enterprises, the central government must act in accordance with the requirements of economic growth and social stability to give active encouragement, while at the same time controlling the rhythm through examination, coordination, instruction and granting rights to conduct experiments at selected places. Macro-economic system reforms which will have a widespread influence and the reform of state-owned enterprises must be carried out gradually in line with the social endurance capacity and the growth of demand so as to create better conditions for self-initiated transformations. In addition, the central government, in accordance with the progress of the reform, needs to accelerate the formulation of economic laws and regulations, and improve economic order.

Some have claimed that the main problem of the current economy is to regulate the market economy through a planned economic approach.

The major problem in China's existing economy revolves around two-way switching. On the one hand, China's planned economy as a whole should be transformed into a market economy. On the other hand, however, the market economy must retain specific aspects of the planned economy, hence the contradiction. We must not underestimate the influence of the planned economy. Over the past decades, we have publicized and carried out the planned economy both theoretically and practically. The planned economy has in fact taken roots in the concepts and habits of the people, and has permeated into theory, policy and systems. In the past, the government would usually softened policies when faced with economic stagnation; the relaxation of policies would often lead to disorders, which again forced the government to tighten its policies. The result was a vicious cycle. Some people contend that finance is the last defense line of the government, and that the government will lose its controlling ability if the line is broken through. This thinking is in fact incorrect. The only way to add vigor to the overall structure is to reform the financial sector.

Yet another viewpoint holds that the most important task of the present economic reform is to carry out reform in accordance with the law.

China has made great achievements in its economic reform since the Third Plenary Session of the 11th Central Committee of the Communist Party of China. But the new structure has often encountered clashes, conflicts and sometimes even disorders. These problems are closely related to the fact that some reforms were not carried out in accordance with the law. In fact, direct administrative methods were used during the reform process. Laws exist only to confirm and consolidate the results of reform. This has seriously weakened the authority of the law, and reduced the law into a weak and passive position unfavorable to the strengthening of legal system. The administrative approach, due to its own limitations, often made the reform incomplete, and brought disorder and even failure to the reform. Therefore, when restructuring the old system, we must pay great heed to reform methods, fully apply legal means in the reform process and ensure that the administrative methods we use must be in compliance with the legal system. The legal system should actively adapt to these requirements in order to fully play a guiding role in safeguarding the reform effort; and the adoption of reform measures, the readjustment of the content of reform and standardization of reform orders must all be done in accordance with the law.

In essence, the market economy is an economy governed by law, and it cannot be properly established without a legal system. The urgent requirement in establishing a socialist market economy is to perfect a corresponding legal system. Therefore, the legal system formed on the basis of the planned economic structure must undergo reform in order to adapt to the socialist market economy.

The most important task for the reform of the legal system is to solve problems related to the position of law.

This question actually involves the relationship between "rule by law" and "rule by man." Numerous discussions on the issue in the past led to a common understanding that "rule by man" must be replaced by "rule by law," and that "state affairs should be handled in accordance with the law and foreign affairs should also be conducted according to law." This in fact is the primary prerequisite for China to realize its modernization program. Since the objective of reform is to establish a socialist market economy, administration according to law has become even more important. With the determination of the central government and the concerted effort from higher levels at the top down to the grassroots units, the bad practice of conducting everything not in accordance with the law but according to the words of individuals in power or administrative orders, must be eliminated ideologically as well as in practice. Meanwhile effective measures should be adopted to ensure the implementation of law, and the handling of everything according to law. After a period of time this effort will lead to a stable society governed by law, and the establishment and perfection of a new order in the market economy.

The most difficult part in the reform of the legal system is to solve the problem of ensuring administration by law and changing government functions.

Administration by law is the key symbol of modern administration. Due to the influence of the traditional economic structure and old habits, China has a long way to go to achieve legalization of its administration. The legalization of administration has become even more important under the new economic structure. To a great extent, the formation of a socialist market economic structure depends on the establishment of the concept of administration by law and an administrative system. However, it will be quite difficult to establish the new economic structure and realize the transformation of the operational mechanism of enterprises if administrative interference with the market, enterprises and specific economic activities is let go unchecked. An important content of administration by law is to transform government functions in accordance with the law. The administrative functions of the government should be redefined so as to meet the requirements of the new economic structure; and strict distinctions should be drawn between administrative, property and enterprise management rights. Government functions in terms of the market and enterprises must be limited to guidance, administration, coordination, and supervision, rather than direct intervention in the production and operational activities of enterprises. With the exception of taxes, the government cannot share in the profits and distribution of enterprises, neither does it bear any responsibility for losses. The government should be prohibited from abusing its power and intervening in areas beyond its purview of power.

Chapter II
Macro-Control of
the Socialist Market Economy

1. Macroeconomic Management: Focus of Economic Reform

(1) Macroeconomic control should be the product of market economic reform and should not simply equate to government management over the economy.

Although the terminology of macro-control has been popular with Chinese economists for less than a decade, it is more frequently used by Chinese government officials, entrepreneurs and economists than in any other country worldwide. It is quite natural that the meaning of the concept entrusted by the people is extensive, and confusing. Under the planned economic system for some 30 years, the national economy was an administrative centralized entity, which we referred to as the "great unified economy." The system had neither independent microeconomic mechanism, nor independent macroeconomic mechanism. The process of economic reform is a process of separating microeconomic mechanism from macroeconomic mechanism, a process remains to be completed.

Economic reform in China has entered the middle and late stages, and the goal we have defined is to establish a socialist market economic structure. Under conditions in which commodities are basically market-oriented, factors of production as a whole is confronted with the market, the non-government owned economy grows increasingly stronger through market competition, and the state-owned economy has no alternative but to enter the market, changes in the functions and methods of government management over the economy have become a key issue. There-fore, macroeconomic management has become the focus of eco-nomic reform in China. It is thus necessary to deepen reform in order to ensure that macro-management is approached scientifi-cally.

Macroeconomic management is the product of market eco-nomic reform. Experience and theory concerning macroeconomic management first came from Western countries. However, it has been somewhat difficult to find a precise definition for macro-economic management in the economic documents of Western countries.

The view accepted by the majority of economists holds that macroeconomic management does not simply equate to economic management by the government. The government participates in the economy from various aspects and, therefore, administers certain aspects of the economy. For example, in order to maintain the order of the market economy, the government draws up laws to ensure fair competition, while at the same time enforcing the law and providing administrative supervision. The government should also establish and administer public facilities and utilities, while supervising the financial ability of state-owned enterprises, and preserving and increasing the value of state assets. In addi-tion, social services directly provided by the government may also be regarded as a special economic sector. These economic or economy-related actions of the government should not be includ-ed in the scope of macroeconomic management.

Then, what kind of actions of the government are regarded as macroeconomic management? Over a long period of time economists hold that the so-called macroeconomic management means management of the economic aggregate such as total consumption, total savings deposits, total investments, the volume of the money supply, financial revenue and international pay-ments. Practice in some countries proves that, in addition to the aggregate, the government should also pay close attention to the structure of primary industries due to the fact that the existing market situation requires improvement. A noteworthy point is that the industrial policies of Japan and the Republic of Korea have recorded noticeable economic achievements. In addition, some economists believe that income distribution is of great socio-economic significance and should not be overlooked by government macro-control. Actually the governments of many countries have taken the income policy as part of the content of macro-control.

While macroeconomic management is being comprehended as management of the aggregate, this is in fact equated to the management of the aggregate demand. In the eyes of many economists, the planned economy is the restricted economy based on resources, while the market economy is a restricted economy based on demands. Therefore, macro-control of the market economy also represents the control over demands. The impact of so-called monetary and financial policies hits precisely the aggregate demand. If macroeconomic policies limit depression and crises by employing means to simply stimulate demand, it will ultimately lead to economic stagnation, or inflation. On the other hand, theoretically speaking, demand and supply cannot be completely separated. Demand can promote supply, while supply can create demand. Today, therefore, many economists believe that macroeconomic management does not mean the control over demands only, but also the control over both demand and supply.

A point closely related to the aforementioned problems is that traditional macroeconomic theory and practice have, in fact, included only short-term economic stability and balance in the tasks of macroeconomic management, while long-term economic development has been excluded from the scope of macroeconomic management. Firstly, with regard to the developing countries with market economy, strategies and guidelines for long-term development are the undeniable responsibilities of the government. They hold that it is more significant to guarantee long-term and sustained stability and rapid growth than to eliminate short-term economic fluctuations. Secondly, as far as developed countries are concerned, any failure to research and consider long-term development trends and adopt corresponding policies will also have adverse effects. Therefore, more and more people agree that macroeconomic management should give equal consideration to both short- and long-term economic problems.

Hence, by macroeconomic management it is meant to adopt appropriate policies and measures to solve problems that will affect the nation's economy as a whole, so as to enable the national economy to develop effectively in a steady and balanced way.

(2) Any delay in macro-management reform will result in adaptation difficulties and contradictions. A striking example is that micro-invigoration has led to confusion in macro-management.

1) The coexisting pattern of dual economic systems and dual economic operational mechanisms has brought contradictions and problems to macro-management.

China's current macro-management method retains distinctively features of the transitional period of mechanisms. On the one hand, it has reserved the traditional methods and means of direct control. On the other hand, it has also adopted new methods and means of indirect control. Therefore, it is a combination of the two mechanisms. New methods and means should not be regarded simply as being necessary and able to play a positive role, while traditional methods and means as being unnecessary and apt to play a negative role. A rational pattern of transition should ensure the continuous growth of the new system and replacement of the old system. Otherwise, the word of "transition" will lose its meaning. The coexistence and rational combination of the two systems are determined by the following two aspects: a) It can ensure basically the stability of the macroeconomy; and b) It is beneficial to the smooth transition of the entire economic system, including the macro-management system itself. This is the fundamental criteria for China's current macromanagement system.

However, the "coexisting pattern" and its continuation over a certain period of time will threaten the effectiveness of macroeconomic management due to the entanglements and contradictions emerged under the new situation when two different mechanisms operate simultaneously side by side. They will even distort, offset and weaken the dynamic role of macroeconomic control. Therefore, how to end as early as possible the situation of "coexistence of two systems operating at the same time " and ease difficulties and frictions resulting from such a situation is an important problem demanding an urgent solution in the process to establish and improve the socialist market economy, and it is also a weak link in the reform of China's economic system.

2) There is currently a wide gap between the macro-control system and the real pattern of China's national economy.

The national economy has basically evolved from a physical economy into a commodity and monetary economy. The management of value has assumed the leading position over physical management. However, the macro-control method still depends too much on traditional planned management and direct administrative control. At the same time, macro-management still places major emphasis on the management of the state-owned economy, which accounts for less than 50 percent of the whole national economy. Therefore, it is not macroeconomic management in its true sense. The scope of mandatory planning currently covers only a smaller half of the management of the state-owned economy. Generally speaking, contracting or the responsibility system has been adopted for this particular part economy under mandatory planning, and the basic means for macro-control include "negotiations" and "bargaining." Other possibly used means has not been duly recognized, such as establishing and improving information system and providing enterprises with better service in information and consultation.

3) The degree of market growth and the market system are incompatible with the transitional macroeconomic management paradigm.

Under existing market economic conditions, macroeconomic management is mainly based on the market. Proceeding from China's present situation, which will most likely prevail for quite a period of time in the future, the market system is imperfect, particularly in terms of the slow development of the production elements market such as funds and labor force. In addition, a price determining system based on the market has not as yet been established. It will also take time to establish and improve market organizations and systems to meet the demands of the market economy. On the one hand, this situation has naturally restricted the basic role of the market in the allocation of resources; on the other hand, transition of the macroeconomic management pattern should be characterized by its progressiveness, so as to better coordinate and match both the previous and present situations. If not handled well, and particularly if the actual conditions and basis of the market are neglected in order to obtain quick results and early transition, it will most likely lead to consequences contrary to the desired results, adversely affecting the state's economic control ability as well as the effectiveness of macro-control. We must proceed from China's actual situation, and previous experience and lessons, and study earnestly the problem of how to make the two situations adapt to each other.

4) Macro-control has not yet shifted to rely mainly on economic and legal means.

Judging from the perspective of effectiveness, administrative means are no longer playing any guiding role in China's macro-control. The main reason for the investment contraction in fixed assets in 1989 was not the strengthening of administrative control, but the tight money situation instead. In fact, price hikes also reduced the actual scale of investments. Administrative means are also needed for macro-control under conditions of the market economy. At present, China retains far too many administrative means based mainly on administrative orders. Generally speaking, economic and legal means have not yet been effectively employed.

Firstly, the legal system leaves much to be desired. For example, the role of finance in the economy has become increasingly conspicuous, but the Bank Law has not yet been formulated so far; and the unreasonable monopolized operation in one or two industries has hampered fair competition, but there is no anti-monopoly law, or a law governing fair competition. The development of infrastructure industries is too slow, but no laws for invigorating and strengthening infrastructure industries have been adopted.

Secondly, the existing legal system lacks coordination. For instance, there are no detailed rules for the implementation of some laws, and some relevant laws fail to accord with each other and sometimes they are even self-contradictory. Hence, people are uncertain as to what to do.

Thirdly, it is almost a prevailing situation under which laws are not observed or cannot be observed. The reasons for the failure to observe laws lies in the drawbacks of the judicial department itself, as well as in external factors such as higher administrative authorities interfering in judicial activities. Some laws, though being promulgated, are not strictly observed because they lack popular support. For example, though the Bankruptcy Law on Enterprises was published quite some time ago, enterprise bankruptcy in its true sense has rarely occurred so far due to the fact that the socio-economic conditions are not ready for a proper arrangement for bankrupt enterprises. All these facts indicate that legal means can not meet the actual requirements of macroeconomic management.

5) There is no change in the situation that the role played by financial departments in terms of macroeconomic control is weakening.

The scale of financial revenues and expenditures, and their proportion in the total national income affect to a great extent the functions of financial macro-control. A case in point is that since the adoption of the policy of reform, the financial revenue has decreased proportionally in the total national income. The proportion of financial revenue of the central government has also dwindled in relation to the total financial revenues. This in fact is the rational and inevitable outcome following the policy of separating the functions of the government from those of the enterprises, and strengthening the practice of independent accounting of enterprises. However, the problem now is that the decrease is too drastic, and the financial revenues going to the central government accounts for less than 50 percent of total financial income. This is extremely irrational, seriously affecting the role of financial macro-control. In most countries, local expenditures actually account for a considerable proportion. The national income is organized by central financial authorities and then allocated to local authorities in various forms, thereby allowing room for the central financial authorities to exercise macro-control over the entire economy.

Also the current irrational structure of financial expenditures has greatly weakened the regulatory role of financial departments in macroeconomy. Firstly, of the total financial expenditures a large proportion goes to administrative expenses, which is growing most rapidly. This naturally reduces proportionally expenditures for educational, scientific and technological undertakings. Secondly, financial subsidies are still granted to ordinary processing industries and the service trades which ought to be operated according to commercial principles. Such subsidies, in accordance with the demand of economic development and reform, should be abolished. Thirdly, an enormous expenditure must go to price subsidies, and an arduous effort has to be made before completely abolishing price subsidies. Other welfare expenditures similar to price subsidies such as rent subsidies and public health service are also a heavy burden on financial departments. Finally, subsidies to cover the deficits of state-owned enterprises account for approximately 20 percent of the total financial expenditure.

6) Many problems exist in tax revenues as a means of macro-control.

a) The contracting system of state-owned enterprises has tied up taxes and profits together. The standard characters of tax revenues have thus been engulfed by the irregular contracting system characterized mainly by bargaining, and the economic regulatory role of tax revenues has undoubtedly been weakened. b) Income taxes for enterprises with different ownerships are different, and the standards used in the collection of turnover taxes are in fact different. And this confused situation naturally leads to the unfairness in tax burdens. c) There is little difference in tax burdens for different industries and taxation have not played an effective role in regulating the industrial structure. And some irrational differences in tax burdens have adversely regulated the industrial structure. For example, the tax burden for some infrastructure industries that should be encouraged for development has been as high as and sometimes even higher than that of ordinary processing industries. d) So far the individual income regulation tax has not played any role in regulating the differences in individual incomes and the citizens' awareness of income statements and tax payment remains weak. In addition, an effective mechanism to ensure that those with high incomes pay taxes has not been established, and thus there are serious losses in terms of individual income tax payments.

The aforementioned facts indicate that the current macro-control method lags far behind objective requirements. Instead of operating smoothly, the two systems when combined together often create contradictions and conflicts, and cannot well coordinate with each other.

(3) Problems involving the deepening of macro-management should be solved in a comprehensive manner.

Some economists hold that at the present stage, China should make the realization of a short-term balance of the aggregate an important aspect of the macroeconomic management.

However, China lacks a clear quantitative concept in its overall annual control. The common understanding is to maintain a basic balance between total supply and total demand. In the economic documents of most Western countries total supply and total demand are automatically balanced in perpetuity. The key is that new inputs, an extremely important variable, have not as yet been duly valued in China's statistics and planned management. Some have suggested that the target for short-term management of the aggregate should be the realization of a balance between the effective total demand and potential total supply. Another understanding, similar to the one above but more commonly expressed, is that consumption and investors should be in conformity with the endurance capability of the national strength.

Even though the government has stressed the importance of increasing supply, its actual overall policies suggest to have attached more importance to the management of requirements. At present, the most highly valued variables have been the investment scale of fixed assets, the scale of bank credit and the balance of import and export trade. Many problems exist in the determination of the true variables and rational quantitative norms. The increased figures, based on the situation in the preceding year, are usually determined by adding an appropriate amount to the previous year's corresponding figure according to perceptions which are then taken as planned targets. In fact, such variables are mutually restrictive and the relationships between them can be clearly expressed in the formula whereby total savings deposits equal to investments in fixed assets, plus the net export volume. However, it was not until recently that people came to understand and began using the concept of total savings deposits. The accounting system for the national economy still lacks a target based on total savings deposits. In addition, the target for the scale of credit has less real significance than the target for the supply quantity of currency. Nonetheless, what the rational money demand should be has become a much disputed issue. A most common understanding is that the increase of the money supply should equal the economic growth rate plus the planned rate in price hikes. An extremely important factor which has been overlooked is the process of monetary integration in developing countries.

The balance of international payments is of special significance in the short-term management. The so-called "balance of international payments" is the unified and complete balance between income and expenditures of current and capital accounts. A strange phenomenon existing in China is that an excessive attention has been paid to current accounts, while neglecting capital accounts. In an effort to ensure its balance of international payments, China has implemented an administrative management system for foreign trade and foreign exchange. People worry very much about deficits in current accounts, but pay little attention to deficits in capital accounts, or precisely the net outflow of capital. The rational structure of China's international payments at the present time should be in fact the other way round.

China actually should and is able to implement an effective long-term strategy. This fact is of great significance indeed for a developing country that has trailed behind but is now matching and even surpassing the economic and technological level of some developed countries, and is especially significant for a country with such a vast territory and huge population. Since 1979, China has extricated itself from the traditional pattern of development, shifting its focus from heavy to light industry and agriculture, from import substitutes to both export trade and import substitutes, and from a unitary state accumulation to various forms of accumulation. The new development strategy has scored great success thanks to the sustained efforts of development and opening to the outside world, and the country has realized its strategic target of doubling its gross national product within 10 years ahead of schedule.

Since the beginning of the 1990s, China has entered a new economic growth period featuring a transition from a low-income to a medium-income level, and from a life with enough to eat and wear to a moderately high standard of living. Today, China is confronted with the task of accelerating the development of infrastructure facilities and basic industries, relaxing and eliminating bottleneck restrictions, rapidly developing its service sector and upgrading technologically its industry and agriculture in an all-round way. This means that while continuing to develop competitive labor-intensive industries, China must also accelerate the development of capital- and technology-intensive industries, accelerate the process of rural urbanization, and more closely combine industrialization with information engineering. Further deepening the reform and opening wider to the outside world should be the basic approach for implementing the aforementioned strategies. China is confronted with many challenges as it attempts to implement such a development strategy. Practices of the 1980s are far from sufficient to cope with the new situation due to the fact that substantive changes have taken place in the economic operating mechanism, the market economy has reached a higher level and China has established closer relations with other countries. A failure to adapt to the new situation will turn China's development strategy into an empty and abstract policy slogan.

While employment has long been regarded as a short-term macro-control issue in Western countries, it has been regarded as a long-term issue in China. Thus far, China's economy is still confronted with a serious potential unemployment. In other words, in factories and particularly in rural areas, at least one-third of the labor force is considered redundant or surplus labor. Chinese society can hardly endure a situation when potential unemployment becomes open unemployment. The basic method of avoiding it is to accelerate the economic development and create more industries and jobs, and this is a road proved effective already.

Whether in terms of short- or long-term macroeconomic management, China has stressed the importance of the industrial structural policies. We have recorded both success and failure in this regard. Due to long-held traditions of a planned economy, when formulating and implementing industrial policies we have been inclined to make them all-embracing to be implemented in an all-round way. Quite obviously, this approach has naturally collided with the general orientation of reform and opening to the outside world. Another important lesson from the past is that we often forgot the fact that unlike China the enterprises in Japan and the Republic of Korea are not owned by the state when we learned willingly from their experiences. In spite of this, we still believe that regulation and control of the industrial structure in the 1990s are an indispensable part for macroeconomic management. Industrial policies will continue to play an important role so long as we earnestly draw lessons and change our approach and methods.

Income distribution is an aspect that cannot be avoided during the present stage of macroeconomic management. Since the introduction of the reform and opening policies in 1979, we have always taken the control of the wage level as an important means for restraining the expansion of the demand and price hikes. While breaking the egalitarian form of distribution, we also hope to restrict and remove unfair income distribution resulting from different competitive conditions. Some people are being allowed to become rich first on the premise of the rational distribution of income according to work and related factors. At the same time, however, common prosperity is encouraged. Income distribution appears to be satisfactory in some rural areas with relatively well developed township enterprises. However, the general situation still leaves much to be desired. The general level of wages and welfare benefits in state-owned enterprises, government institutions and various collective enterprises has skyrocketed much faster than the economic growth rate. All things considered, egalitarianism remains the main trend, and unreasonable income distribution has affected the improvement in economic returns, while at the same time quite naturally leading to the emergence of various social problems. At present, economists are generally concerned about another problem based on the fact that regional income gaps have become increasingly prominent along with the growing imbalances in the development of regional economies. The old practice of "trimming the fat to pad the lean" and bringing regional income gaps to the same level must not be repeated, and neither must this undesired trend be allowed to run its own course.

In addition to the above factors, China's government departments still have power to control and interfere in the operations of enterprises, particularly state-owned enterprises, including appointments and dismissals of factory directors and managers, determination of contracted operational targets, and supervision over the preservation and increment of state-owned assets. We firmly believe that these should be in no way regarded as activities related to macroeconomic management.

Protecting and improving the economic order, particularly the market order, are perhaps the most important responsibilities of macro-control at the present stage. Economic order in a mature market economy is mainly safeguarded by law, agreements, habits and ethics. However, the economic system in China is in a transition period and comprehensive economic departments of the government are forced to rely on certain administrative methods to supervise and examine market activities. It goes without saying that the process leading to rule by law must be accelerated.

With regard to inflation, some specialists contend that the current price rise does not necessarily indicate inflation, and that it is largely due to price reform. They say, price reforms are designed to replace state planned prices with market regulated prices. Therefore, prices are bound to move upwards, so price hikes do not always indicate inflation. Price hikes have in fact spurred many active factors such as promoting the development of production and the establishment of the market system.

The current problem centers on the fact that the relationship between reform and development has not been appropriately handled. Our economy developed rapidly under the condition when the old system was still playing a major role, but the old system was unable to bear the pressure of high-speed development. A number of problems emerged under such circumstances, including speculation in real estate and stocks, and the establishment of an excessive number of economic development zones. All these problems resulted from the interfering behaviours of the government.

Some specialists contend that the "double-track" economic system demands simultaneously a "double-track" regulatory means.

China's economy has witnessed three major fluctuations since 1978, and is now entering the fourth high tide. When we look back we should draw experience and useful lessons. Stress should be placed on the relationship between micro-reform and macro-stability. The progressive reform is characterized by the fact that as far as the relationship of profits and the redistribution of interests are concerned top priority is given to the vested interests under the old system; however, when the vested interests protected by the old system remain unchanged, development of at least part of the new system is allowed, thus forming the so-called double-track system. China's reform at present is basically a transition to a double-track system. The most important double-track system is the one adopted in the ownership structure, governing the relationship between the state-owned and non-state economies. The basic reform method for state-owned economy based on the premise of not changing the ownership system is to delegate power to enterprises and grant them more profits. The goal is to give greater encouragement and greater decision-making power to enterprises, enabling them to seek their own interests. To some extent this has changed the operational approach of enterprises and has raised their production efficiency. On the other hand, however, it has been an important factor causing macro instability.

Two reasons have contributed to fluctuations prevalent in China: a) The central government's plan for rapid growth; and, b) competition under the state-owned system between local governments and enterprises within the budgetary restrictions. Competitive relationships exist when such entities have their own decision-making power. However, instead of market competitions, the competitive relationships between them are still subject to budgetary restrictions. The central government's plan for rapid growth was the reason for the economic fluctuation between 1978 and 1980, though the later two fluctuations (1983-1985) and (1987-1991) were not caused by the same reason. In 1985 and 1986, the central government adopted the deflation policy and curtailed total economic demands. However, there was still the possibility that the economy would be confronted with a overheated development, because under the system of decentralization of power competition was prevalent between state-owned enterprises and local governments. There were thus two different forms of fluctuations—inflation in the investment sector and inflation in both investment and consumption simultaneously. Once granted ownership enterprises not only seized more resources and investments, but also expanded various forms of consumption by making use of their controlling power over income distribution and expenditures, including increasing individual income, consumption of public funds, bonuses, wages and management expenses. Therefore, the overheated growth in economy was accompanied by inflations in other sectors at that time. Similar methods were adopted when attempts were made to cool

. the economy down during the first three fluctuations. It was all through direct control by using administrative means instead of indirect control based on the market regulation and control of policy variables. Direct administrative methods were adopted to control the credit scale and the investment scale. An analysis of the first two fluctuations has revealed that the means for controlling finance and credit produced little tangible result, while direct curtailment had effectively brought the investment scale and number of investment projects under control. The reason why the indirect means to control finance failed to produce any effect lies not only in the financial system, but also in the structure of the economic system. On the one hand, the regulation of the interest rates was confronted with great obstructions during its formulation and implementation. On the other hand, even though interest rates were regulated, when enterprises which were still under the budgetary restrictions and local governments were still based on the public ownership, the state-owned economy responded very weakly to regulated interest rates; and indirect means which are effective for the market economy cannot be used. Even though we employed direct means to control the credit scale and the amount of money in circulation, we still could not prevent the collaboration of local governments and enterprises in the state-owned banking system, using various methods to break through the planned targets of the central government. In the past, the amount of actual credit always exceeded planned credit, and sometimes by as much as 200 percent.

Under these circumstances, local governments have many methods to bypass the credit control of the central authorities. Therefore, it is quite obvious that control measures over investments have played a major role in retrenchment. For example, economic retrenchment began in 1988, with finance and credit were under tight control in the second half of the year. However, enterprises maintained a fairly high economic growth rate by way of the so-called "external cycle" and "chain debt." Measures were taken to control investments in early 1988, and the economy began to cool down and the growth rate declined, thereby leading to the sluggish market. In the second half of 1989, the central government noticed the sluggish economy and lifted lightly its control over money supply. However, the effort failed to produce positive results. It was not until the second half of 1990 when the government relaxed its control over investments that the national economy as a whole was able to rise from the slump because the investment scale of the state-owned enterprises had expanded extensively. Up to today the control over investments by administrative means remains as the most effective way, though we wish very much to adopt indirect control. In addition, the control over finance has first of all affected the interest of the non-state economy while state-owned enterprises can seek new methods. Therefore, the conclusion can be drawn that since we are in the transitional stage of the double-track system, market regulation should be actively promoted as far as macro-control is concerned. On the other hand, we must adopt different administrative methods in order to stabilize the economy. So long as the economy has a double-track system, we must likewise have double-track regulation and control means. All administrative measures still in use today have a positive effect so long as they are beneficial to creating the market, developing a favourable environment for the market economy as well as the non-state economy.

Some economists believe that we should strictly control the issuance of money, while at the same time effectively improving macroeconomic control and reforming the management system of the total demand.

China's economy has developed at a high speed since its adoption of the policy of establishing a socialist market economy. However, rapid economic development requires the control over the total social demand so as to ensure economic stability and high efficiency. Therefore, currently the most urgent task is to reform the management system of the total demand and improve existing policies.

The control over the total demand is a major component of macroeconomic control. At present, China is in the transition stage to a market economy, a period characterized by the tendency of expansion of investment. Therefore, we must proceed in a prudent manner, adopt conservative financial policies and rely on restrictive financial policies to control the total demand.

The Central Bank is the state's macroeconomic management organization, responsible for financial policies. Its targets, financial policies, methods, as well as its organizational and operational mechanisms have played an important role in the implementation of the policy for the total demand. Due to the influence of the traditional macroeconomic management system, the Central Bank's existing system needs to solve a number of urgent problems in its management of the total demand, including the generalized monetary policy and the distribution policy for the scale of credit ceiling. To this end, the concept of total demand must be clearly defined and problems which may easily cause confusion must be clarified. We must concentrate our efforts on discussing and analyzing the merits and demerits of the credit ceiling system.

At present, the Central Bank controls total demand by setting credit ceiling, a method feasible under the traditional financial market system monopolized by the Central Bank. However, under the current financial system the Central Bank is separated from specialized banks. Commercial credits have developed rapidly and non-banking financial organizations and the capital market have constantly moved to the forefront. The control over the scale of credit does not necessarily mean the control over the volume of money placed in circulation. Surplus savings deposits are expanding and are being transformed into purchasing power by the following methods and channels: Loans are granted to non-banking organizations; banks and enterprises have joint accounts; increases in loans from government revenue; short-term debts are transformed into long-term loans; and some non-banking financial organizations have adopted various means to evade the control of credit ceiling. All these methods and channels have rendered the control of credit ceiling ineffective. Therefore, it is impossible for the control of credit ceiling to attain the goal of effectively controlling the total social demand.

Simultaneously, the practice of using administrative methods to allocate the scale of credit to specialized banks has undermined their initiative, thus reducing their efficiency.

Economic development demands reformation of the existing system of the total demand. However, such reform requires market mechanisms. At present, as China's market mechanisms are still imperfect, indirect means will be employed as much as possible to reform the total demand management system. An important aspect is that the Central Bank must restrict its economic loan scale and effectively control the issuance of currency. Available indirect means can be adopted include: The Central Bank should strengthen its management over funds raised by specialized banks; funds raised by the Central Bank should include mortgages for government bonds; funds can be raised by issuing short-term bonds; raise interest rates; examine source of funds of financial organizations; the Central Bank is forbidden to grant loans to enterprises directly; and accelerate the transformation of specialized banks into commercial banks.

During the discussion of the administrative means for macro-control and economic levers, some economists pointed out that the planned economy was controlled by administrative means, i.e. mandatory planning, while the market economy is regulated by economic levers. While advancing from the planned economy to the market economy, China faces the risk that the administrative means are becoming more and more ineffective while conditions for employing economic levers have not yet matured.

Fifteen years of reform have brought about essential changes in the macro-control mechanisms of the Chinese economy. An analysis of the figures since China began its reform reveals that following the founding of the Central Bank in 1984, China has gradually established money supply mechanisms centered on the basic currency and related multiples. The amount of currency in circulation in the Chinese economy has changed from the passive variable prevalent prior to the reform into a variable which exerts a major impact on economic fluctuations. Hence, the true relationship between currency in circulation and economic activities has emerged. This means that once the volume of the money supply is increased, the output, or in other words, the demand, will go up after six months, and vice versa. Here it refers to the time relationship between the money supply and industrial output, and does not mean any increase in currency in circulation. The aforementioned aspects are in fact characteristics of the market economy.

The result of China's effort to regulate the macroeconomy by economic levers leaves much to be desired, with the failure in macro-control between 1985 and 1988 being a case in point. The main reason for the successful economic retrenchment between 1989 and 1991 rests in the fact that the government employed administrative means.

There are basically two fundamental reasons for the ineffectiveness of economic levers. Firstly, a large number of state-owned losing enterprises depend totally on the banking system. Secondly, banks have to issue bank notes to offset the financial deficits of the central government. During the economic rectification between 1989 and 1991, over 3 million township enterprises declared bankruptcy, while only few state-owned enterprises followed suit. Hence, as far as state-owned enterprises are concerned, the economic retrenchment failed to accomplish the goal of adjusting the economic structure and eliminating backward enterprises, resulting in the ineffectiveness of economic levers. The pressure on the banking system from the central government deficits is obvious. Domestic and overseas loans can offset only a minor portion of the government deficits. Following the adoption of the reform policy in 1979, with the exception of 1985, the central government has recouped a portion of its deficits by relying on banks to issue bank notes, making it difficult for the banks to independently implement monetary policy.

At the same time, the administrative means of macro-control has become less effective, because local governments have greatly strengthened their control over resources during reform, and the proportion of resources under the control of the central government has dropped on an annual basis. Under the pressure of local governments, local branch banks have tended towards localization. In recent years, multiple ownership and the emergence of a large number of non-banking financial institutions have led to multiplicity and complication in the currency circulation links. With more and more circulation links out of its control, the control power of the central government over the banking system is weakening.

Only by deepening reform that necessary conditions can be prepared to use economic levers in macro-regulation. China is internationally recognized for its success in the progressive reform. But the next round of its reform calls for many other necessary auxiliary reforms. The runaway currency circulation may appear to be a failure in macroeconomic control, but it is in fact a problem existing in micro-control because the root cause rests with enterprises. Hence, it is very difficult for any reform to be carried out simultaneously in enterprises and taxation system to yield any positive result. Reforms in enterprises must be accompanied by follow-up moves in the social security system. Nonetheless, several decades of reform has greatly strengthened the endurance capability of the Chinese people and their economy, thus conditions are ready for supporting reforms even on a very limited scale.

The whole range of reforms is an extremely complicated and arduous systems engineering. Economists and central government departments concerned have long studied and proposed specific programs. However, designing a national program represents the same degree of difficulty as ascending to the heavens. The central government should formulate a detailed program for reforms in the financial and taxation systems and establish nationwide, unified and standard financial and taxation systems. Central authorities need only to formulate principles for the reform in enterprise and social security system, and leave the specific programs under the care of the provincial authorities. For example, in order to facilitate the nationwide circulation of labour force, central authorities can stipulate itemized individual retirement pensions, and pensions should be transferable when the pensioner has moved from one locality to another. Local authorities will determine details for the establishment of retirement funds and the appropriate withholding rate from the wages of the employee. Local authorities have boundless creative ability and are capable enough to do a good job in planning. Guangdong Province has already made promising moves in this regard.

Successful auxiliary reforms in finance, taxation, enterprises and social security system in the next three to five years will enable China to make substantial progress in its overall reform effort, and China's market economy will take shape initially.

Some specialists hold that development of the market economy should bring the functions of the government into better play.

Past practice of all countries with market economies shows that to some extent government interference exists unexceptionally in the modern market economy. However, due to the differences in the development of market and economy in different countries, the functions, scope and level of the market economy also differ. Generally speaking, they involve the following eight aspects:

First, laws and regulations are an inevitable demand for the market economy and are in fact the premise for fair competition. However, actual operation of the market economy has sometimes restricted and negated itself. Therefore, a complete set of laws and regulations are of great importance in guaranteeing the smooth operation of the market economy. After 100 years of accumulation, countries with modern market economies have already formed a complete legal system; and compared with them China still has a long way to go. The legal framework needed for the planned economy differs completely from that of the market economy.

Second, China's planned economy has operated for many years, and the plan for economic reform in line with the market economy has not been quite in shape. Countries with market economies such as France, Switzerland, Japan and the Republic of Korea have all employed the method of planning in economic management. However, their plans differ from the planned economy of ours. A point well worth mentioning is that the content, functions and targets of their economic plans change along with market growth, economic development and changes in competition. For instance, France first adopted a guidance plan, which was replaced later by an indicative plan, and recently it has changed once again to a strategic plan.

Third, the government can play an active role in allocating

resources in limited areas. In fact, the market economy serves as the foundation and an important means for the allocation of resources. In departments with their market mechanisms in good operation, the government has no need to participate in the allocation of resources. The function of the government should be concentrated mainly on the following areas: a) providing infrastructure facilities indispensable for the development of resources; b) providing indispensable materials and services for the development of resources such as education, vocational training and medical care, because these important aspects in the economic development require government participation; and c) organizing macro strategic studies, including basic research and development, development of new departments, development of underdeveloped regions, and helping industries requiring government support and create conditions so as to bring their potentialities into full play.

Fourth, the function of the government lies in macro-control which is utmost important for the stable operation of the market economy and reducing the range of periodical economic fluctuations.

Fifth, the government should promote an easy exchange of information. Limited facilities and inadequate access to economic information may bring certain losses to the national economy. Therefore, information delivery, telecommunications and transportation are very important. Shortly after the merger of East and West Germany, the German Government invested massive funds in a state previously belonged to East Germany. The investment, equal to China's annual investment in fixed assets, was mainly used to improve information, telecommunications and transportation facilities.

Sixth, market system should be further cultivated and improved. China has initially established a market economy and the government is responsible for promoting market growth and establishing the order for market competition, a fact which will enable the rapid growth of the market. After the Second World War, the experiences of some new industrial countries and regions which had successfully cultivated a market economy has proved that this is particularly important for China. A unified market should be established to supervise and protect the management of enterprises according to law, ensure the operations of the market free from interference.

Seventh, unreasonable aspects arising from market distribution should be corrected and the social security system should be established and improved. With regard to the coordinated development of society, the role of market mechanisms has its limitations. The market economy cannot automatically ensure the fairness in the social income distribution and the regional development in a coordinated way, and the government bears responsibility in these areas. China's effort to reform and improve the social security system is more urgent today.

Finally, greater efforts should be made to promote the establishment and improvement of the socialized service system. In the past, many enterprises ran social welfare facilities. In countries with market economies, measures were taken to reform and improve public welfare facilities related to enterprises so as to reduce social burdens borne by enterprises. For example, encouragements are given to the development of accounting and auditing firms, employment agencies, and legal and consulting offices. In China, it is necessary to improve the service system for labour and employment, train personnel and provide employment services, perfect the labour dispute handling system and protect the legal rights and interests of enterprises and workers and staff. The aforementioned are the main aspects of the government functions. Judging from China's current situation, changing government mechanisms is an important content of the economic structural reform, as well as one of the major factors for supporting reforms. Only by defining the government functions is it possible to straighten out the relationship between enterprises, the government and the market, as well as relations between central and local authorities.

Specialists stress that the transition from the traditional system to a socialist market economic structure requires necessary administrative means in macro-control, and that economic and legal means must be fully employed. The legal system based on the planned economy must undergo reformation and the legal system for the socialist market economy must be established and improved.

Economic laws, regulations and systems should comply with the demands of the market economy, and should be implemented in coordination with the transfer of the macro-management system and the regulatory and control forms.

Economic management and operations under the condition of the market economy should be standardized and restricted by related economic laws, regulations and systems. This is an important aspect and necessary means for enhancing the state's macroeconomic management capacity. Viewed either theoretically or practically, the market economy is an economy based on the market and governed by laws and regulations. Without the latter there will be no order and economic operations are bound to be chaotic. However, during the process of establishing a socialist market economy, the establishment of economic laws, regulations and systems will inevitably undergo a process of gradual improvement before reaching maturity and perfection. China has long been subject to "rule by man," and many of its past economic laws and regulations will be revised or otherwise abandoned. Due to the fact that many people from high levels to the grassroots have little knowledge of legal systems, it may take a long time to accomplish the arduous task of creating an institutionalized environment with established systems required by the socialist market economy. Therefore, the transfer of the macroeconomic management should be coordinated with the progress of the economic legal system. This aspect is in fact a weak link in the establishment of a socialist market economy in China, and represents a major problem which requires an urgent solution to ensure the gradual strengthening and improvement of China's macroeconomic management and to accelerate the transfer of the form of macro-control and regulation. Judging from the actual situation and existing contradictions in China, the following countermeasures should be adopted:

a) Both comprehensive management and specialized economic departments should examine thoroughly at the earliest possible date, a large number of systems, economic laws and regulations promulgated and implemented in the past. All systems, laws and regulations inappropriate to the current situation or contradictory to the construction of the socialist market economic system should be abolished, and reform measures proved by many years of practice to be effective and relatively mature should be standardized timely as a system or adopted as legislation so as to remove confusion, and clarify and improve the legal environment.

b) In line with major problems and weak links, emphasis should be placed on accelerating the establishment of economic and legal construction, and gradually preparing legal guarantees for overall management under the market economy. For example, regarding the standardization of various basic economic relations, stress should be placed on the research and formulation of enterprise laws, property law, banking and the budget laws. With regard to defining operational rules for the market and standardizing market activities, attention should be paid to in-depth research and the formulation of the anti-monopoly and anti-illegitimate competition law, as well as the trademark law and patent law. In the formulation of laws governing specified economic behaviours, the establishment and perfection of the accounting laws, law of cost and auditing law, will be of primary importance.

c) We must effectively strengthen economic supervision and economic judicial systems and the building up of the rank of personnel in these fields. We must extend a determined effort to solve those serious, long-standing, common problems in social and economic life, including laws are not fully observed or enforced, knowingly violation of the law, and prohibition orders are not carried out. Only by so doing can the law become a truly powerful deterrent force terrifying to all, thus creating conditions necessary for the realization of an institutionalized economy and the improvement of the marco-management effectiveness.

Experts stress that macro-management requires that the government should properly interfere in the market, and it should leave the matters which can be handled by the market itself under the care of the market, so as to let the market play its due role. We must make sure not to use the methods for the planned economy to regulate the market economy.

Some economists contend that China should guard against companies run by institutions and mass organizations to abuse their powers to obstruct fair market competition in seeking for their own interests.

China's reform in the last fifteen years has been a process of replacing the old economic structure with a new organizational structure. In the course of establishing the new structure, many township enterprises emerged side by side with enterprises run jointly by the government and mass organizations (GOES), totalling 125,000 in 1992.

Various GOES in fact existed in the initial stages of China's economic reform, including the China International Trust and Investment Corporation. However, the number of such organizations increased rapidly after 1985. The dual-price system has provided conditions and opportunities for GOES to earn generous profits, thus forming the so-called official commerce and official speculation. In 1989, the government began the rectification of GOES, and following the remarks made by Deng Xiaoping during his tour to south China in 1992, the government instituted organizational reforms and streamlined government departments. The surplus staff and departments from government establishments organized themselves into companies to try a new way out.

GOES can be classified into three categories according to their different functions—mere skeletons, restructured companies and economic entities. Skeleton companies do not engage in commercial activities and simply charge some fees by providing consulting services and coordination for their subordinate enterprises. Restructured companies refer to former government departments at various levels that have retained their former power and now can directly engage in commercial activities. New economic entities refer to former government organizations that have basically abandoned their former administrative power and are now engaged solely in various commercial activities. Strictly speaking, the GOES here are mainly referring to economic entities based on profits earning. They have decision-making power, the right to do business, and strict budgetary restrictions, enjoying some relative advantages.

Since Chinese GOES are still at the primary stage of development, it is much too early to draw any conclusions concerning their role and their impact on the course of the economic reform. But an analysis of GOES reveals that they have greatly promoted the reform of state-owned enterprises, development of the labour force market, and the transformation of the economic structure.

At this point we will cite the situation in Singapore as a reference. In Singapore there exist a large number of enterprises related to the government, known as GLCS. Like private enterprises, GLCS participate in the market competition on an equal footing; and if they suffer from poor management the government does not provide them with any special protection, so they have to close down. Also, the government has formulated clear rules and regulations to restrict their power, and they do not enjoy any special privilege. Singapore's experience tells clearly that ownership is not the decisive factor in the operation of an enterprise, the success of an enterprise is based on its performance. The distinction between China's GOES and Singapore's GLCS lies in their different practices and the institutional environments.

The Chinese Government should appropriately control the behaviour and practice of GOES so as to prevent them from taking advantage of their power and engaging in unfair competitions. From a long-term point of view, China should adopt a distinct legal system designed to properly regulate the cooperative relations between officials and merchants.

Some economists stress that Taiwan's experience in economic development can serve as a reference to other parts of China.

China has for many years sought a development form suitable for its economic modernization.

Since World War II, developing countries and regions have adopted various economic development patterns, including the Soviet pattern characterized by centrally planned economy, the Western laissez-faire pattern and the East Asian pattern. The practice in the former Soviet Union, East European countries and some developing countries and regions has proved that the former two patterns do not work. And only the East Asian pattern has proved successful. The East Asian pattern stresses the importance of foreign investment, technology, exports and education, while at the same time laying due emphasis on the authoritative role of the government. At first, this pattern enabled Japan to become the first non-Westernized modern country. Later, some other East Asian countries and regions, including Hong Kong, the Republic of Korea, Singapore and Taiwan which have also scored success by following the same pattern.

As early as in 1976 a heated and sustained discussion began in China as to the goals of its development and what road it should take. Some people adhere to the concept of the centrally planned economy, while others prefer the adoption of the Western laissez-faire approach. China's experience in the past 30 years has proved that the inefficient centrally planned system for the allocation of resources cannot meet the requirements of modern economic development. The lessons learned by East European countries and China from the 1989 political turbulence indicate that a totally laissez-faire approach will simply bring chaos to China, and thus leaving the East Asian pattern as the only approach that China can follow. However, among the five East Asian countries and regions that have developed their economies successfully by following a similar pattern, the cultural background of Japan and the Republic of Korea differs greatly from that of China, while Hong Kong and Singapore do not have as vast rural areas like China, so their experiences are not very suitable for us. Taiwan alone represents a completely pure Chinese society which has successfully realized modernization under similar conditions. In this sense, the Taiwan pattern is most directly related to the other parts of China.

Nonetheless, some people doubt that the Taiwan pattern will truly suit the other parts of China, because they have different systems. An analysis of the primary stages of Taiwan's economic system and the current economic system in other parts of the country reveals that the situation in the distribution system of the resources and the degree of macro-interference is very similar. In terms of the structure of ownership in the 1950s and 1960s, the industrial production owned by the Taiwan authorities accounted for a fairly high proportion. Currently, in industrial production the proportion of China's state-owned enterprises is falling and the growth rate of the private economy and other economic sectors is higher than that of the state-owned economy. Therefore, the analysis indicates that the current economic system on China's mainland is in many ways similar to that of Taiwan Province in its early stages of development.

Many economists believe it is feasible to use Taiwan's experience in economic development as a reference. However, the economy in China's mainland has its own characteristics, and after abandoning the centrally planned system, the government should in no way neglect the management of public property, and should place great emphasis on formulating the rules and regulations for the protection of property rights. Simultaneously, the government should attach importance to the market situation. Once these conditions are ready—the establishment of fledging industries, market mechanisms have developed and the new mechanisms have been accepted by the people—it is possible to gradually delegate power and realize the further promotion of economic development.

Some experts say that at present close attention should be given to practical operations in microeconomic management.

Experiences over the past decade have proved that we will be faced with a serious contradiction during the course of implementing macroeconomic management. In other words, economic growth and reform of the economic structure sometimes call for different oriented macroeconomic policies. Theoretically speaking, reform is based on long-term economic development and should be regarded as the central issue. In practice, however, people are unwilling to sacrifice short-term economic returns and refuse to abandon the immediate achievements from economic growth.

However, the more complex problem lies in the fact that at the present stage economic structural reform involves both external and internal macro-control. This means that if we are to reach a certain macro-control target, we not only need to adopt ordinary policies and means, but also special policies and means including some reform measures. Remarkable and effective experiences have gained by employing the two means simultaneously in the readjustment of the industrial structure and the improvement of the balance of international payments.

With regard to the ways and means of macro-control, the problem which often calls for solutions is how to best coordinate direct and indirect control methods. The need of the economic reform and the frequent changes in the situation make it even more difficult to handle the problem.

Great changes have taken place the in the present situation. Regardless of whether people have recognized it or not, direct planning or administrative orders for production and sales of commodities as well as investment activities have lost their effectiveness on many occasions. If the government intends to realize its influence on the national economy it can rely mainly on the following means, including credit, finance, taxation and other measures based on its monopoly of the productive factors such as interest rate, exchange rate and land rental costs, as well as the examination and approval of the scale of security issuance, and import and export trade. All things considered, it is quite obvious that China's current macroeconomic management, to a great extent, has become indirect.

2. Financial System Reform: Key Issues for Deepening the Reform

(1) The chaotic financial order reveals that a strong Central Bank is required for effective macro-management.

Many economists hold that China needs a strong Central Bank, considering its establishment as an urgent task to enhance macroeconomic control. They say that the Central Bank should not only have the power, responsibility and ability to regulate and control the currency, but also the ability to analyze and judge the macroeconomy. At the same time, the system of profit retention for the Central Bank should be abolished in order to avoid the expanded issuance of basic currency for profit-making purposes.

China's Central Bank currently lacks the responsibility, ability and power to regulate the currency independently. For example, in early 1988, central authorities decided to adopt a retrenchment policy and recover Central Bank loans of 25 billion yuan (basic currency). That same year, a series of measures designed to accelerate the reform aroused the enthusiasm of various sectors and promoted a higher growth rate in production. Such circumstances led to the rapid growth in loans, and the Central Bank failed to recover 25 billion yuan of loans. Under such a situation the question arose as to whether should the Central Bank implement the set monetary policy or should it continue to expand the issuance of currency along with economic growth? The government had no intention to reduce the rate of economic growth and the Central Bank was unable to recover and curtail loans as planned. For all practical purposes the bank actually implemented an expansion policy which led to inflation in credit. Between October 1988 and October 1989, curtailment of social demand was once again restrained, thereby leading to negative growth. In order to reduce the ranks of the unemployed and effectively put an end to negative growth, the government demanded that banks expand their credit scale. The Central Bank continued to expand loans when faced with the sluggish market and slumping demand. As a result, factories produced a great deal of overstocking products, which in turn tied up their funds. In the second half of 1990, the government realized the need to stimulate social demand and instructed banks to issue fixed assets loans. Thereafter, banks transferred loans for ordinary circulating funds to loans for fixed assets, and within only a few months granted around 50 billion yuan of loans, which stimulated the demand and promoted production. The aforementioned examples reveal that the Central Bank must obey the instructions of the government passively as to what policies it should implement.

The flow of massive funds into local markets and stock markets, and the emergence of the "real estate craze" and "stock craze" were all closely related to the chaotic disorder in finance. Other countries have enforced strict control over banks engaged in activities related to the securities and real estate sectors. However, China's banks including the Central Bank have in fact invested in securities companies. This situation must be changed.

(2) It is necessary to standardize relations between the Central Bank and the government, so as to prevent banks from being overwhelmed by the influence from local governments.

Some experts have cited the 1988 and 1989 examples to illustrate the necessity for the Central Bank to have independent power. Other experts hold that it was not because the Central Bank was not powerful enough that problems occurred in 1988 and 1989, but because the central government had misjudged the economic situation and failed to implement effective economic measures. The Central Bank is a nonprofit-making organization, and its main goal is not to earn profits, but instead to serve as a tool of the government. In cases when the Central Bank fails to agree with the main economic policy decisions and economic judgements of the government, it should nonetheless obey all the same. Under different systems in different countries, including countries with market economies, the arrangement of financial organizations is also different. For example, although the Bank of England is a department under the Treasury, it plays a major role in making decisions and regulating the market. Therefore, the main problem in China is that the relationship between local branches of the Central Bank and local governments should be standardized so as to avoid the excessive impact of local governments on local banks. In this way local banks were able to implement the economic policies of the central government. On the other hand, the relationship between the Central Bank and the primary decision-making departments of the central government should be standardized. For instance, the Central Bank implements only the decisions of the Premier of the State Council.

(3) The macro-financial system has acquired initially the features of the market economy and the deepening of the reform in finance must be conducted in a coordinated way.

According to some experts, we should have an overall assessment of China's macro-financial system. Over the past more than a decade of reform, China's macro-financial system has initially acquired the features of the market economy. An analysis of China's money supply mechanisms shows that the proportion of the multiplier effect of monetary operations conforms basically with the economic theory in the West. The money supply is in fact closely related to economic growth. Statistics prior to 1978 show that money supply at that time was passive and currency was only a tool of the planned economy. Money supply then was entirely determined by material distribution and currency itself was passive. However, currency has become active since the government adopted the policy of reform and opening to the outside world in 1979. And monetary changes can lead to changes in the entire economic situation.

Non-state-owned enterprises in China have reacted rationally to the situation of the money supply. With many companies in Hainan Province feeling the pinch, however, companies capable of moving fast in importing and exporting products have acquired huge cash reserves and are doing quite well. Some people who invested heavily in Beihai City, the Guangxi Zhuang Autonomous Region, have been unable to recoup their funds due to the slump in the local real estate industry. A major portion of policy loans granted by the central government to enterprises have gone to township enterprises, which have also begun to react to the money supply situation. These aspects have provided the Central Bank with a material basis in using economic levers to regulate the economy.

China has scored marked progress in monetization, even though the process slowed down after 1985 along with the emergence of inflation. At present, however, China's reform is headed for a new stage. A famous economic theory in the West is called financial deepening which is based on the ratio between total financial assets and the total national assets. Using an equation based on financial assets as the numerator and national assets as the denominator, the ratio will grow in the course of the marketization and development of economy. If China's reform has reached a new stage, will the large amount of currency and loans issued in 1992 lead to the monetization of China's economy? Will it in fact represent a phenomenon in financial deepening? If so, this is a new demand for economic development, and we needn't feel panic. There are also people who believe that the current inflation is extremely serious and must be put under control immediately. This new development requires further analysis as to what impact these non-banking organizations will have on the economy and whether or not they represent characteristics of the market economy in finance. Past experience shows that the financial levers in regulating the economy could not function under China's old system due to the fact that state-owned enterprises depended totally on the government. Our economic levers will not be able to function as long as we don't sever the blood relationship between state-owned enterprises and banks, and continue to grant to state-owned enterprises huge policy loans.

At present, China has a double-track ownership system based on the joint ownership by the state and non-state-owned units. Non-state units can employ economic levers, while state-owned units can only rely on administrative levers. The Chinese economy is now in a transition period. The market economy demands the use of economic levers to regulate the economy, while state-owned enterprises continue to use administrative levers as a regulatory device. There is danger in allowing such a situation to continue. In the course of marketization, the power of local governments is expanding greatly, more and more non-banking financial organizations have been established, and the efficiency of administrative levers has been weakened. At present, conditions are not yet ready for market economic levers to function effectively. When inflation occurs it will be very difficult for either economic or administrative levers to bring the situation under control, because some decisions made by non-financial organizations of local governments may go beyond the control of administrative levers while economic levers will not work for state-owned enterprises need policy loans. The only way to alleviate the problem is to accelerate the reform, adopt comprehensive supporting measures and conduct coordinated reforms of the social security system.

Thanks to years of reform, the endurance of our economy has been strengthened. Therefore, auxiliary reform programs can be considered. Nonetheless, we are still faced with the pressure of inflation, and the overall environment leaves much to be desired. The Central Bank must make every effort to bring inflation under control. The long-term drawbacks of inflation will create anticipatory confusions among the people, leaving them with a bad psychological outlook. The Central Bank must adopt effective measures to control inflation. If such measures fail to work effectively, it must then find new methods to ensure that inflation is brought under control within nine months to one year. The smooth implementation of reform measures requires a liberal environment, a fact proved by experiences in 1989, 1990 and 1991. Under a liberal environment, auxiliary reforms should be implemented to ensure that in three years of time our economic reform will be truly upgraded to a new stage and that the market economy will initially take shape.

(4) Policies for the establishment of banks run by local people and foreign-funded banks should be liberalized.

Some experts have pointed out that the government and the market are currently competing for two scarce resources—personnel and funds. A large number of qualified personnel have flowed from government organizations into the market, thereby indicating its attractiveness. At present, the first-class market for state treasury bonds is sluggish, while there is great demand on the first-class stock market. These facts show clearly that the government and the market are scrambling for the two aforementioned resources.

There are two solutions to the problem, one is to accelerate the reform, the other is to return to the old track of the planned economy, and the latter will lead to nowhere. With regard to funds, it is necessary to accelerate the reform of the financial system and correctly handle the following three relationships: the relationship between the government and enterprises, the relationship between the public and private enterprises, and the relationship between China and other countries. In the past, we classified banks as government organizations or as government monopoly organizations. Such a classification was improper. With the exception of the Central Bank, other specialized banks should be commercialized. Commercial banks should be run like enterprises and bank activities should be carried out like that of the market. We should not only allow individuals to run enterprises, but also allow local people to operate banks. Banks should be operated under the shareholding system. We should not only allow foreign enterprises to invest in China, but also allow foreign banks to open branches in China. In this way we will be able not only to make use of foreign banks to attract foreign capital, but also to start competition between foreign and Chinese banks so as to promote the transformation of the country's banking system.

(5) The goal of the Central Bank should be to control the issuance of currency, and not to earn profit.

Some experts contend that in addition to reforming existing commercial banks, it is necessary to abolish or reduce restrictions on the establishment of commercial banks by individuals or non-state groups. This involves two major aspects: 1) abolishing restrictions on establishing banks; 2) abolishing various restrictions on foreign exchange businesses and other related activities. Of course, this does not mean that all restrictions should be abolished all at once, instead they should be annulled in a planned manner. On the other hand, it does not mean either that the government will relinquish its control completely. On the contrary, the government should see to such activities in accordance with rules and regulations. In recent years, private credit banks have emerged in the country's rural areas, and some of them have become sizeable commercial banks. Once all private banks operate under the principle of earning profits, they will be put under good and proper management. They can bring their initiative into play in at least the following areas. Firstly, they will support small and medium-sized township enterprises. Under the present circumstances, small enterprises are not as highly valued as state-owned enterprises. With their support this problem can be solved. Secondly, these banks operate in line with the principle of earning profits, so they will not tolerate any loan defaults by enterprises. Thirdly, commercial banks established by individuals or non-state enterprises will exert competitive pressure on state-owned banks and reduce the proportion of policy loans. Fourthly, the establishment of such banks will help restrain the growing demand for stocks and real estate. Fifthly, these new banks will help improve financial management. At present, state-owned banks are unable to meet all the financial demands of enterprises, particularly small and medium-sized enterprises as well as township enterprises. Partially illegal banks have opened in many localities, particularly in rural areas, and it is very difficult for the state to manage such banks. An urgent task facing the government is to stipulate the rights of private banks and enhance the awareness of depositors of the intensified risks if they deposit money in private banks while borrow money from state-owned banks. Management of the Central Bank over commercial banks, including both private and state-owned commercial banks must be based on the principle of openness.

(6) Interest rates should be the focus of attention, and any reform in interest rates must first of all maintain a positive interest rate.

Many experts have pointed to the dangers resulting from a negative interest rate.

As shown by statistics that the total savings deposits had reached 1,300 billion yuan in the past period. So one percent raise in interest rate of the total savings deposits equals 13 billion yuan. Before the raise of the interest rate, if we wanted to change a negative interest rate into a positive interest rate, the interest rate must be raised by 10 percent. The banks would have to pay an annual interest of 130 billion yuan on savings deposits, an amount far in excess of the state financial figure of 20-30 billion yuan today. It is thus quite obvious that the expenditure on the raise of interest rates is a very heavy burden on the state. How about a raise in the interest rate of loans? At present, the bulk of bank loans has been granted to loss-making enterprises. Therefore, the problem of the negative interest rate is closely related to the bad performance of enterprises. The failure to resolve this problems will in turn make it very difficult to raise the interest rate. Chinese banks are established by the state, while banks in the United States are owned by individuals. While loss-making banks in the United States will be forced into bankruptcy, Chinese banks established by the state never need to declare bankruptcy, because state financial departments will cover any losses sustained by banks.

(7) Commercial banks are still considered the pillar in fund-raising. The core of financial reform is the reorganization of commercial banks and the establishment of various non-state-owned banks to serve small and medium-sized enterprises.

Currently there is a misunderstanding in the country that under the market economy the pillar of the financial system is the stock market. This is in fact incorrect. Over the past decade, many banking, market and financial experts have conducted in-depth studies and reached the following conclusions:

Firstly, the role of the stock market in raising funds varies in different developed countries. In Britain and the United States, funds raised through the stock market account for a larger proportion relatively, about 10 percent of all newly-raised funds. At present, only in the United States that bonds issued by enterprises are in good operation.

Secondly, in fund raising commercial bank loans are still the main external method used in many developed countries, including countries in Europe, Japan and various developing countries. Commercial banks are the pillar of the financial sector, with the banking system in Japan being a case in point.

Thirdly, unofficial financial institutions have played an important role, particularly in supporting the small and medium-sized enterprises in developing countries and regions. Taiwan is a good example in this regard, and over a long period of time funds raised by non-governmental organizations or unofficial financial institutions accounted for 30-50 percent of the total. Therefore, in terms of financial system reform in China, reform and reorganization of commercial banks are a key aspect of the financial reform effort. Commercial banks in the United States provide a unique example, because banks there exercise little supervision over enterprises. However, such a system is inappropriate for China as the country moves towards the market economy. Banks have played a major supervisory role in Japan and Germany. The reason why banks can play such a major role in these countries lies in the fact that banks have access to many unique means. For example, banks are concerned with whether or not loans can be recovered, and thus placing great stress on the supervision over the accounts. In addition, banks have access to means not available to other financial institutions.

China is currently witnessing a craze for stocks and bonds. The craze is based on a number of factors, including: a) Due to the limitations in the traditional pattern in the control of loan scales, many localities have bypassed restrictions to development various new methods in fund-raising. b) Stock markets have developed from scratch, and many of them have recorded notable achievements. It is therefore correct for enterprises to employ direct methods to raise funds. c) People lack enough knowledge of investment risks. d) The enthusiasm for direct fund-raising comes from the understanding of difficulties in reforming the existing banking system. According to experts, direct fund-raising will not be the main orientation over the next five to ten years, and perhaps even longer. They say that the traditional commercial banking system should be established instead.

Prior to 1978 the state financial departments monopolized the system and the role of banks was very limited. Now, however, it appears the reverse extreme is prevalent. The banking sector currently has replaced the state financial departments, monopolizing everything. Now, policy-related loans (subsidies), commercial loans and development loans, are all mixed up, amounting to about 40 percent of financial loans, including subsidies for farm produce and sideline products as well as state-owned enterprises. Therefore, China's financial allowances are in fact much higher than the figures listed in reports, between 20-30 percent. When all policy-related loans granted through the banking system are included, the actual financial figure is most likely to rise as high as 80 to 90 percent, a problem which is extremely difficult to avoid. In addition, all kinds of loans are mixed together, and banks are unable to exercise any supervision. All the while, some banks have pursued their own goals by making use of the confused situation. A point well worth mentioning is that some enterprise banks are opposed to the separation of policy-related loans from commercial loans. The correct method is to substantially reduce policy-related loans, because they represent one of the root causes leading to the restrictions of the soft budget and the issuance of bank notes by the Central Bank. We should either separate policy-related loans from commercial and development loans, or specialized commercial banks. The state financial departments should take care of matters related to finance. Loans for development such as those for infrastructure facilities and energy projects should be handled by special development banks similar to the Japanese Development Bank. It should be pointed out, however, that such development banks should be subject to specific stipulations. Speaking of development banks, many departments want to establish their own banks. This is a phenomenon contrary to the purpose of development banks. With regard to commercial banks, the experience of major banks in Japan can serve as a reference. There were a great deal of bad debts in Japan following World War II, a similar situation confronting many Chinese enterprises today. In readjusting the relations between enterprises and banks, a practical approach is to turn bonds into equity capital and strengthen the supervision of banks over enterprises. In addition, Taiwan's experience has shown the importance of unofficial banks and financial institutions. Though small and medium-sized enterprises are extremely important to China, it is very difficult for them to raise any fund through official financial institutions.

(8) Confusions in the financial order indicate that the Central Bank should strengthen its supervision and audits of financial institutions.

One of the major responsibilities of the Central Bank is to supervise financial institutions. Therefore, a supervisory and management system based on caution should be established. At present, the People's Bank of China is actively developing its auditing ability, but still lacks cautious management. Audit procedures should ensure that financial institutions operate in a steady and sound manner, and such procedures should focus on the risk management of financial institutions. At the same time, the People's Banks should be granted necessary authority and administrative power, enabling them to correct the unstable operational behaviors of financial institutions and establish reserve funds securing the assets of financial institutions and limit the risks resulting from losses on loans. Tens of thousands of auditors working for the People's Banks require further professional training.

Some economists have suggested that China establish a credit committee responsible for credit control targets and supervision so as to avoid credit fluctuations.

Other experts have pointed out that the banking system in Viet Nam is not responsible for covering the financial deficits and losses of enterprises, and they say this experience should be served as a reference to us.

3. Accelerate the Reform in the Financial and Tax Systems

(1) The financial and tax relationships between the central and local governments should be changed from the financial contract system into a tax distribution system.

Many experts contend that it is necessary to standardize the distribution relations between the central and local financial departments and between the government and enterprises. Tax distribution system whereby tax revenues are shared by central and local authorities should be adopted to replace the current practice of contracted financial responsibility system. Other experts have suggested that the practice of dividing financial revenues between the central and local authorities can be adopted first. Then the tax distribution system should be adopted as the second step. A system whereby taxes are separated from profits should be adopted to replace the contract system of financial responsibilities for the distribution between the government and enterprises.

At present, financial relations between the central and local authorities, and between the government and enterprises are far from being standardized. Since 1988, the contract system of financial responsibilities has been widely implemented and has played a positive role in mobilizing local governments to appropriately organize financial revenues. However, this system has its drawbacks. The contract system is based mainly on localities. The base quota is sometimes modified by a progressive increase. Take a province for example. Its contracted tax quota to be paid to the central government includes the base quota and a progressive increase of 9 percent over the previous year's figure. A drawback to the system is that the inflation rate sometimes has exceeded 9 percent, and thus the total taxes the province has actually paid to the central government represent a negative growth. This system has thus constantly reduced the total financial revenues of the central authorities. This particular contract system at the same time has an unfavorable influence on the formation of a unified market and also hinders the progress in readjustment of the industrial structure. China's financial revenues are based mainly on indirect taxes, with the tax rate usually defined according to prices. For example, the price of coal is comparatively low and enterprises engaged in coal production are unable to earn high profits, and hence taxes are low. However, the prices of cigarettes and wine are comparatively higher, and likewise tax rates are higher. In order to increase revenues, local governments prefer to develop industries with high tax rates, while industries with low tax rates, although in urgent need of development, remain as weak links. Under an irrational pricing system, the local financial contract system will result in the deformation of the industrial structure. Therefore, an urgent task is to replace the financial contract system with the tax distribution system. We have adopted the contract method in terms of the distribution relationship between the central government and enterprises. Far from being standardized, the base quota is usually determined through negotiations with a specified progressive rate. Under such circumstances, the financial revenues of the government cannot be guaranteed. Therefore, the proportion of government financial revenues continues to fall. This is another important reason why we are conducting a series of taxation reforms, including expanding the value-added tax (VAT), unifying the income tax rate on enterprises and establishing the individual income tax. In addition, land and property taxes must also be levied.

Emphasis should be placed on the implementation of tax distribution system in the future reforms, rationalizing the interest pattern between the state, localities, enterprises and individuals and creating a favorable environment for the formation of a unified market in China. However, this will require the following:

a) Abolishing the system which combines profits and taxes together, establishing a new system which separates taxes from profits, and eliminating the substitution of taxes for profits, the expansion of taxes at the expense of profits and the phenomenon of making no distinction between profits and taxes.

b) Stipulating the same income tax rate for enterprises with different forms of ownership so as to create conditions for fair competition between all enterprises. The trend towards a relatively high income tax for enterprises should be corrected so as to enable enterprises to increase the retention level of funds, help them overcome difficulties resulting from the shortage of funds and reduce their operational cost.

c) Promoting product tax and value-added tax throughout industrial enterprises to resolve contradictions and improve the turnover tax system.

d) The overlapping in tax collection related to the income distribution of enterprises and individual income must be eliminated and the regulatory tax for enterprises must be abolished. The regulatory tax will be implemented for individual income only so as to rationalize the burden.

e) Enterprises should all repay loans after they have paid taxes. This new practice will urge enterprises to use funds sparingly and restrain overheated investment.

f) The tax collecting scope of resources should be expanded so as to regulate differential incomes and promote the rational use of resources.

The effective implementation of tax distribution system requires the completion of the following tasks as preconditions:

a) Based on the clearly defined tasks of the central and local authorities, it is necessary to distinguish the scope of the financial and administrative power of the central authorities from those of the localities, determine separate taxes and tax items for both of them respectively, and fix separate limitations of income and expenditures for the two. Enterprises should pay taxes to both the central and local authorities in accordance with the law. At present, the scope of local taxation power are comparatively limited. Local authorities should be granted a greater tax collection scope which will increase local taxes and their proportion in the total tax revenue.

b) Local governments should be granted certain legislative power to enable them to stipulate some taxes and issue bonds, thereby providing them with new economic resources required for economic development.

c) In coordination with the strategy for economic development, the formulation of medium- and long-term financial strategies should include the balance of budgeted revenues and expenditures based on the balance of the total social supply and total demand. It is also necessary to improve laws and regulations related to finance and taxes, and realize scientific management.

d) It is necessary to actively develop financial and credit activities, increase the variety of revolving funds, open securities markets, and examine and approve allowable foreign debts at different levels. A funding system for the debt repayment, and financial and credit institutions should be established. Regarding the financial funds in the existing revolving fund system, special government credit can be issued, including low interest loans and discount loans in support of specified production and service projects. At the same time, the depreciation of the assets of state-owned enterprises should be accelerated and new products development fund should be established. In addition to retirement insurance funds, social security tax should also be established, so as to provide financial support for the new products development fund.

e) It is also necessary to improve the overall macro coordination systems for the Ministry of Finance, the State Planning Commission, and the Central Bank. In comprehensive planning for finance and credit, the Ministry of Finance and the Central Bank must extend great effort to restrict the overall scale of key state construction projects which must be arranged by the State Planning Commission, both in terms of total funds and total supply. At the same time, practices should accord with market-oriented industrial policies, technical policies and regional development policies so as to ensure the rationalization of the economic structure.

(2) Following a comprehensive analysis of the mechanisms of the China's financial contract system and its effect on revenues and expenditures, an expert from the World Bank noted that the next step of China's financial reform should be the improvement of its taxation system.

The financial contract system between enterprises and the government, and between local governments and the central government is an important content in China's economic reform and has played a significant role in boosting the economy.

China has implemented the financial contract system combining taxes with profits. Private enterprises and enterprises with foreign investments pay both the industrial and commercial consolidated tax and income tax, while state-owned enterprises and collectively-owned enterprises pay only the former. Financial revenues local governments pay to central authorities are predetermined in accordance with the financial contract system. The system is based on the following characteristics: a) The formulation of the tax law is separated from tax management. The central government formulates the tax law, while local governments control all tax management responsibilities, with the exception of customs duties. b) The system features dual factors based on the distribution of both financial revenues and budgeted expenditures. c) Activities in different regions and industries lack unity and stability.

Problems resulting from the financial contract system include: a) The proportion of tax income to output is falling along with the rising economic growth rate. b) Regardless of different circumstances, the proportion of the financial revenue of the central government to the national income will fall along with the increase of the national income.

Although the mechanisms have promoted development of China's economy, they have also created a number of unfavorable consequences, including: a) The proportion of state financial revenue to the national income has dropped sharply. b) Tax burdens on different industrial sectors are unbalanced and transregional financial burdens are uneven. c) It is quite difficult to implement central government macroeconomic regulation policies for the national economy. d) The situation has led to unfair tax burdens on inland provinces, with taxes being much higher than for those comparatively well-off coastal provinces.

Due to its drawbacks this system, while offering only the weakest guarantee for a certain level of financial revenue, has created havoc in terms of the overall tax revenue and financial system, thereby leading eventually to massive financial deficits, serious inflation and an unstable macroeconomic environment, and affecting the continued development of the economy.

Therefore, China should take follow-up measures for its financial reform to improve the tax system and ensure the realization of the goal of implementing macro financial policies leading to steady economic development. The central government should not only control the formulation of the tax law, but more importantly, should further control the implementation of the tax law and the management of tax collection.

(3) The fundamental principle in the reform of China's tax system is to open the market and unify tax laws.

Some experts stress that tax system reform must conform with the basic features and laws of the market economy. The unified market must be based on unified tax laws. The market is open and the structure of the tax system, as well as the collection and management of taxes should suit the demands of the open market, and develop gradually to gear with generally accepted international practices related to tax revenues. The market is competitive and tax revenues should embody the principle of fair tax burdens. The market operates in line with macroeconomic laws and tax revenues should play a greater role in strengthening macro-control and promoting the microeconomy. Judging from China's past practices and international experience, the reform and construction of the tax system under the conditions of the market economy should abide by the following fundamental principles:

1) The principle of efficiency. A scientific tax system is the basis for correctly and effectively bringing taxation into full play. The direction for tax system reform should meet development demands for the market economy so that tax revenue will effectively promote the economic operations. At the same time, authorities in tax system should raise their efficiency and reduce costs in administrative work.

2) The principle of fairness. Taxpayers should be treated fairly, both horizontally and vertically. By horizontally it refers to the principle that taxpayers with same economic capability should pay same amount of tax. In other words, the same criterion applies to people under the same conditions. By vertically it refers to different taxes should be paid by people with different economic capabilities, and different criteria should be applied for people under different conditions.

3) The principle of standardization. The essence of taxation

requires standardization of the tax system, and the standardization is an important precondition for realizing a legalized tax system and ensuring fair tax burdens. Therefore, standardization should be the starting point for the overall design of the tax system, the determination of various tax factors and managerial methods for tax collection. Effort should be made to attain unity, comprehensiveness and scientific approaches in standardizing the tax system, while adhering to generally accepted international practices that conform with the conditions in China. Efforts should be made to avoid as much as possible substituting policy readjustments for structural readjustments. The aforementioned aspects should ultimately find expression in tax laws and regulations.

4) Functional financial principle, also known as stable economic principle. Taxation is a lever the government employs to regulate economy; it should give guidance for the economic development, and maintain full employment and the relative stability of prices. When the economy approaches to the point of full employment and is experiencing inflation, the tax rate can be raised accordingly so as to reduce inflationary pressures. On the other hand, when the economy is in stagnation and the unemployment rate rises, the tax rate can be reduced so as to restrain the trend towards recession in economy.

5) The principle of neutrality. Under the condition of the market economy, market plays a guiding role in allocating resources after the average social profit rate was basically established. To this end, taxation should as far as possible be based on the principle of neutrality taxation and should not interfere or hinder the effective operation of market mechanisms.

(4) The guiding principle for tax system reform is to expand the tax sources, rationalize tax burdens, reduce favourable terms and tighten the control over taxation.

The guiding ideology for the reform in the tax system should be in accordance with unified tax laws and based on fair tax burdens, a simplified tax system, rational division of power, standardized distribution methods, and distribution relationships being brought into better balance. Tax system reform should expand the tax sources, rationalize tax burdens, reduce favourable terms and tighten the control over taxation. The tasks facing the reform of tax policies include the popularization of the value-added tax, unifying the income taxes of enterprises, expansion of the tax resources, and initiate the collection of land tax, property tax and individual income tax. The specific content will include:

1) China is a developing country with a relatively low productivity and lower individual income. According to present circumstances, it will be quite difficult for China to provide conditions necessary for implementing a tax structure based on direct tax payments in recent years.

In line with actual conditions in China, the selection of main tax categories in the structure of the tax system should give due consideration to the requirements of state finance and economic regulations.

During the process of social reproduction, circulation and production are the two links for creating and realizing national income. Tax funds in these links are comparatively rich and are easy to control. The taxes set in these links help to ensure a steady growth of tax revenue, playing a marked regulatory role in production, circulation, distribution, consumption and other links. In addition, the distribution link of China's national income mainly covers the distribution link of the actual income of enterprises, i.e. the distribution link of the profits of enterprises. With relatively more concentrated tax funds tax categories established in this link will to some extent help regulate the economy, and their regulatory role in distribution in particular is even greater. Proceeding from the country's actual conditions, in the production and circulation links it is appropriate to select the turnover tax based on the circulation volume of commodities. In the distribution link, the income tax of enterprises based on their profits can be regarded as main tax category or bulk tax category. In addition, various auxiliary tax categories will be added in order to coordinate and supplement main tax items and enable taxation to fully play its role in various sectors of social enonomy.

Currently, revenue from China's turnover tax (including the value-added, product, business and consolidated industrial and commercial taxes) accounts for over two thirds of total tax revenues. Such a high proportion will exert certain pressure on future tax system reform. Therefore, with regard to tax system reform, great attention should be placed on properly readjusting the structure of tax revenue. As mentioned above, in line with China's economic development level and the actual situation of its economic system, the turnover tax will continue to account for a relatively big proportion in a fairly long period of time. It is fully necessary and in conformity with China's actual conditions to follow a compound tax structure with the turnover as main tax category and other tax categories as supplement.

2) In the reform of income tax of enterprises, the short-term goal is to unify the income taxes of enterprises with only domestic investment. Later efforts should center on unifying the income taxes of enterprises with both domestic and foreign investments and formulate the Income Tax Law for Enterprises of the People's Republic of China, applicable to all enterprises. Establishment of a unified and standard income tax system for enterprises with domestic investment only will not only help remove a major obstacle to the transformation of the operational mechanisms of enterprises, and facilitate enterprises to gear themselves to the market for fair competition, but will also standardize the distribution relationship between the state and enterprises.

Main proposals for unifying the income taxes of enterprises with domestic investment only include:

—Merging the existing income tax rate of state-owned enterprises, implementing the 33 percent tax rate in a unified manner and giving due consideration to small enterprises during this period; pre-tax deduction items and listed payment standards for the income tax of enterprises should be unified and standardized. In addition, pre-tax deductions should be based on the stipulations of the tax law so as to protect the tax base from erosion.

—With regard to supporting measures for unifying the income tax of enterprises with domestic funding only, the method of repaying loans prior to taxation shall be changed to after-tax repayment of loans. Construction and budgetary regulation funds for key energy and transportation projects collected from enterprises should be abolished accordingly.

The state, as the sole owner of state assets, has the right to share in the after-tax profits of state-owned enterprises. In consideration of the actual conditions of enterprises, with the exception of a few enterprises, most existing enterprises will be exempt from paying after-tax profits for a specified number of years.

Unifying the income tax of enterprises with domestic funding will be of great significance for deepening the reform of economic system and will involve a series of major reforms of the enterprise system, including the depreciation system for enterprises, the investment and financial system, wage and bonus system, and the social security system of workers and staff members. The income tax system reform of enterprises and these related reforms are mutually conditioned and mutually beneficial. The gradual implementation of the aforementioned reform measures will provide structural guarantees for transforming the operational mechanisms of enterprises.

The method of changing the pre-tax repayment of loans to the after-tax repayment of loans is an important aspect of unifying the income tax of enterprises with domestic funding. In summary, the method of pre-tax repayment of loans retains the vestiges of the state unified control over income and expenditure, including: a) Investment loans of enterprises are mainly guaranteed by the tax revenue of the state. Hence, both enterprises and banks face little risks. The inevitable outcome of such a risk-free investment mechanism is an irrational investment structure and poor returns for investment. b) Over expansion of the investment scale resulted from blind investments is unfavourable to state macro-control. c) The badly-eroded taxation base of the income tax of the enterprises has created a relatively wide gap between the nominal tax rate and the actual tax burden as far as the income tax of enterprises are concerned and the state revenue is not guaranteed for a steady growth. The implementation of after-tax repayment of loans will help enterprises establish a risk mechanism in their investment system, enhance their investment and economic returns and enable enterprises to develop within themselves mechanisms of self-restraint. This is an extremely important link in promoting enterprises to transform their operational mechanisms. If enterprises are not required to undertake risks for their investment behaviour, transformation of their operational mechanisms will be out of the question.

3) The goal for the reform of the turnover tax is to establish a taxation pattern featuring the simultaneous existence of the value-added tax (VAT), product and business taxes which will be regulated by a two-tiered system. This means the VAT will play an overall regulatory role in commodity production and circulation, while the product tax will be used as a special regulatory tool for some consumer goods such as cigarettes, wine, petrol and automobiles. With the exception of wholesale and retail commerce, the tertiary sector will continue to implement the business tax. One of the primary views accompanying the first introduction of the VAT into China was that the VAT could only be implemented in industrial production, mainly as a solution to problems of overlapping taxation. Practice over the years has proved that we have only introduced the calculating method of the VAT but failed to pay due attention to the inherent demands of the VAT in overall taxation and simplifying the tax rates. In addition to obstacles created by the irrational pricing system, problems have emerged during the course of implementing the VAT, including complicated tax calculations and distortion in tax reductions. Future reform should be carried out in line with the generally-accepted international practices, and establish a standardized principle for the VAT ensuring that it will adequately cover the entire process of commodity production and circulation. At the same time, the tax rate should be simplified. This is in fact the only way that all functions of the VAT can be brought into full play. First of all, the implementation of the VAT throughout the process of commodity production and circulation can ensure the true deduction from tax payments as indicated by receipts. This in turn will solve problems of distortion of tax deductions, losses of tax payments, and the current practice of tax deduction according to purchase costs, so as to ensure the reali-

zation of mutual restriction and supervision of taxpayers in taxation. Second, this new method will greatly simplify taxation, provide convenience for both taxpayers in paying taxes according to law and tax authorities in the collection and management of taxes. Third, it will effectively solve the long-standing difficult problem of how to distinguish wholesale from retail sales in business tax. Simultaneously, by raising the standard tax rate of the VAT the retail sales will be brought under control and tax evasion will be reduced accordingly.

Specific proposals for the reform of the turnover tax include:

—Expanding the collection scope of the VAT. First, the VAT will be promoted in an all-round way in industrial production, and will then be expanded to commodity retail sales.

—Simplifying the tax rates of the VAT. Three to four grades of tax rates will be established first. However, the four-grade tax rates will become one or two grades when the VAT is expanded to commodity retail sales.

—Implementing productive VAT so as to encourage enterprises to conduct technical transformations and expand production. In other words, tax payments on the fixed assets of enterprises will be taken into the scope of tax deductions of the VAT.

—Simplifying the method for calculating and collecting the VAT. The method of tax deductions for purchases, and the system of tax deduction according to tax payments on the receipts will be put into practice in a comprehensive manner.

—With regard to certain special commodities and some high-grade and luxurious consumer goods, in addition to the VAT as a tool for general regulation, product tax should be collected as required for special regulations. As tax burden for some products has been reduced, to ensure the financial revenue it is necessary to expand the scope of the product tax to include certain final consumer goods and some intermediate products as well. Along with the growth of financial revenue, the improvement in market mechanisms and reform of the price system, product tax on intermediate products will be gradually reduced until being abolished completely. Thereafter, only part of final consumer goods will pay product tax.

—The business tax will play its due role mainly in the tertiary sector. In line with the industrial policy and the existing situation of the reform of the tertiary industry, the business tax rate will be adjusted accordingly.

—On the basis of reforming and improving the turnover tax, the tax system for both domestic- and foreign-funded enterprises will be unified.

4) Reform of individual income tax.

Fair income distribution is an important social target in a socialist country. However, it is impossible for the market economy to automatically materialize this goal. Therefore, the state should maintain fair distribution by implementing appropriate income and tax policies.

Currently, the individual income tax, individual income regulatory tax, and income tax for self-operated industrial and commercial households in urban and rural areas exist simultaneously side by side. The lack of strict legislation, well-defined standards and coordinated policies has resulted in the emergence of a series of contradictions. In order to effectively implement overall control over taxation in income distribution, a new individual income tax system will be established recently to suit the income distribution pattern based mainly on the principle of to each according to his work, with other distribution methods as supplements. While giving expression to the principle that the socialist market economy must take into consideration of both fairness and efficiency, this distribution pattern recognizes reasonable gaps in individual incomes but opposes polarization. Specific proposals for the reform of individual income tax include:

—The existing individual income tax, individual income regulatory tax and income tax for self-operated industrial and commercial households in urban and rural areas should be combined together to formulate a unified individual income law of the People's Republic of China.

—In line with the generally-accepted international practices, the scope of individual income tax should be expanded and tax on income from private business will be added.

—The progressive tax rate for individual income tax will be implemented. The level of the tax burden will be determined in line with actual conditions in China, with the situation abroad, mainly the situation in other developing countries as a reference.

—Different standards of taxation will be applied to Chinese and foreign personnel.

(5) Reform of local taxes.

The deepening of the reform in the economic system has revealed drawbacks in the current financial contract system. The relationship between the central and local governments urgently requires readjustment. The reform is oriented to establish the tax distribution system whereby tax revenues are shared by central and local authorities. Accordingly, tax system reform should also be in accord with the demands of the tax distribution system.

—A localized tax system should be established. The central government should put under the control of the local governments tax items which have little impact on the overall economy, but are closely related to local economic development, and are convenient for local governments in collection and management. These tax items will be regarded as fixed income of local finance. Tentative proposals for reform include: Categorize business tax as a local tax in addition to existing local tax items; expand the scope and income scale of resource tax and categorize resource tax as a local tax item; and categorize the tax on property and real estate as a local tax.

—The local tax revenue should be expanded and the proportion of local taxes should be increased by a wide margin so as to ensure that the bulk of the expenditures of local governments will be covered by themselves.

—Based on the premise of concentrated macro-control necessary, the relationship between the centralization of power and the decentralization of power in the management of taxation should be handled properly so as to change the confusion existed currently in the division of power over the management of taxation. With regard to tax items already set as fixed income for local governments, most of the management power over such tax items should be delegated to local governments.

—Except for local tax items which must be implemented nationwide uniformly, legislative power for local taxation should be delegated to the legislative bodies of provinces, autonomous regions and municipalities directly under the central authorities.

—It is necessary to reform and improve local tax items and optimize the structure of the tax system. China has already established the framework for a compound tax system. However, the category of tax remains to be more rationalized. As far as local tax items are concerned, some should be abolished or merged, while others should be reformed and improved. In addition, some new tax items should be established.

(5) State tax bureaus must be established, management of taxation must be strengthened, and taxation must be standardized according to law.

In regard to China's existing tax system, only the income tax law for foreign-funded enterprises and foreign enterprises, individual income tax law, and procedural laws (law on the collection and management of tax revenues) have been officially adopted by the National People's Congress. Most of other tax items don't have full official legal bases in support. In fact, some of them are provisional regulations, some regulations lack detailed rules for implementation, and some tax items that have been implemented in draft form on trial basis for many years. The establishment of a market economy not only calls for the reform in the tax system and legislation for the tax system to go simultaneously, but also requires legislation of taxation to provide guarantee for the reform in the tax system. It is necessary to establish state tax bureaus so as to intensify management of tax collection. It is also necessary to strengthen the legal system building in taxation. Efforts to reform the tax system should also include the completion of official legislation in line with legal procedures. Under the condition of market economy taxation should be standardized according to law.

Supporting methods for the collection and management of tax are required. In essence, the management of taxation is the process of enforcing the law. Therefore, a taxation system based on strong management and in conformity with the market economy should be established. The intensification of management of taxation should be carried out according to law. Close attention should be paid to tax evasion and those who refuse to pay taxes by violent means should be dealt with severely according to law. The principle of stern punishment should be reflected in handling such cases so as to strengthen the legal deterrent of the tax law. Strict tax collection and management, standard market transaction behaviour and market order, prevention of illegal competition and eradication of behaviours disturbing market order will guarantee the implementation of the tax law and policies for taxation. Over the next few years, great effort should be made to bring distribution relationships of tax revenue into better balance. Improvements of the tax system will be of great significance for the development of the market economy. The reform of tax system is an extremely complicated problem involving major readjustments in macroeconomic policies, as well as the redistribution and readjustment of economic interests in various sectors. Therefore, while pursuing reforms, it is necessary to have strong and coordinated leadership, along with an equally strong and coordinated macro-control system. The planning of reform must include full investigations and studies. Opinions from various sectors must be solicited and international experiences should be earnestly studied. The aforementioned reform will simplify China's tax system, while at the same time making it more rational in structure and more effective.

Chapter III
Reform of the State-Owned Enterprises

1. Conceptual Issues Concerning Reform of the State-Owned Enterprises

(1) The key to successful reform of enterprises depends on various factors; opinions differ on whether or not the key lies in the reform of the ownership system.

The representative view holds that the key to the success of enterprises does not lie in ownership system.

Most people, including experts from the World Bank, are of the opinion that many facts have demonstrated that there are successes and failures among both public and private enterprises. The key to the success of an enterprise does not lie in ownership system, but rather in whether or not the enterprise dares to face the pressures of market competition and has a flexible management mechanism. Appropriate structural and managerial policies can improve significantly the economic returns of publicly-owned enterprises. This fact is fully proved by the World Bank's booklet entitled *Factors for the Success of Publicly-Owned Enterprises*. It is a general view that the basic problem for China's long-term economic development is how to improve the efficiency, innovative ability and competitiveness of public enterprises. Reform of China's state-owned enterprises is mainly designed to find a practical form for the public economy which will enable it to cooperate with the market economy, and not to practice privatization.

Some experts point out the need to clarify the term of privatization.

Is structural reform meant privatization? We should first of all clarify the meaning of privatization. The narrowest meaning of the word is to allow individuals to own public property. In this sense, structural reform does not mean privatization. This is true due to the fact that in modern economies, even in a capitalist country, major shareholders of large corporations are all legal persons and not individuals. In the English language, the word of privatization can be interpreted in a broader sense as well as in a narrow sense. According to Chinese economist Liu Guoguang, the translation of the word "privatization" as *si you hua* (owned entirely by individuals) is not accurate; rather, according to him, it should be translated as *min ying hua* (civilian management). The world's most famous advocate of privatization is Milton Friedman, an American professor and Nobel Prize winner. During a 1988 lecture tour in China, Professor Friedman mentioned privatization in the broad sense. While we can accept the content of his lecture, we can't accept his term of "private system." He insisted on using the term, because it is opposed to state monopoly and government monopoly, and can be transferred freely, thus called privatization. Due to the language barrier, the original meaning is still quite vague. Somewhat later, Professor Friedman said the word "privatization" should be interpreted as the public ownership we referred to. Since the term of thorough privatization means that something is owned by everybody, and if each person has a share, isn't it a public ownership or ownership by all? This is not meant that Professor Friedman's concept is entirely identical to ours. The point I wish to clarify is that the concept of public ownership and private ownership should be understood in light of actual conditions, and we should not rigidly stick to our original views.

Marxist theory on the socialization of the relationship of property rights is correct, and, therefore, it is also correct to say that public ownership is the main body. However, the form of public ownership and the form of socialization cannot be tied to the old dogma, as set by the former Soviet Union and by Stalin. We should develop the system according to our own conditions.

(2) The fundamental principle of taking the socialist publicly-

owned economy as the main body should remain unchanged, but its connotation and role should be reevaluated.

Up to the end of 1992, China's total state-owned assets valued RMB 3,069.7 billion yuan, 72 percent of which were operational assets. State-owned assets played a leading role in social and economic development, with large and medium-sized state-owned enterprises serving as the pillar of the national economy. The structural reform of the state-owned enterprises is doubtlessly the central link in the reform of China's economic system.

Experts, during their discussions, agreed that the focus of the reform of the state-owned enterprise system rests on the reform of the property rights system, while the crucial issue related to the latter reform is how to understand the socialist public ownership system.

The traditional viewpoint maintains that the fundamental principle of taking the public economy as the main body must be firmly adhered to.

The reason why we must always adhere to the principle of taking the public economy as the main body during the reform is determined by the superiority of public ownership, its economic position and the role it plays in the national economy.

Firstly, public ownership is the basic characteristic of the socialist economic system. The basic goal of socialism is to apply the distribution principle of "to each according to his work," eliminate exploitation and polarization, and finally to accomplish common prosperity. This lofty goal can only be achieved through the system of public ownership.

Secondly, public ownership system facilitates the development of productive forces.

The system of public ownership has altered the nature of labour, and freed it from a position of enslavement. Therefore, it is quite different from the historical state of labour based on slavery, corvée labour and hired labour, and it has achieved new value. In addition to being simply a means of livelihood, it has evolved into a right. Politically conscious people view labour as a need for displaying one's talent, while voluntarily contributing to the state and working for the interests of the public.

Public ownership system facilitates the concentration of human and material resources, thereby making it possible to greatly shorten the primitive accumulation of funds and accelerate the collection of funds. At the same time it helps in the expansion of reproduction and the construction of key projects, production bases and industrial zones.

Public ownership alone has provided the conditions necessary to achieve the maximum integration of planned management and market regulation. Therefore, so long as there are no major mistakes in policy decisions, it is entirely possible to reduce to the greatest extent waste caused by redundant construction and blind production, while maintaining a balance between various major proportional relationships, ensuring the sustained and coordinated development of the national economy, and avoiding the emergence of various types of capitalist economic crises.

Public ownership facilitates overall planning and rational distribution, while harmonizing relationships between regions, enterprises and various links in economic operation. It thus contributes to technological exchanges and development, the rational allocation of resources, lowers investment burdens and reduces investment risk. It also augments the success rate of opening up new markets and helps to strengthen the competitiveness of products on the international market.

Thirdly, China's public economy controls the nation's economic lifeline from all aspects and influences the economic situation. Following decades of a common effort by the Chinese people, the public economy has gained greater strength, with its development having a direct impact on the fundamental interests of the people, and the future and destiny of the state.

Fourthly, the public economy is the foundation and objective basis for socialist cultural and ethical progress. The striking manifestation of this lies in the fact that without the public economy there would be no socialist ideology or the socialist superstructure it determines and the latter in turn serves the public economy.

Fifthly, public ownership has special and highly important significance in China. If China, a vast country with a large population, but relatively limited natural resources, fails to take the public economy as the main body, many of its people will inevitably be deprived of a source of livelihood and the social consequences will be inconceivable.

The reason we must persistently adhere to the fundamental principle of taking the public economy as the mainstay in reform is determined by the nature, tasks and goals of reform.

On the one hand, reform is self-improvement, and not a fundamental negation of the socialist system. Only by adhering to the fundamental principle of taking the public economy as the mainstay can we grasp the correct orientation of reform. Otherwise, any significant reform will be out of the question, and will simply represent historical retrogression.

On the other hand, the fundamental aim of reform is to liberate productive forces, and whether or not this can be achieved mainly depends on whether the public economy, which is considered as the main body, is full of vigor and vitality.

Adhering to the fundamental principle of taking the public economy as the main body requires drawing a clear line of demarcation for privatization, while at the same time correctly understanding and handling the relationship between the public and private economies. In the wake of the implementation of reform and opening, we have relaxed policies which allow the private economy to exist and develop within a specified limit. We have also affirmed in principle the policy that the private economy is a necessary supplement to the socialist public economy, an affirmation which is without any doubt correct. After all, the private economy and public economy are different in nature and will differ in future development. Moreover, the private economy has a dual character under circumstances in which it coexists with the public economy. Generally speaking, the private economy has both positive and negative aspects, and whether or not advantages outweigh disadvantages, or vice versa, depends on how it is guided and managed. We must never place the private economy on a par with the public economy, and nor should we reverse the positions of the "main body" and "supplement."

The typical view is that we should reevaluate the connotation and role of socialist public ownership.

1) "Public ownership" under the planned economic system referred to the public ownership of the means of production, i.e., public ownership in the physical form, while the system of personal ownership can be applied to the means of livelihood. This is determined by the requirements of the planned economy. According to Engels that society will allocate all of these factors on the basis of the plan made in accordance with available resources and overall social demand, and money will become useless.

The characteristics of the socialist market economic structure include: a) In most cases, the physical form of public ownership has appeared unnecessary, and the measurement of assets is realized through the value of commodities and the external form of currency. b) Under circumstances featuring the coexistence of and competition between various economic sectors, the state cannot completely control ordinary means of production, and public ownership of all means of production no longer exist. c) The market economy demands the reallocation of available resources within the scope of the society as a whole in accordance with market law, and public ownership of means of production in physical form obviously is thus contrary to market law. Therefore, socialist public ownership should not simply be the traditional public ownership of means of production, but should instead be public ownership of commodities in value form.

Transformation from the physical form to the value form will not change the foundation of the system of socialist public ownership. Transformation of the physical form of state assets into the value form is carried out in accordance with the principle of exchanges at equal value, with the state recovering capital of the same value while maintaining ownership of the asset in its value form, thereby preventing loss of the asset. The state reinvests the capital in other areas which yield high returns, and thus achieves even greater asset value than that of the original asset. The foundation of socialist public ownership not only will remain unchanged, but will also continually consolidate, develop and expand.

2) The basic role of public ownership under the traditional planned economic system rested with its function as the main body. The mainstay role means that the public economy occupies a dominant position, and exhibits its absolute superiority in terms of the overall national economy. According to Engels, all capital, agriculture, industry, transport services and all business exchanges are increasingly concentrated in the hands of the state. At most, the non-public economy is only a supplement to socioeconomy.

The basic role of public ownership under the conditions of socialist market economy should in fact be its leading role. a) Trades and industries which affect the national economy, the livelihood of the people and social public utilities, as well as those in which it is inadvisable to launch competition, shall be placed under state control and management. b) Ordinary trades and industries shall be developed and managed jointly by the public economy and various non-public economic sectors, with such sectors engaging in equal competition resulting in the promotion of the efficient and elimination of the inefficient. The influence of the public economy should be brought into full play by constantly improving management and raising efficiency. c) In the past, the mainstay role of public ownership was demonstrated mainly by its absolute quantitative superiority in terms of publicly-owned enterprises. In fact, the role of public ownership should not rest in quantity, but rather in quality, i.e., efficiency and competitive capacity. So long as public ownership holds a qualitative dominant position, it is possible to bring its due role into full play. d) The role of the public economy is, in fact, determined by the leading role of the state-owned economy. And, so long as the state-owned economy plays a leading role, public ownership will naturally function its role.

The leading role of public ownership conforms with the theory on the primary stage of socialism. The primary stage of socialism is characterized by the situation which allows the coexistence of a variety of economic sectors with different ownership systems in order to fully develop the socialist market economy and upgrade socialist productive forces. Non-public economies not only supplement the national economy, but are also an economic form which has enjoyed long-term coexistence and common development with the public economy, in spite of the fact that taken as a whole they do not occupy a leading position. Excessive stress on the mainstay position of the public economy, while concentrating everything in the hands of the state and restricting equal competition amongst various economic sectors would greatly weaken the positive role of the non-public economy. This in turn would be disadvantageous to the development of the socialist market economy, and would fail to meet the requirements of the theory and practice of socialism at its primary stage.

Another supplementary viewpoint holds that the dominance of public ownership is not a goal, but simply a means.

The proportion of public ownership and the form it adopts should depend on whether or not it facilitates the development of productive forces.

Traditional public ownership differs in concept from public ownership under the market economy, with changes taken place in both intention and extension. The traditional system stipulated two forms of public ownership—state and collective ownership. In the future, the form of public ownership system will be diversified, with the state ownership as one form in addition to other forms of public ownership such as the shareholding system, institutional and cooperative ownership systems.

Taking public ownership as the leading factor is not a question of quantity, but instead a question of quality.

In the past, we overstressed the proportion of public ownership, thinking that the larger in size and higher the degree, the more advanced it would be, a view which is in fact incomplete. Taking public ownership as the dominant factor should not be reflected in its quantitative proportion only, but rather in the quality of public ownership. Establishing public ownership as the dominant factor means that it has adopted the most advanced technology, it holds the most important position in the national economy, has the highest level of management, and enjoys great vitality and highest economic returns. Should public ownership incur heavy losses like some existing state-owned enterprises, then the larger the proportion of public ownership, the heavier the burden on the government and taxpayers. This form of public ownership as the main body is unacceptable.

The dominance of public ownership is neither self-styled or artificial, nor is it determined by the government. It should be acquired through market competition. If public ownership proves itself to be superior to other forms of ownership in the competition and with more vigor, then its dominant position is well established. The dominant position of public ownership is not solid if it is supported by protectionism or by specially-granted privileges from the government.

The proportion of public ownership changes, sometimes larger and sometimes smaller. Property is fluid, and the main methods of fluidity include: a) transfer of property rights; b) market transactions of public corporate shares; and c) adoption of the system of enterprise bankruptcy.

At present, we should make it clear that under the condition of public ownership as the mainstay, the private economy is "socialist." We should not only protect public property, but also protect legal private property from encroachment.

Enterprise should focus on efficiency, placing efficiency first and fairness second. Enterprises are responsible for efficiency while society should be in charge of fairness. This in fact is the only possible way to enhance the vitality of enterprises.

Yet a third viewpoint centers around the fact that we should develop diversified ownership structures, with multifarious public ownership as the leading factor.

The development of diversified ownership structures with multifarious public ownership as the leading factor is required by the development of the socialist market economy. Individual ownership, the private economy, and various foreign-funded enterprises are not only compatible with the market, but also require the existence and normal operations of the market as preconditions for their existence and development. Individual economies based on autarkies are yet another case. Economy based on cooperative ownership in its real sense, the collectively-owned economy and various economies based on mixed ownership are all compatible with the market to varying degrees. The economy centering on the shareholding system, including the shareholding system based mainly on public corporate shares, is quite naturally all the more inseparably linked with the development and operation of the market. Therefore, developing an economy of diversified ownership is the objective requirement for establishing a socialist market economy. How then does "socialism" in the socialist market economic structure express itself? It is in fact expressed in the structure of diversified ownership dominated by public ownership. The dominance of public ownership does not require that public ownership, especially state ownership, hold proportionally an overwhelming percentage of the national economy. Allowing public ownership, especially state ownership, to hold an overwhelming percentage will be disadvantageous to the growth, and normal and effective operation of the market. What we refer to as "public ownership taken as the leading factor" means that the public economy holds a leading position and plays a leading role in the national economy; it is not required to hold proportionally an overwhelming percentage. So long as departments with natural monopolies, departments target the public good, various departments seeking to meet the common needs of society, others involved in infrastructure facilities, and those which earn little or no profits within a short period of time but are highly significant to the national economy, as well as those departments holding economic lifelines are subject to the control, or basic control of the economy based on public ownership, such an economy will hold the dominant position, play the leading role in economic development and maintain the socialist nature of the national economy. Under these circumstances, the government has sufficient power to direct, guide and regulate market operations, correct the possible loss of the effectiveness of the market, and thus the market can effectively regulate the economy and allocate resources. Here, public ownership is not based solely on state ownership, but instead on diverse forms of public ownership. Developing diversified ownership structures dominated by various forms of public ownership is required by the establishment of a socialist market economy. Such an ownership structure will allow the socialist market economy to operate normally and effectively.

A fourth view holds that changes have already taken place in the traditional concepts of public ownership and private ownership.

There is a great difference between the present public and private ownerships and the classic public and private ownerships of a century ago. In terms of private ownership, Marx pointed out that the socialization of production had resulted in great changes in the development of private ownership from private capitalism to a social capitalist system, or the shareholding company system. The classic private system was carried out by individuals. At present, whether in the United States, Britain, Germany, France and Japan, major shareholders of large companies are corporations. Of course, the situation in different countries varies. In the United States, legal entities are mainly non-banking financiers, such as old-age pension funds, investment companies and foundations. In Japan, over 70 percent of enterprises hold shares of other enterprises, and thus it is sometimes hard to easily tell the owner of a company. Marx pointed out as early as a century ago that the shareholding system had undergone changes, along with changes in the concept of public ownership. According to Marx, public ownership means common ownership by the entire society, without exclusivity. Therefore no one loses his share rights, with everyone having an equal share in communes and common shares being held by society as a whole. Therefore, in his book *Anti-Dühring*, Engels criticized Dühring's commune for the fact that it was not publicly owned, but was instead owned by specific groups. Since the commune was essentially exclusive, the groups had the right to exclude others. The concept of public ownership advanced by Marx changed at the time of Stalin, with the change surfacing at the time of Lenin, who said that a cooperative system could be integrated with the socialist system. As a result, the entire view of socialism changed. How then did it change? The change resulted from Lenin's recognition of collective ownership as public ownership. Stalin added yet another point that the society as a whole with a common share should be realized by the organization of the state. Therefore, it is quite obvious that the concept of public ownership changes all the time.

A major breakthrough achieved during the 14th National Congress of the Communist Party of China is the decision it has made that socialism can have a market economy, and likewise there should be major advances in the understanding of ownership.

After analysing relationship between modern productive forces and the relationship of production, Marx pointed out: Socialization of ownership should be realized along with the socialization of productive forces. This principle is correct and remains true even today. Of course, the productive forces of a society are found at multiple levels, and not all are highly socialized. For example, shoe repair is less socialized. In terms of socialized productive forces, there should be a socialized relationship of production to control productive forces. Therefore, ownership should also be socialized. However, in light of the practice of modern society, we can see that the socialization of the property right relationship is diversified in form. New forms of ownership have emerged in addition to existing state ownership, collective ownership and cooperative ownership.

(3) Marketization of state assets is not tantamount to privatization.

During discussions, many experts spoke in favour of marketization of state assets. They held this view because the key point in enterprise reform is the question of property rights, a question which is not only an issue of clarification, but also an issue concerning internal mechanisms. Under conditions of a market economy, this issue involves a series of questions, including the ownership of property rights, definition, circulation and the operation of property rights. In fact, it includes how to effectively manage, allocate and operate state assets as a whole. A mere effort to push state-owned enterprises to the market is not powerful enough to escape the traditional framework in the management of state assets and free from the shackles of administrative mechanisms. This will eventually lead to a restoration of the old system. The correct solution to the question is to steer state assets to the market. This is the fundamental issue regarding property rights and also the fundamental requirement of the socialist market economy.

Implications related to marketizing state assets include:

a) State assets enjoy full circulation on the capital market, property rights can be transferred and regrouped in accordance with the law of market competition so as to realize the optimum allocation of resources.

b) In the market circulation state assets pursue the maximum monetary value to realize maximum economic returns. The value of state assets not only must be maintained, but should yield even greater value.

c) State assets are allowed to operate independently on the market. Generally speaking, the state is not directly involved in the management of such assets. State assets are mainly under the operation of enterprise corporations, which enjoy corporate ownership of state assets.

d) State assets should be put under a unified management, a combination of centralized and decentralized management. Generally speaking, the management of state assets should be indirectly conducted through intermediate operational organizations, so as to guarantee that such assets operate independently on the market, free from direct administrative interference.

Some people have expressed either doubt or worry about this approach, asking whether the marketization of state assets will lead to privatization.

However, the general view is that marketization of state assets is not tantamount to privatization.

The circulation and transfer of state assets and related property rights on the market are not compensation free, but instead such assets are transferred at equal value and with compensation. These assets are still owned by the state. Therefore, under conditions of the socialist market economy, public ownership in physical form has changed into the value form, but it remains unchanged in nature.

However, when pushing state assets into the market, we should adhere to the following principles:

a) A small group of trades and industries under state monopoly should not be guided into the market, but should be placed under state management directly.

b) In general, state-owned shareholding enterprises should retain their state shareholding position. In accordance with traditional theory, shareholdings should reach 51 percent of all shares. In fact, under circumstances wherein stock rights are fairly scattered, the figure can be much lower than the traditionally stock split.

c) When transferring state assets and related property rights, we should consider the leading role of public ownership in important economic sectors so as to ensure that the economy based on non-public ownership will not completely monopolize or control certain important economic areas.

d) In terms of concrete operations, we should guard against any loss of state assets, strengthen supervision mechanisms and enforce strict evaluations of state assets.

(4) Economy based on management by individuals does not mean "turning public into private," it provides a way out in the reform of state-owned enterprises

An important operational form for marketizing state assets is to retain state ownership of such assets but under civilian management so as to meet the requirements of the development of the market economy, while at the same time allowing some state assets to be owned by the people and under their management.

Some people cringe at the mention of civilian management, thinking it means heading for privatization. The following example cited during discussions fully illustrates the point. In early 1993, the media carried widespread reports on the practice of state ownership and civilian management in several thousand small commercial enterprises in Beijing. One report warned that Beijing, the capital, should pay attention to the issue, and should refrain from arbitrarily advocating "civilian management." This particular view was highly representative of the thinking of some people, who insisted that "civilian management" equates to "turning public into private" and "privatization."

Most people maintain that "civilian management" does not mean "privatization," so "turning public into private" is simply out of the question.

Regarding enterprises based on state ownership but under civilian management, the property rights of the enterprises are still owned by the state, and there is simply a change in the form of management. Even with some state-owned enterprises whose property rights are bought or incorporated by collectives or individuals, such transfers in property rights do not equate to "turning public into private." The reasons for this are as follows: First, the property rights are sold for equal value and they are not transferred without compensation. Therefore it is only a change in the form of assets, a change from their physical form to their monetary form, which are then invested in infrastructure facilities, basic industries and other areas in which the state is in dire need of investment. Such changes facilitate the readjustment of structure and improvements in efficiency. Second, such transfers of property rights may appear to be a change from public to private, but are, in essence, the best form for revitalizing operational mechanisms. It is effective for both sides when individuals purchase the property rights of state-owned enterprise. On the one hand, the value of property rights is fully retained in the hands of the state which can thus rid itself of problems resulting from the exclusive rights of assets, and the state can again place itself in an equal or even more advantageous position with its rivals. On the other hand, the reason the particular use value of property rights comes to an individual entrepreneur in an enterprise under management by individuals is because he has already made specific considerations and plans in terms of transaction expenses and concrete production arrangement. Upon assuming the control of machinery and equipment, the entrepreneur can make an all-out effort. Third, we must draw a clear line of demarcation between value and use value. Marxist economists hold that the value of commodities reflects and determines the relationship of production, while use value is the natural attribute of commodities, and it does not specify the relationship of production. As mentioned earlier that the exchange is based on equal values, a situation in which neither the state loses nor the individual gains, a single penny. Moreover, even if the buyer later uses the assets to engage in business and reap huge profits, this has nothing to do with the state (the seller).

Experts contend that one way out for the reform of state-owned enterprises is to retain state ownership but place them under civilian management, or change both ownership and management by individuals, while at the same time efforts should be made to fully develop the economy run by individuals, and truly transform the operational mechanisms of enterprises.

In this case, the concept should be clarified first of all that socialist economy is made up by the economy of the whole people, the collective economy and private economy plus other forms of economies. One cannot think that one type of economy alone or a certain types of economies as socialist economy, let alone regarding one or several types of economies as being closer to capitalism, and other types of economies as being closer to socialism. Nor can one think all state-owned assets as being superior to others. In the final analysis, superiority should be based on three standards—facilitating the development of productive forces, enhancing the overall national strength and improving the living standards of the people—a concept advanced by Deng Xiaoping. The correct approach is to provide everybody with equal opportunity under the circumstance of a socialist market economy. Besides, the concept of the "natural leading position" of state-owned enterprises must be abandoned. In other words, the leading position of state-owned enterprises is neither "natural" nor inherent. Like all other enterprises, the key to whether or not state-owned enterprises can play a leading role in the development of national economy depends on whether or not they can gain superiority over others through equal competitions on the market. Special favours granted previously to the state-owned enterprises through planning and administrative methods in investment funds, price setting, taxation and credit loans will become fewer and fewer as the market economy matures. As a result, the leading position of state-owned enterprises based on administrative means and state planning will gradually die out. This in turn will gradually place both the economy run by individuals and state-owned economy in an equal position of free competition. On the other hand, some non-standard practices of the economy run by individuals during the first few years will be gradually eliminated along with the gradual improvement of the legal system. A further analysis reveals that it would be inappropriate to say now that this economic sector is "supplementary," holding only an "auxiliary" position and playing only a "secondary" role. This is not only incompatible with the aforementioned argument concerning equal competition amongst various economic sectors, but also with facts. For example, in China today, the state-run economy is the largest in terms of scale, but in terms of economic returns the economy run by individuals comes first. During the 11 years of reform and opening carried out between 1980 and 1991, the economic returns of this economic sector grew by 38-fold, an inconceivable figure for the state-run economy.

(5) Legal entities of state-owned enterprises should hold ownership and enterprise corporations should be the assemblage of all members.

The current theory on the structure of property rights of state-owned enterprises holds that the relationship between the state and enterprises is one that separates ownership from management. The state retains the ownership of state-owned enterprises, while state-owned enterprise corporations have managerial rights over enterprise property as independent economic entities, and retain their predominant position in terms of independent management.

According to this theory of separating the two rights, the state and state-owned enterprise become two legally independent mainstays. In terms of state-owned enterprises, it represents the separation of two rights existing outside enterprises. Therefore it is called "external" structure that separates the two rights, different from the "internal" separation of rights within the enterprise corporation. This includes the structure that separates ownership and managerial rights between the board of shareholders and the board of directors (limited stock companies), or between the board of directors and the general manager of a limited liability company within the corporation. It also separates internal organizations of the company which are not independent legal main bodies. Experts maintain that the current doctrine on the separation of ownership from managerial rights was adopted as an important theory and measure at the very beginning of reform, and that achievements gained under its guidance should be fully affirmed. However, many difficulties emerged between theory and the practice of the socialist market economy, and it was quite difficult to meet the requirements of the new system. For example, it was impossible to gain a concrete grasp of the concept and connotation of managerial rights and it was theoretically vague. The result will likely be either that there are little differences between managerial rights and ownership, or that it may become ownership merely. Besides, under the condition of the market economy, the mainstay of the market economy must be independent owners of commodities, and the exchange and transfer of commodities will inevitably result in a shift in ownership. Otherwise it will violate the market economic law, and is thus inconceivable in terms of market economic activities. Finally, it is difficult to solve the following questions: How to separate the two rights? What is the substantive standard for the separation? Where is the dividing line? Theoretically it is quite difficult to give a clear explanation to all those questions, and it is also impossible to handle correctly in practice. The many difficult problems existing in the theory of separation of the two rights should be regarded as important reasons for the difficulties faced by the reform in state-owned enterprises.

Experts proposed that under the condition of socialist market economy, we should transform the separation of two rights from externally to internally. This means to transform the separation of the two rights currently existing only outside state-owned enterprises into separation of the two rights inside enterprises, while at the same time recognizing and establishing corporate ownership of state-owned enterprises in order to meet the internal requirements of the market economy.

The question remains: Will the change from external into internal separation structure of the two rights and the establishment of the corporate ownership of enterprises mean that the state will lose ownership of enterprise property, and thus the ownership by the whole people will change into collective ownership or generate "privatization"?

Even though experts are in unanimous agreement that the answer is negative, they hold two different view in regard to theoretical basis.

The first viewpoint centers on an exploration of the theory of a legal person.

Enterprise corporations are a form of a corporate aggregate composed of all members of the corporation. Enterprise corporations are not fictitious legal civilian mainstays, but instead are based on a mass organization as the legally stipulated foundation. As the major shareholder of state-owned companies and a member of their corporate aggregate, the state decides on how best to exercise a company's corporate ownership. State ownership of a company's stocks is legally intermingled with the company's corporate ownership, which is in essence ownership by all of the company's corporate members, including the ownership of the state. The establishment of the ownership of an enterprise corporation will not lead to the state's loss of ownership of enterprise property, but instead improves the effectiveness of the state in exercising its ownership. A point well worth noting is that the ownership of enterprise corporations is not tantamount to "enterprise ownership." Enterprise ownership is in fact an ambiguous concept, which is understood either as ownership by the enterprise collective organization, or as ownership of the director and manager of the enterprise. The difference between enterprise corporate ownership and enterprise ownership lies in the fact that the ownership mainstay of the former is the enterprise corporation which is an assemblage of all members. It is thus different from enterprise workers and staff, director and manager, and it is also different from any individual corporate members. Therefore, enterprise corporate ownership will not result in changing enterprise property into either collective ownership by workers and staff or personal ownership by the director or manager.

The second viewpoint is based on theory on state economic ownership, according to which state ownership is divided into state economic ownership and enterprise corporate ownership.

Corporate ownership of state-owned enterprises is in fact state ownership of property. The corporation is created by relying on others and engages in external activities in its own name. Once the investors complete the funding process, the corporation is established and becomes independent of the investor with autonomy to act in its own name, with the investor having no right to withdraw his property, nor to allocate, use and dispose of enterprise property. Corporate ownership cannot be inherited as can ownership of the natural man. Along with the loss of the status as a legal person, the property ownership of the corporation is also lost, with remaining property returning to the original investor. Corporate ownership is in fact exercised by the legal representative recruited and appointed by the owner of the enterprise, i.e. shareholders, or by a legal institution organized by shareholders.

Under conditions of a modern market economy, the enterprise is the main body of market operation, while the state provides macro-control outside normal market operations. The precondition for an enterprise to become the main body of market operations is possession of the rights to independently dispose of property and to be able to undertake legal liabilities based on such rights. This requires that the various functions of state ownership to be exercised by the enterprise. As an investor in the state-owned enterprise, the state possesses the capital and rights and interests of the enterprise, and based on the strength of funds contributed enjoys the right to recruit management staff of the enterprise and the right to claim the property of a defunct corporation. While in existence, a state-owned enterprise enjoys the right to independently hold, use, profit from and dispose of property.

Precisely because the state enjoys economic ownership of the property of state-owned enterprises, the establishment of corporate ownership of state-owned enterprises will not lead to the loss of ownership by the state. In terms of actual operations, the question remains as to whether or not the division of state ownership into ultimate ownership and corporate ownership will lead to the existence of state ownership in name only, or to the actual transformation of enterprise ownership worthy of the name. These questions must be resolved when establishing enterprise corporate ownership.

Protecting the ultimate ownership of the state, while at the same time refraining from interfering in the property rights of enterprise corporations, requires that we proceed in light of the separation of the dual functions of the government, and establish a set of comprehensive and effective organizational systems for specialized management of ownership. Specialized ownership management institutions have four responsibilities: basic management of ownership, management of new forms of ownership, management of profit, and management of the selection and appraisal of corporate leaders of state-owned enterprises.

When considering the country's hundreds of thousands of state-owned enterprises, it will be far from an easy matter for the final ownership management institution at the government level to fulfill the aforementioned responsibilities which have been subject to repeated alternations, refinements and simplifications. At present, we should encourage annexation, mergers and cross shareholding between corporations of state-owned enterprises through various economic and administrative means. Certain enterprises with interconnections should be incorporated into a large company in line with necessary administrative authorization which will make them fully-funded subsidiaries or associated companies. Trade corporations should be transformed into corporations without government functions. Various small state-owned enterprises should be sold in order to recover capital, or should be reorganized into state shareholding companies or asset operating companies. The central government can easily manage 1,000 large enterprises, while various provincial and municipal local governments can manage 100 medium-sized enterprises each. At the same time, certain functions of ultimate state ownership can be entrusted to large companies to ensure that final ownership remains in the right hands.

2. Methods for Reforming Property Rights of State-Owned Enterprises

With regard to the reform of the property rights of state-owned enterprises, experts agree that existing enterprises should be transformed in accordance with their specific type, and different forms and methods should be adopted for the transformation of different types of enterprises. However, some minor differences emerge with regard to concrete ways and specific methods to be adopted for classifying transformations.

The typical view is that state-owned enterprises should be classified into state-owned and managed enterprises, enterprises owned by the state but run by other entities, state-owned shareholding enterprises, and state-owned enterprises run by individuals.

1) State-owned and managed enterprises

This category refers to enterprises directly managed by state organizations, or by institutions directly associated with competent departments. Included in this category are a small number of trades and industries subject to state monopoly, where free competition is considered inappropriate.

These enterprises are not encouraged to enter the market and their property rights are not transferable. However, there are examples of such enterprises abroad having adopted the shareholding system.

2) State-owned enterprises run by other entities

Enterprises under this category include the following: a) Infrastructure facilities and other key projects controlled by the state, as well as enterprises implementing mandatory planning, and enterprises suffering serious losses but cannot declare bankruptcy, nor to be abandoned. Such enterprises need not be managed by the state itself, they can be entrusted, contracted or leased to other economic entities which possess relative strength and operational capabilities, for the purpose of improving management. b) Enterprises which need not adopt the shareholding system or enterprises which operate better by other entities than under the shareholding system. These include small retail commercial ventures, small industrial enterprises and tertiary industries. Enterprises such as these, small in staff and funds, but far-reaching in services, are suitable for decentralized management and are allowed to adopt contract and leasing systems in management.

Generally speaking, the management rights of these enterprises should be transferred through the market. They can adopt entrusted management, contracting and leasing management.

When necessary, such enterprises can be transformed into shareholding enterprises or enterprises based on civilian management.

3) State-owned shareholding enterprises

In addition to situations suitable for the aforementioned state-owned enterprises, other large and medium-sized state-owned enterprises can be reorganized by adopting the shareholding system, i.e., transforming them into companies. Legal forms of shareholding enterprises include limited stock companies and limited liability companies, as well as special "one-person companies," also known as exclusively funded limited companies.

State-owned shareholding enterprises enjoy corporate ownership of companies and have the right to dispose of enterprise property according to operational requirements. They have the right to sell fixed assets, dispose of surplus idle assets, mutually regulate property, mutually hold or transfer stock rights, engage in stock transactions, and in some cases auction or annex entire enterprises. Corporate ownership of a company in no way contradicts state ownership, because the state, as the largest shareholder and a member of the corporation aggregate of the company, decides on how to exercise corporate ownership of the company. State ownership of company stock is legally merged with the corporate ownership of the company, and, in essence, corporate ownership of the company is the ownership of all corporate members of the company, including state ownership itself.

4) Enterprises run by individuals

This category refers to state-owned enterprises changed into non-state enterprises based on management by individuals. They include mainly some small and medium-sized state-owned enterprises insignificant to the national economy, and state-owned enterprises which incur serious losses and need not be retained. Hence, transforming them into enterprises run by individuals is conducive to promoting economic development and improving productive forces, and the change will not affect the leading position of the public economy.

Placing state-owned enterprises under management by individuals is usually accomplished through property rights transactions market, incorporation or auctions.

Others contend that property right reform consists of five methods—authorized management, stock management, ownership and management by individuals, state ownership and management by individuals, and grafted management.

While China's economic reform over the last dozen of years has achieved successes in a number of aspects, reform of state-owned enterprises has been unsuccessful. Numerous methods have been adopted for the reform of state-owned enterprises and great effort has been extended to carry out the process. However, state-owned enterprises have not as yet been able to adapt to the development of the market economy. Why has such a situation emerged? The main reason lies in the failure to rationalize the relationship of property rights. Firstly, we are unclear about the asset value of enterprises, with currently bookkeeping including only the original and net value of fixed assets, and not the current value of enterprise assets. Nor are we clear about the proportion of fixed assets belonging to the state and that belonging to non-state entities. We have not yet established a set of rational property right organizations or a system of administration and management. In fact, state-owned enterprises are nominally referred to as "state ownership by the masses," with no one has been assigned to bear responsibility. This is especially true when enterprises are still under direct government management as appendages of government departments which are under no restraints in terms of restricting and interfering in operations of enterprises, but which at the same time bear no responsibility. On the other hand, enterprises can simply "eat from the same big pot." Today, however, many people have come to realize that the first requirement for solving problems of enterprises is to solve problems related to enterprise property rights. They understand that this is the only possible way to separate the government from enterprises, while at the same time separating the two rights of management and administration in order to allow enterprises to engage in independent management and assume sole responsibility for their own profits and losses. The following ideas have been advanced for resolving problems related to property rights:

1) For a small number of state-owned enterprises, including mainly enterprises under relative monopolies or key enterprises, we can introduce a responsibility system under which state assets can be placed under authorized or entrusted management. In this way the state retains final ownership of the enterprise property, and assigns the day-to-day management and allocations right over to the enterprise. For example, this method is used at the Capital Iron and Steel Co. The adoption of this form must meet the following requirements:

a) in conformity with state industrial policies;
b) with relatively stable resources and demand conditions;
c) with outstanding and authoritative managers.

2) Property rights must be clearly defined due to the fact that most enterprises can only be transformed into limited liability companies. Property rights must also be delineated for enterprises in which the state has the major share, especially if they are not managed by a single state department, but by several departments which the state has entrusted management and administration. Enterprises should be free of direct government interference, and should have a board of directors, separ-

ate the government from the enterprise. The two rights are separated by management methods featured in the shareholding system. When taken as a unit, an enterprise should engage in independent management and assume sole responsibility for profits and losses.

3) Auctioning large numbers of small state-owned enterprises, thereby transforming them into enterprises run by individuals.

4) State ownership and individual management. Contracting state assets to individuals with the state collecting rent.

5) Grafted management. Foreign investors and township enterprises are allowed to invest in state-owned enterprises, with state assets in turn converting into funds of either of the two entities. Original methods cannot be used once this form of joint venture is adopted, a fact will automatically alter the situation in which there is no distinction between the government and enterprises.

A third view holds that methods for the transformation of state-owned property rights include the shareholding system, enterprise ownership, the sale of property rights, and ownership and management by individuals.

A method of pincer attack from both within and without can be used in transforming the property rights of state ownership. One method is to use the shareholding system to transform state-owned enterprises, a method commonly known as "blending with sand" or altering the original management method by absorbing foreign capital, domestic private capital and township enterprise capital. This in turn would generate a mechanism characterized by independent management, self-responsibility for profits and losses, self-development and self-restraint. While this is indeed a good method, we should understand that the universal introduction of the shareholding system for state-owned enterprises in China will be a long process and that its experimentation has just started.

Therefore, we can adopt a second method based on the establishment of "enterprise ownership" in state-owned enterprises. The current value of state assets originally controlled by state-owned enterprises should be determined through clearing and appraisal of assets before being placed under enterprises for use with due compensation. Enterprises shall pay asset taxes (rental) to the state in accordance with the current interest rates. After-tax profits will revert to enterprises and will be used to establish development, risk and welfare funds to which enterprises then have the full right of allocation. This in turn provides enterprises with a solid economic foundation for generating mechanisms characterized by independent management, self-responsibility for profits and losses, self-development and self-restraint, and creates conditions necessary for developing the shareholding system. Investing and purchasing shares is insignificant between state asset holders, and a genuine shareholding system can only be established through mutual investment and purchases of shares between owners of enterprises with independent property rights.

We can also sell a large number of small enterprises, including their property rights. One method is to sell an enterprise to the workers and staff, enabling them to establish a cooperative system in which all workers and staff provide labour and hold shares. A second method is to sell an enterprise to individuals, in the primary stage of socialism private economy should be allowed to have a relatively big development.

Some state-owned enterprises can be retained, including non-profitable public utilities, extra large projects (such as the Three Gorges Project) or high-tech industries which involve large investments and require long construction periods, but yield slow returns. While such projects are suited during construction to use primarily state investment, once completed they can be transformed into projects based on management by individuals with shares issued to society.

The transformation of state-owned property rights is an extremely complicated matter which can in no way be properly completed for at least several decades.

3. The Issue of Transforming State-Owned Enterprises into Companies

The general view of experts concerning existing state-owned enterprises is that those to be retained or transformed into enterprises owned and managed by the state itself, or owned by the state but managed by others or managed by individuals will be small in number. Numerous large and medium-sized state-owned enterprises should be reorganized into shareholding enterprises, namely, they should be transformed into companies. The mainstay of the modern market economy is based largely on various forms of companies. Nonetheless, transforming state-owned enterprises into companies will be an arduous task.

Discussions have yielded a number of concrete opinions regarding just which organizational forms should be adopted for transforming state-owned enterprises into companies, as well as the concrete method for the transformation.

One view holds that the transformation of state-owned enterprises into companies should include the following three forms:

1) Stock limited companies. This form applies to enterprises which need to raise massive funding from the public, while at the same time decentralizing risks. Such companies can list their stocks on the market, while directional fund-raising limited stock companies can transfer stock rights on the stock market.

2) Limited liability companies. This form applies to joint ventures, as well as cooperative, associated and group enterprises, and relatively closed enterprises which mutually hold and purchase shares. This particular type of companies do not openly issue stock to the society, but their stocks can be transferred on the stock market with approval of the board of shareholders or board of directors.

3) Exclusively funded limited companies, also known as "one-person companies," are a special form of the shareholding system involving only one shareholder who assumes limited responsibility. This particular form applies to exclusively state-funded enterprises. With the exception of the aforementioned

situations applicable to stock limited companies and limited liability companies, all remaining large and medium-sized state-owned enterprises which will be transformed into shareholding enterprises can adopt the form of exclusively funded limited companies, and as such can introduce a leadership system based on a board of directors. Exclusively funded companies are allowed to transfer all stock rights on the stock market. If only limited portion of stock rights are transferred, the enterprise will be classified as limited liability companies.

A similar viewpoint holds that the organizational form of companies includes exclusively state-funded companies, and limited liability companies in which shares are held by a corporation based on public ownership and stock companies based mainly on public ownership.

With regard to the transformation of state-owned enterprises in line with a specific company structure, it is necessary to distinguish the specific situations of enterprises and adopt different organizational forms of companies. These mainly include exclusively state-funded companies, limited liability companies wherein shares are held by publicly owned corporations and stock limited companies based mainly on public ownership.

—The form based on exclusively state-funded companies can be adopted for certain enterprises whose establishment depends on state investments such as large infrastructure facilities, enterprises with a poor prospects of profitability and individuals are unwilling to invest, but which at the same time must be developed, as well as other enterprises in which individuals lack the ability to invest.

—Most large and medium-sized state-owned enterprises can be reorganized into limited liability companies, wherein shares are held by publicly owned corporations.

—Certain large and medium-sized state-owned enterprises can be reorganized into stock companies based mainly on public ownership where shares are held either by corporations or by workers and staff. This system allows workers and staff to hold shares, with the corporation being responsible for the directional collection of shares.

—A small number of enterprises can be reorganized into limited collective stock companies based mainly on public ownership through the open issue of stocks to raise funds. And a small portion of these enterprises can be transformed into listed stock companies.

At present, a series of policy documents related to China's limited liability and stock companies provide an initial policy basis and standards for the transformation of state-owned enterprises in line with the shareholding system. Notwithstanding, it is necessary to clarify that policies concerning the transformation of state-owned enterprises into exclusively state-funded companies must emphasize the following points:

Firstly, exclusively state-funded companies can adopt a variety of organizational forms, including the single company form oriented directly towards the government. Other company forms include state holding, investment, and group companies. These particular types of companies can adopt various forms such as shareholding, purchasing shares, mergers and investments to promote the transformation of the operational mechanisms of a large batch of state-owned enterprises, making them subsidiary shareholding companies. Another form involves the government entrusting the management of exclusively state-funded companies to group companies or state asset management companies, thereby making them solely funded subsidiaries under state holding companies.

Secondly, in the early stages of transformation and in line with the form of the company, more trades and enterprises can be transformed into exclusively state-funded companies. The transformation of state-owned enterprises into exclusively state-funded companies will enable enterprises to operate on the basis of the existing Corporation Law, a move which is in turn conducive to the separation of the government from enterprises, granting enterprises independent management and self-responsibility for profits and losses, and laying a solid foundation for further promoting the transformation in line with the shareholding system. From a long-term point of view, the state mainly controls some holding companies and group companies which are in the minority, they nonetheless have enormous strength which will in turn promote the development of a large group of small and medium-sized enterprises subject to either state or mixed ownership.

Thirdly, the board of directors, a system which will be instituted in exclusively state-funded companies and is regarded as the ownership organization of these companies, will have the right to make major decisions relating to production and management. Members of the board of directors are selected, seated, appointed or dismissed by the state asset ownership agency authorized by the government.

Fourthly, special laws, regulations and policies should be implemented to standardize the relationship of the responsibility, rights and interests of the government and boards of directors and respective members. They are laws similar to those various foreign countries have enacted to deal specifically with state-owned companies. For example, the Renault Co. of France and the Iri Co. of Italy act in accordance with special regulations formulated by their respective governments, with said regulations determining the relationship between the government and enterprises. The basic characteristics of the laws will be formed by the government acting in its capacity as owner, and will mainly be designed to readjust the relationship between the state as the final owner and the board of directors, which in itself is in fact the management responsibility system of the board of directors. Companies themselves are established and operate in accordance with the unified principles of the Corporation Law.

Fifthly, in the absence of the aforementioned laws, we have the option to adopt relatively comprehensive contract forms such as the management and contracting of assets which are designed to handle the relationship between the government and the company in order to provide effective incentives and restrictive mechanisms.

A third view is that we should establish public stock companies with reorganized ownership.

Many people are of the opinion that the shareholding system is acceptable for state-owned enterprises. An expert who formerly worked for the World Bank provided the following systematic analysis of this particular question. Firstly, we should reorganize state-owned enterprises into stock companies, a standard practice under the market economy which can be completed in one to two years. Reorganization will in turn allow enterprises to raise their economic returns. Thereafter, the ownership structure should be rearranged by transforming government-controlled enterprises into enterprises controlled by certain public organizations which show concern for profits and exercise effective supervision over management.

Reorganization of the ownership of public stock companies refers to the rearrangement of state-owned property rights, and distributing the effective property rights of enterprises to several different public organizations, each of which is concerned solely with enterprise profits, and not with output value, purchases or marketing, nor with the industrial wages of the enterprise. In principle, state-owned enterprises are owned by the people as a whole. However, in accordance with past practices in China, each state-owned enterprise has been regarded as property exclusively owned by a central department, or by respective local governments. Some people believe that state-owned enterprises actually belong to the workers and staff of the enterprise. This particular tendency has emerged in practice in recent years in order to grant greater decision-making power to enterprises and provide stronger material incentives to workers. However, neither past practices nor recent changes have yet yielded satisfactory results. Moreover, in terms of performance and competitiveness, the sharp contrast between China's state-owned and non-state enterprises has caused an increasing number of people to regard the question of ownership as the key issue related to publicly owned enterprises. However, due to the fact that non-state enterprises themselves are also publicly owned by township and village governments, the contrasts also indicate that structural reform of public ownership can play an important role in solving the problems of state-owned enterprises.

One proposal suggests reorganizing the current pattern of state ownership so as to allow enterprises to rid themselves of their current status as appendages of certain departments or local governments, and distribute their ownership into the hands of several public organizations which will mainly be concerned with profits, rather than with output value, volume of purchases, employment or wages of the enterprises. This type of organizations include administrative bureaus responsible for state assets both at the central and local levels, banks, old-age pension funds and insurance companies. Implementing the proposal will present no apparent difficulties, and we simply need to transform each state-owned enterprise into a stock company, thereafter allowing related institutions to hold a certain proportion of shares in the company. Using legal methods to manage state-owned enterprises is a common practice in other countries. Even in cases where all shares in an enterprise are held by one public organization, such as the Ministry of Finance, or by a certain state holding company, implementation of the proposal will help transform state-owned enterprises, which in turn will yield economic achievements. While the method of distributing the ownership of public enterprises into the hands of several institutions is seldom used, it is nonetheless quite common and highly successful in Germany.

It is quite important that we must clarify the implications of the term of "being concerned with profits," and clearly define the necessity of the motive in regard to state-owned enterprises. In fact, the Chinese economy emphasizes the fact that state-owned enterprises should assume sole responsibility for profits and losses.

At this point, we will proceed from this now familiar topic to an even more common subject, i.e. the profit rate. In our judgment the most appropriate target for determining the efficiency and innovative ability of an enterprise is its profit rate, taking into consideration the deduction of capital, interest and depreciation. However, determinations of this type are dependent on three basic specified conditions. Firstly, it is necessary to reform prices and strengthen competition to ensure profit rates will become a relatively accurate efficiency index in China. Secondly, the term refers to China's long-term, rather than short-term or speculative profits. Finally, certain key state-owned enterprises, such as public welfare enterprises and national defence industries, should refrain from the sole pursuit of profits. However, this in no way implies that such enterprises should neglect profits.

China has a relatively solid foundation for the establishment of public stock companies with reorganized ownership. Although China's state-owned enterprises have seen little change in ownership or the management system over the past decade or so, tremendous changes have nonetheless taken place in many other aspects which have had sufficient impact to affect future development. These include: a) The gradual decline in the proportion of the scale of state-owned enterprises to their industrial output which has compelled them to raise efficiency and improve management, while at the same time the state is given the condition to gradually and carefully consider problems related to reform. b) The practice of establishing joint-stock companies has been widely accepted and useful experiences have been gained, thereby laying a solid foundation for large-scale implementation of the practice. c) The establishment of stock markets has provided Chinese shareholders with a strong sense in stock purchases. Although the government permits individuals and foreigners to hold stocks in various state-owned enterprises, it prohibits the large-scale privatization of such enterprises. d) Implementation of reforms of the unemployment insurance, pension and housing systems, as well as the policy on separating profits from taxes have gradually clarified the demarcation line of state-owned enterprises.

The above analysis has led us to the conclusion that while further deepening reforms in various sectors, other reforms should be carried out with regard to large and medium-sized state-owned enterprises in the industrial and commercial sectors. They include: a) Establishing joint-stock companies, with ownership placed initially under the control of the country's state-owned assets administrative bureaus, with final ownership to be determined at a later date. While such companies are applicable to all types of market economies, they are naturally applicable to the socialist market economy. b) Rearranging ownership, with the major shares being distributed to organizations which are important to the interest relationships of the enterprise and which have the capacity to control the behaviour of enterprise management. Remaining shares can be distributed to middlemen of enterprises and other investors. c) Continuing with self-improvement by further drawing on experiences from the reform of state-owned enterprises in East European countries, as well as from the development of holding companies in other countries, and also from China's own reform practices.

A fourth opinion holds that we should actively promote the reform by adopting the shareholding system based mainly on non-monopolistic holding of stocks.

Proposals for large and medium-sized state-owned enterprises to adopt the shareholding system have gained increasing approval along with the establishment of the socialist market economy and the debate over whether the shareholding system is by nature socialist or capitalist. However, there are different views as to whether or not, and how the shareholding system should be implemented in most large and medium-sized state-owned enterprises during a short- or medium-term period. Specific theoretical problems and those actually encountered in practice include: a) At least two-thirds of state-owned enterprises are, in fact, suffering losses, and it is thus impracticable to directly introduce the shareholding system to such enterprises, for no one is interested in purchasing stock rights in loss-making enterprises. b) It is highly possible that enterprises will be subject to even tighter control if fundamental reform of government organizations is not carried out and original competent departments retain control of state shares. c) Sole reliance on the shareholding system will not solve problems such as no workers or staff are allowed to be unemployed and enterprises have to support society. d) Due to the fact that the Corporation Law and the Securities Law have not as yet been promulgated, and the accounting system has not been brought into line with generally accepted international practices, the implementation of the shareholding system on a large scale could lead to chaos. e) Viewed from the fact that many problems exist during the experimentation of the shareholding system, including underestimates of state assets and discrimination against the state share in profits distribution, implementation of the shareholding system on a large scale could possibly lead to the serious loss of state assets. A point well worth mentioning in regard to the aforementioned problems is that even though they actually exist or are likely to appear to varying degrees, they do not, however, constitute an excuse for refraining from adoption of shareholding system. They simply indicate the complexity and arduousness in the adoption of the shareholding system. Implementation of the shareholding system represents fundamental reform of the traditional enterprise system. Therefore, it involves every aspect of the enterprise system and even the entire economic structure, and the selection of tactics for the implementation, as well as the time schedule and the design of concrete operational methods are vitally important. At the same time, the adoption of the shareholding system will inevitably affect the existing interest pattern and will most likely bring about profit-making opportunities. Therefore, we must pay attention to readjusting the interest relationship and accelerate the process of reform by making good use of the orientation of interests.

The focal points and time schedule for the implementation of the shareholding system include:

1) Establishing special state assets management organizations directly under the standing committee of people's congresses at various levels based on existing state assets management organizations and personnel of the specialized competent departments. In consideration of the large amount of work required during the period of reform, a number of special working committees should be formed in state assets management committees on a departmental basis. The number and size of committees can be appropriately reduced following the successful conclusion of the reform effort. State assets management committees will be the legal representatives and management organizations of state assets at

various levels. Their main responsibilities will be to formulate state assets management plans, audit and supervise the preservation and increases in the value of state assets, determine allocations of state assets, and appoint and dismiss leading personnel in state assets operational organizations.

2) Dividing property rights. The existing enterprise property is divided into the property rights of the central and local governments at various levels, as well as other types of property rights. Prior to any division, we should undertake a thorough clearing and a comprehensive appraisal of the assets of enterprises. When doing so we should adopt an extensive and simple rather than intensive and complicated approach, and solve disputes through consultations. In the division of property rights we can formulate either unified implementation rules for the whole country or detailed rules for the localities. As representatives controlling property rights, state assets management committees at various levels should actively participate in the division of such rights.

Questions related to the division of state property rights between the central and local authorities require further in-depth study. Existing options are based on two formulas: The first formula is based on the proposition that the final ownership of state assets belongs to the central government, while local property rights are a concrete form of the management of state assets which the central government entrusts to local legislatures. The second formula is based on clarifying the fact that the final ownership of state assets should be distributed to central government and local legislatures.

3) Organizing an appropriate number of state assets operational organizations. An appropriate number of corporate institutions specialized in the operation of state assets should be organized under state asset management committees at various levels. Such institutions, which will operate similarly to an enterprise and follow the principle of independent management and sole responsibility for profits and losses, should be completely severed from administrative organizations and should not undertake administrative management functions. In order to avoid the emergence of problems resulting from "fan pai gong si," a company

127

changing its name but continuing to use the same technology to produce the same products, we should adopt detailed and concrete restrictive regulations to impose effective restraints enforced by supervisory organizations, encouraging reports of misconduct and analyzing public opinions.

By way of clarification, the aforementioned operational institutions, in some regions, are not the only entities responsible for state assets operational functions. In fact, other corporations based on public ownership, including investment companies, banks, unemployment insurance and old-age pension funds, as well as other appropriate corporate institutions, can also undertake operational functions. Therefore, the number of newly-established state assets management institutions at various levels will be determined in accordance with the number and quality of other existing corporate institutions capable of undertaking operational functions.

4) Auctions of enterprise stock rights. We should set limits on the holding of stock rights in order to prevent the monopolistic possession of the stock rights of shareholding enterprises. Concrete quota standards should be determined in accordance with the scale of enterprises, with quotas for larger enterprises a bit lower, say between 10-20 percent, with those for smaller enterprises a bit higher, between 20-30 percent. If stock rights held by a state assets management committee under the reshaped property right structure are higher than quota standards, said stock rights should be auctioned, with the new division being lower than stipulated standards. For example, if a state assets management committee holds 80 percent of the stock rights of a certain enterprise, and the quota standard is 25 percent, prior to the auction, the committee should divide the rights into four blocks lower than 25 percent.

Auctions of stock rights will be a vitally important link in the adoption of the shareholding system by enterprises owned by the state. Guaranteeing openness, justice and full competition in the auction process requires the establishment of auction rules and supervisory regulations conformed to the usual practices of the market economy and, at the same time, a stable auction (trading) center should be established gradually. Appropriate stipulations should be formulated to determine the qualifications of those competitive buyers. In addition to the assets operational organizations and other corporate institutions in the aforementioned region, corporate institutions outside the region, including those overseas, will be allowed to participate in auctions. While stipulations on restricting the entry of certain institutions can be adopted when some special enterprises to be auctioned, the number of such stipulations should be limited.

Auctions are advantageous in many aspects to state assets and the reform of the property rights system, including: a) preventing underestimates of state assets, and ensuring a relatively rational estimate of current value; b) enhancing management efficiency through competition; c) urging assets management committees to shift their management methods to value management mainly, substantially increasing the fluidity of assets, thereby ensuring that state assets can be flexibly allocated to highly efficient areas.

5) Organizing limited liability companies. Following the completion of auctions, the successful bidder for asset management rights or ownership will become a shareholder of the enterprise. Thereafter, a limited liability company can be organized in accordance with related regulations. The company's board of directors, composed of representatives of various shareholders and related representatives, will be responsible for strategic planning and decision-making. The board of directors will appoint a general manager responsible for daily business activities. The first step appropriate for most enterprises undergoing the adoption of the shareholding system will be to organize a limited liability company. This will help reduce and avoid chaos resulting from the imperfect system and the lack of experience in organizing limited stock companies by the open issue of stocks to raise funds directly from society. Along with the perfection in organization and system, as well as the accumulation of experience and of business achievements, some limited liability companies can gradually be transformed into limited stock companies for directional fund-raising, while those meeting required conditions can become

listed companies.

The adoption of the shareholding system by state-owned enterprises will inevitably encounter conflicts of interest and questions related to interest compensation. It is thus necessary to establish and rationally use supporting funds for the reorganization of state-owned enterprises. Some concrete problems, including how to make proper use of such funds during the process of adoption of the shareholding system, need to be explained.

1) Fund-raising. Such funds will consist mainly of the capital from financial departments at various levels to subsidize loss-making state-owned enterprises and bank loans to ensure the operation of such enterprises, as well as income gained from the sale of state-owned small enterprises and a portion of the stock rights of large and medium-sized state-owned enterprises, in addition to possible international funds. State assets management committees at various levels will raise funds for their own use.

2) The major uses of the funds in the process of adoption of the shareholding system include: a) Providing employment subsidies to enterprises with excessively redundant personnel. The amount of subsidies will be determined in accordance with the ratio between the current value of enterprise assets based on the appraisal set during the auction of the enterprise and the number of on-job personnel and subsidies are granted in excess of the prescribed ratio, the subsidies increase as the ratio goes up. b) Subsidies shall be provided to enterprises burdened with excessive social security responsibilities. The subsidization method will be similar to that for employment subsidies, but should be based on the ratio between the current value of enterprise assets and personnel at work, as well as on the ratio between the current value of enterprise assets and the number of retirees. c) Funds will be earmarked for expenditures on activities such as auctions and negotiations held in the process of adoption of the shareholding system, as well as other related activities.

An important aspect in the implementation of the shareholding system is to avoid the state shareholders from exercising administrative interference prevalent under the old system. The aforementioned administrative interference will be unavoidable if state shares are being held by existing specialized competent departments or other government administrative organizations, and especially when the possession of shares is monopolistic in nature. To avert such a situation it requires: a) allowing corporate institutions operating in the form of enterprises that assume sole responsibility for profits and losses rather than existing government administrative departments to hold shares; b) stock rights purchased at auctions; c) limiting the proportion of shares held by a single shareholder and prohibiting monopolistic shareholding; d) encouraging corporate institutions from other regions to participate in auctions and become shareholders. Although such requirements appear to be somewhat complicated, they are nonetheless necessary. Hopefully these requirements will minimize the possible administrative interference characteristic under the old system.

We must first select cities for trial implementation in order to reduce possible problems and mistakes in the course of implementing the shareholding system. The arrangement of the time schedule should not require that the implementation be launched on a full scale, but instead it can be carried out one group at a time. Nonetheless, great effort should be extended to complete the process within three to five years. Regarding the ideological understanding, the policy environment and economic situation, especially the existing status of large and medium-sized state-owned enterprises, a favorable opportunity is readily available for the adoption of the shareholding system. We should proceed with a sense of urgency in this regard because a favorable opportunity like this rarely exists. The situation is comparatively suitable for the reform in the auxiliary labour system and social security system when conditions are ready for accelerated economic development. Then there will be more employment opportunities, thus both the cost and risks of the reform will be reduced.

4. Enterprise Reform and the Change of Government Functions

Experts unanimously agree that a fundamental issue concerning the reform of state-owned enterprises is to change government functions and reform the enterprise management system. Without reform of the entire management system, reform of state-owned enterprises won't be successful, an issue that has been fully proved by China's enterprise reform over the past more than a dozen of years. To this experts have voiced many opinions and put forward some formulas.

(1) Establishing a three-level management system related to state assets, separating the government from state assets and enterprises.

The key link in reforming the economic system is to invigorate enterprises. Therefore, a series of "delegating power" measures have been adopted since the initiation of reform. Practice has proved that the result is not ideal. Because, as a systems engineering, invigorating the enterprise cannot be accomplished by the enterprise itself. As far as the enterprise is concerned, property right is a fundamental issue for the enterprise. Unless this issue is resolved, it would be difficult for the enterprise to really be revitalized.

Steering state-owned enterprises to the market and transforming the enterprise operational mechanism is, without doubt, highly necessary. But this alone is far from enough. Because the enterprise property rights stand out obviously as a question involving not only just enterprise internal mechanism. Under the conditions of the market economy, it involves a series of problems related to the ownership, delineation, circulation and management of property rights, in fact, it includes the question of how to effectively manage, allocate and operate the entire state assets. By steering state-owned enterprises to the market merely, it is still difficult for the management of state assets to rid itself from the traditional framework and the restraint of the administrative mechanism. As a result it will eventually return to the old system. The solution to the issue lies in pushing state assets to the market. This is a fundamental issue concerning property rights, and also the fundamental requirement of the socialist market economy.

The property rights serve as the prerequisite for the micro foundation based on which the socialist market economy is re-created, it is also the foundation and basic content of the macro-system reform. And the property right issue affects the whole situation, or to put it metaphorically, pulling one hair and the whole body is affected. Therefore, property right reform is highly significant.

In China's reform practice, the marketization of state assets has undergone further experimentation, as evidenced by the establishment of stock markets, the emergence of property right exchanges in some localities, the authorized management of state assets and the extensive experimentation of the enterprise share-holding system. Although systematic and thorough reform in property rights has not taken shape, full preparations have been made for the systematic and full-scale reform in steering state assets to the market.

At present, China is faced with the transition from the old to the new system and a quick establishment of a socialist market economic structure; it requires urgently a thorough reform in the existing property right system, pushing state assets to the market and promoting an in-depth reform of the entire economic system. It is highly practical and urgent to push state assets to the market, because both the time and conditions are basically ready for the reform.

It is the inherent requirement of the socialist market economy to push state assets to the market, a situation featured by new characteristics different from the conditions of state assets under the traditional economic system.

1) Change from the form of material to the form of value. State assets under the planned economy were represented in the form of materials and the state exercised direct material control over capital goods and products. Under the condition of the socialist market economy, state assets are represented in the form

of value, the assets and economic returns are measured by the amount of the commodity value. Except in a few cases the state monopoly is required, there is no need for the state to apply direct control over materials.

2) Change from the form of solidity to the form of fluidity. Under the old system, state assets, under direct administrative control, had a relative solidity and could not circulate on its own. The socialist market economy calls for the full independent circulation of state assets on the market and the development of competitive management.

3) Property rights change from being vague to being clarified. Under the old system, state assets were nominally owned by the state. Due to the diversified management system and the numerous administrative investment channels, however, the ownership of state assets was ambiguous and not clearly delineated. Under the new system, most of the state assets are placed under the shareholding system and operate in accordance with the corporate system, the company's legal person enjoys ownership, thus clarifying state-owned property rights.

4) Change from single management to diversified management. Under the traditional system, state assets were placed under direct state monopolistic management. Under the new system, with the exception of a few trades and industries which are directly managed by the state, most state assets are managed in a diversified way through intermediate operational institutions.

5) Change from the integration of the government with state assets and the government with enterprises to the separation of the government from state assets and enterprises. Under the traditional system, in order to guarantee the realization of the planned economy, the general administrative functions of the government, its functions as the owner of state assets and its operational functions were integrated into one entity exercised by the competent government departments. Under the socialist market economic structure, the following practices are adopted: a) separating the government from state assets, i.e., the general administrative functions of the government are separated from

the managerial functions of state assets; b) separating the government from enterprises, i.e., managerial functions over state assets are separated from the operation of the state assets.

The framework and basic formulas of the three-level management system of state assets are as follows:

1) State assets management center.

The State Council is responsible for the administrative management of state assets on behalf of the state. A dual management structure is adopted for the administrative management of state assets, which combines unified management and independent management: In the first level, the state asset management committee is responsible for unified coordination and supervision; in the second level, level-to-level management, decentralized management and centralized management are integrated.

The State Council sets up a state assets management committee composed of leading members of various related departments, which is responsible to formulate and coordinate the principles, policies, plans and regulations for the management and operation of state assets and supervise their implementation. The existing State Administration of State Property is abolished.

Level-to-level management is adopted for state assets, so as to integrate centralized and decentralized management: a) Trades and industries monopolized and controlled by the state, such as post and telecommunications, railways, banks, armament, major mineral resources as well as public utilities, are placed under the concrete management of various competent departments under the State Council and accept the policy coordination of the State Assets Management Committee. b) General competitive trades and industries which are unsuitable for decentralized management by multiple departments should be placed under the unified management of the State-Owned Enterprises Administrative Bureau set up under the State Assets Management Committee. The existing general trade competent departments no longer directly lead state-owned enterprises, but instead they are only responsible for formulating the trade policy and will, in the future, gradually be replaced by semi-official trade associations.

2) State assets investment center.

Except for a few state monopolized departments which are under the direct operation and management of the competent departments under the State Council, specialized investment intermediate institutions should be responsible for the operation of other state assets. State assets management departments do not directly participate in the asset business, they only send representatives into the board of directors or management committee of the investment intermediate institutions to participate in making business decisions and exercising supervision.

State assets investment intermediate institutions, only responsible for the capital (assets) investment and income, do not engage directly in the concrete business operation, but possess an independent enterprise corporation status as the mainstay of the state assets market.

State assets investment intermediate institutions include investment companies, holding companies, enterprise group companies, insurance companies, commercial banks and various foundations.

An investment intermediate institution should not become an organization of the whole trade, if a trade has only one investment company or holding company, it will lead to economic monopoly and hinder competition; an investment intermediate institution itself should not be too large, because that would lead to slow decision-making and low efficiency.

3) State assets business operation center.

The concrete operational business of state assets is placed under the charge of vocational state-owned enterprises. They are responsible for concrete production and operational activities, and for lowering costs, raising efficiency and increasing profits, they are also the mainstay of the state assets market. Most of the existing state-owned enterprises should belong to such vocational enterprises.

(2) Changing government functions is the key to transforming the mechanisms of enterprises and shaping the microeconomic base.

A basic task for economic reform is to shape a microeconomic base.

If the mainstay of the planned economy is the state or the government, then the mainstay of the market economy should be enterprises. In terms of the public economy, only state-owned enterprises engaged in independent management can become the mainstay of the market economy or the microeconomic base of the socialist market economy. What is the basis for this statement?

The average person understands the microeconomic base as grass-roots level production or operational units. This understanding is in fact extremely inadequate and inaccurate. The microbase must be an independent, dynamic and responsible economic performer. It must, in fact, have its own economic interests and make independent operational decisions, and must be either driven by or restricted by the interest relationship. Only economic units with independent management status can be considered as "economy-minded persons," and serve as either the mainstay of the market economy, or the microbase of the national economy. Hence, it is quite appropriate to say that the status of independent management should be the soul or source of life of the microeconomic base. Whether or not a production and operational unit at the grass-roots level can actually become the microeconomic base depends on whether it has genuine independent management autonomy.

The traditional planned economy lacked a microbase because grass-roots production and operational units lacked genuine independent management autonomy. Under the old system, the government was integrated with enterprises, the state had overall control of the income and expenditures of enterprises, and the principle of exchange of equal values was replaced by the principle of uncompensated allocation. At the same time, economic means were replaced by administrative means, horizontal economic links were partitioned by administrative divisions, and the commodity economy was replaced by the product economy, or the natural economy. An enterprise without the status of independent management lacked internal economic dynamics and depended entirely on the mandates from its superiors. Enterprises thus became grass-roots units in an administrative sense, no longer representing a true "microeconomy." As a result, micro-economic laws such as laws governing exchanges of equal value, economic accounting and equal competition disappeared. More-over, there was no distinction between macroeconomy and mi-croeconomy. The principal microeconomic activities of en-terprises, including production, supply and marketing, were incorporated into the state's mandatory planning, and the overall national economic management became a large microcosm. In addition to engaging in production and management, enterprises were also required to provide extensive social services, including assuming the responsibility for providing food, clothing, housing and transport for all workers and staff, and in some cases even the residents of entire communities. Not only that, they were also required to provide cradle to grave services, including medical care and old age pensions, with some even assuming the functions of a grass-roots government. As a result, enterprise management became a "small macrocosm." However, macroeconomic manage-ment cannot exist without a microeconomic base, because the two are closely related. Therefore, the absence of independent status for enterprises and a microbase for the national economy is the fatal flaw in the planned economy.

Therefore, under conditions of public ownership, one of the main tasks of economic reform is to shape microeconomic bas-is and transform state-owned enterprises into independent pro-ducers and managers.

Whether or not state-run enterprises can gain independent management status depends on whether or not the functions of government economic departments can be transformed.

From the very beginning of its urban economic reform China stressed the separation of the government from enterprises and that state-owned enterprises should become independent produ-cers and managers engaging in independent management and assuming sole responsibility for profits and losses. However, this is an arduous task which cannot be accomplished in one stroke. Firstly, enterprise reform requires the support of other supple-mentary measures such as price reform, and reform of the social security system. Secondly, it is necessary to conscientiously separate the government from enterprises, and the power necessary for independent management should be shifted from the government to enterprises. The first task can be carried out easily, while the second task will progress slowly and it will be very difficult to make a move forward. Although adopted quite some time ago, the Enterprise Bankruptcy Law has been faced with many difficulties in implementation due to the fact that enterprise mechanisms have not as yet been transformed. In addition, though the Enterprise Law has been approved, it is not put into practice yet. In order to accelerate the transformation of the mechanisms of state-owned enterprises the regulations promulgated in recent years have clearly stipulated 14 rights to be granted to enterprises. However, it has been extremely difficult to carry out these regulations. A recent State Council survey of the implementation of the regulations revealed that a considerable portion of the 14 rights granted by the regulations were not as yet in place, and most of the rights remained still in the hands of competent business departments. These departments refuse to grant enterprises decision-making autonomy stipulated in the regulations in terms of operational policies, the selection of supply and marketing units, the establishment of organizations within enterprises, and the right to determine wages and the distribution of bonuses. For example, some factories which want to undertake renovation projects have been forced to undergo examinations by more than 10 organizations, including planning department, city construction planning department, environmental protection department, water and electricity supply department, transportation authorities and banks before receiving an approval. One factory director said that although the regulations had granted enterprises the right to proceed with productive construction within the factory, his factory was given a fine of 22,500 yuan when an old wall of its original warehouse was replaced by iron railings. The department concerned insisted that the factory "had violated the rules and regulations for construction." Another example, a factory, in an effort to streamline its administrative structure, abolished the department of the people's armed force (PAF), incorporating it into the factory's security section. Alarmed by this move leaders of PAF departments at all levels—province, city and district—all came out to intervene. The result was that the factory was not only forced to restore the PAF department, but also made its director serve concurrently as the head the PAF department. There are numerous similar cases like these. The 14 rights granted by the regulations to enterprises do not include the personnel right to appoint or dismiss factory directors or managers. Under such circumstances, it is extremely difficult to guarantee enterprises' independent management status.

What has made it so difficult to readjust the relationship between the state and enterprises? The main reasons lie in the following aspects: a) The approaches and concepts of related government departments and personnel in charge lag far behind the rapidly developing situation, and it is difficult to change within a short period of time these approaches and concepts formed under the prolonged existence of the planned economic system. b) An even more important reason lies in the fact that reform itself involves readjustments in the interest relationship, and it is very difficult for people to give up their vested interests and power. The fact that the government has not as yet changed its functions is responsible for the difficulties encountered during the process of transforming existing mechanisms of state-owned enterprises and establishment of microeconomic basis. At present, various social circles are concerned about the transformation of the mechanisms of state-owned enterprises. However, it seems a misconception has formed which blames enterprises for the failure in the transformation of their mechanisms. Enterprises are repeatedly urged to transform their mechanisms. This is indeed unfair to most state-owned enterprises. Even though they are anxious to transform mechanisms and to gain their independent status for self-management, it is very difficult for them to do so. Enterprises cannot gain independent status for self-management and transform their mechanisms unless the functions of government economic departments are changed, and the yokes brought about by the various types of administrative interference in enterprise activities removed. As one Chinese saying goes: "It is better for the doer to undo what he has done." The failure of enterprises to transform their mechanisms is only a "phenomenon," while the failure of government economic departments to change their functions is the "root cause." In analyzing the problem we should begin with the failure to transform the mechanisms of enterprises. However, to solve the problem we should focus mainly on the transformation of government functions. We should on the one hand arouse public awareness of the transformation of the mechanisms of enterprises, and on the other hand call urgently for the transformation of the functions of government economic departments. Only when government functions are properly transformed in compliance with the requirements of the socialist market economy, can we truly turn state-owned enterprises into independent producers and managers based on public ownership, and create on the basis of public ownership microeconomic basis full of vitality.

We should persist in implementing the principle of separating the government from enterprises, separating the state as a political entity from the state as an economic entity.

The key to transforming the functions of government economic departments lies in conscientiously implementing the principle of separating the government from enterprises. In China today ownership by the whole people is still based on the form of state ownership; so it is necessary to separate the state as a political entity from the state as an economic entity, because the two entities are different in nature and follow different laws. The state has existed as a political entity throughout history, and its economic pillar is national finance which has all along followed a noneconomic principle characterized by uncompensated levies and allocations. At the same time, since China is still in the primary stage of socialism, the ownership by the whole people has unavoidably adopted the form of state ownership. Therefore, the state controls social assets on behalf of the whole people and thus becomes an economic entity which must follow the principles of economic accounting, and exchanges or compensation of equal values. Under the system of the integration of the political and economic entities over the past decades, the economy was subordinated to politics, and subordinated to a political system of highly centralized management, thereby stifling the formation of the microbase. The on-going effort to shape a microbase requires separating the government from enterprises, and the state as a political entity from the state as an economic entity and liberating the economy owned by the whole people, with the state as its agent, from the yokes of administration, ensuring it to operate in line with market economic mechanisms.

There are two different views concerning how to separate the state as an economic entity from the state as a political entity. One view holds that economic and political entities should be separated organizationally, placing the economic entity under the people's congress.

The state as an economic entity is represented organizationally by all the state assets management committees set up from the central down to the local levels. These committees are responsible to and accept the leadership and supervision of standing committees of people's congresses at various levels or special committees, but are free of interference from government administrative departments. The main responsibilities of the state assets management committees include guiding and supervising the business activities of various state assets operational companies (state-run investment companies). The tasks of various state assets operational companies, which operate like enterprises completely, include investing in enterprises and controlling state assets on behalf of the whole people. Enterprises should bear responsibility for investments made by related investment companies and engage in independent management in the capacity as independent corporations. In this way, the owner/manager relationship formed between the state assets management committees (state assets operational companies) and enterprises facilitates the implementation of the principle of separating the two rights.

Governments at various levels represent organizationally the state as a political entity. In terms of its relationship with state-owned enterprises, as well as with other enterprises, including private, cooperative and foreign enterprises, the state exercises only economic administrative and management functions and powers, in addition to providing various social services. State functions include: a) industrial and commercial administrative management and state assets registration; b) macro-control by financial and monetary means; c) drafting medium- and long-term development programs and industrial policies and providing guidance for enterprise investments; d) making preparations for the construction of infrastructure facilities related to communications, transportation, post and telecommunications, energy resources and hydroelectric power; e) preparing and establishing some basic industries, high technology and basic research; f) developing human resource and education; g) fostering and developing a market system; h) running social security undertakings; i) establishing various economic regulations; and j) implementing income policies and other means to regulate income distribution. Briefly, the basic economic functions of the government center on creating a favourable and stable macroeconomic environment for all enterprises, ensuring equal competition, preventing unfair income distribution and eliminating disparities. Under the new system wherein the government is separated from enterprises, all local governments will have no right to contend for investment and projects, and instead must devote all efforts to developing infrastructure facilities, improving the investment environment so as to attract more domestic and foreign funds.

Most people disagree with separating the economic entity from the government, thinking it is both impossible and unnecessary. They feel the crucial point is to separate the economic entity from the political entity within the government, including relative separation both in organization and function. For example, we could set up a state assets management committee under the government, as well as a subordinate state-owned enterprise administrative bureau, placing state assets under centralized management. Other government functional departments could exercise the due functions of the political entity.

In recent years, the nation as a whole has witnessed an upsurge in the establishment of a socialist market economy. However, certain chaotic phenomena have appeared due to circumstances resulting from the lack of clear understanding and imperfect regulations. On the one hand, it has been difficult to carry out the separation of the government from state-owned enterprises; on the other hand, various Party and government departments, including army and police organizations, taxation and, industrial and commercial administrative departments, have established various types of companies and enterprises by abusing their power. At the same time, the reform of the banking and financial systems has made little progress, but banks, including the People's Bank, the country's central bank, have, taking advantage of their financial position, established various trust and investment corporations, and have directly participated in transactions of securities and real estate. Under the market economy, the role of enterprises is like that of the athletes on a sportsfield while government departments play the role of umpires and linesmen. However, most umpires and linesmen in China today have abandoned their positions and also become athletes, thereby causing chaos. The phenomenon of indistinction between the government and enterprises is in a sense much more serious than before. Nevertheless, one point which must be stressed is that some existing abnormal phenomena represent just problems emerging along the road of progress. Such problems can and must be completely corrected, a pursuit which can only be accomplished by further deepening the reform.

(3) Effective solution to the most difficult problem of indistinctions between the government and enterprises is the implementation of the shareholding system.

Though there has been very little progress in the reform of large and medium-sized state-owned enterprises, we have nevertheless recorded various achievements, especially in our understanding of enterprise reform. Along with the deepening of reform, we have formulated the Enterprise Law and Regulations Concerning the Transformation of the Operational Mechanisms of Enterprises, specifying decision-making power of enterprises. In this sense our reform has achieved notable results. In fact, how could we have these regulations formulated if we haven't made substantial progress in our understanding? However, it goes without saying that many problems still exist. Such problems are manifested in a number of ways. For instance, there is still a wide gap between what is stipulated in the regulations and how they are actually implementated, especially in large and medium-sized enterprises. In addition, the regulations themselves contain considerable limitations. For example, large and medium-sized enterprises should have the right to handle imports and exports. But according to the current regulations, enterprises are required to have the approval by the department concerned for imports and exports. Besides, the present regulations have left out what should have been included. For example, the corporate ownership of state-owned enterprises has not yet been recognized by the present regulations. How then can enterprises as legal entities but with no property rights to assume sole responsibility for profits and losses?

What is the correct road for the reform of China's enterprises? The present contract system cannot achieve the goal of transforming the operational mechanisms of state-run enterprises. The existing system embodies the so-called "mother-in-law and daughter-in-law relationship," and therefore it is impossible to eliminate the defects resulting from the indistinction between the government and enterprises. The contract system has in fact placed various restrictions on the ever-changing enterprises. While it may enable enterprises to yield short-term benefits, it can not promote all enterprises to develop as a whole in the long run. The contract system requires that all enterprises increase production and earn profits. This is contrary to the market law according to which the rise of some trades is always accompanied by the fall of some other trades and the success of some enterprises is always accompanied by the failure of some other enterprises. Therefore, the contract system cannot be the goal for enterprise reform. Hence, the implementation of the shareholding system is our way forward.

At present, the most difficult aspect of enterprise reform lies in the separation of the government from enterprises, because it involves issues related to interests and methods.

However, enterprise reform also faces numerous other difficulties such as development of the market system, finding a solution to the problem of property rights and improving the internal management of enterprises. While all of the above will be advantageous to the reform of the economic environment and altering existing ideologies and concepts, the reform effort will still be faced with many difficulties. For example, in terms of the property rights it is necessary to uphold state ownership, while at the same time providing enterprises with corporate ownership. Athough the shareholding system undoubtedly can solve this contradiction, it is not so easy to achieve unity in people's understanding and in concrete operational methods. Some people believe that the shareholding system will render state ownership impractical. In fact, the state will still hold stock rights in enterprises and can participate in enterprise management in accordance with the law, and share profits based on the capital contributed. How then can this be described as "rendering state ownership impractical"? Problems also exist in the internal management of enterprises. If poor management exists in individual enterprises, the responsibility then rests with the enterprises themselves. But if poor management exists universally in all enterprises, then the problem lies not only with individual enterprises, but mainly with the economic system. This, in fact, is exactly the current prevailing situation in China.

Although enterprise reform faces many difficulties, we should realize that the indistinction between the government and enterprises remains the most difficult problem. The indistinction between the government and enterprises will result in failure to form a market system, and the failure of enterprises to engage in independent management and assume sole responsibility for their own profits and losses, thereby making it impossible for enterprises to achieve an effective internal management. Under this circumstance, it would all but impossible to bring the superiority of the shareholding system into full play, even if it was put into practice. This is currently the case with some shareholding enterprises in Shanghai. The key to deepening enterprise reform centres on separating the government from enterprises. The functions of the government should be correctly stipulated, and the government must focus on governing only what it should, and refrain from interfering in other areas. If it engages in pursuit of the latter, it will not be able to properly manage the former. Such a phenomenon must not be allowed to continue.

The main reason why township enterprises and foreign-funded enterprises are well-managed lies in little interference from the government. Some township enterprises established by township governments, are different from state-owned enterprises. Government stipulations apply to state-owned enterprises in their production, exchanges and distribution, while township enterprises are free from such restrictions. Moreover, bankruptcy is the only avenue for township enterprises when they sustain recurring losses, because township governments could not afford to assume responsibility. However, loss-making state-owned enterprises can be propped up by the state financial departments. These discrepancies are enough to reveal the differences between township and state-owned enterprises. This is especially true in terms of foreign-funded enterprises. Joint ventures, including sham ventures, are prevalent in some localities. The government will not "dare" to control an enterprise classified as a joint venture, and hence the productive forces there are "liberated."

We must stress that the failure to properly transform state-owned enterprises may possibly lead to the spread of many defects existing in state-owned enterprises to township enterprises. Therefore, the significance of reforming state-owned enterprises lies not only in invigorating such enterprises, but also in ensuring the sound development of all Chinese enterprises.

Enterprises have common points irrespective of national boundaries; as commodity producers and managers they all possess features as follows. Enterprises are market-oriented and their production is designed for exchange. In addition, enterprises under independent management assume sole responsibility for their own profits and losses and can engage in expanded reproduction. The operations of enterprises are targeted at earning profits, and the responsibilities and functions of the government and that of enterprises are clearly separated.

On the basis of the aforementioned common features, the

future model for Chinese enterprises will retain their own characteristics based mainly on public ownership and the coexistence of diversified economic sectors. It is predicted that by the year 2000, the state-owned, collective, and non-public economic sectors will each account for one-third of the Chinese economy. Such a situation will be beneficial to the operation and development of the socialist market economy. Will state-owned enterprises be outdistanced by private enterprises? The answer to this question depends on the results of market competition. However, we firmly believe that so long as state-owned enterprises rid themselves of the yokes of the traditional system and engage in fair competition, they will by no means be inferior to private enterprises. There is no need to fear the development of private enterprises so long as we properly operate and invigorate publicly-owned enterprises.

(4) State property ownership should be separated from administrative authority to ensure implementation of the shareholding system.

Our basic choice is to introduce the shareholding system to most enterprises undergoing reform. The shareholding system is an organizational form for enterprises required by the modern market economy. Since we have decided to adopt a market economic system, we must therefore adopt a modern organizational system for enterprises.

However, before the question concerning property rights is properly solved it is impossible to implement the shareholding system. The focus for solving the property rights issue is to change the system of state ownership, which is currently in the form of public ownership, and realizing primarily a change in people's understanding. In the past we considered state ownership the highest and ultimate form of social ownership. This view does not conform with current reality. Whether under capitalism or socialism, state ownership has been proved to be incapable to integrate fairness with efficiency. Under state ownership, so-called fairness was achieved at the expense of efficiency. When public ownership is separated from the form by which it is realized, we found that neither state nor collective ownership has the capacity to propel the development of productive forces. They are by no means superior forms and therefore must be subject to reform. What is the key to the reform of state ownership? Quite simply, the government. The property rights based on state ownership must be separated from the administrative rights of the government, and failure to accomplish this will make it impossible to achieve all other objectives. In addition, failure to achieve the separation will make it impossible to separate ownership from managerial rights. Since property rights currently belong to the government, it will be impossible for the government to refrain from interfering with enterprises. Those with vested interests are unwilling to relinquish such rights. This is a tough obstacle lying ahead of us and no one can bypass it. Though we have tried for more than 10 years but failed to bypass the obstacle. We must dare to face and make every attempt to solve this most difficult problem. Finding a solution to the problem is the only possible way to clearly define property rights. Theoretically, including Marxist theory, property rights stand for an economic relationship, a relationship of interests rather than a kind of function or power in the superstructure under the control of the state power and are subject to its direct interference. Separating property ownership from administrative rights is the only possible way to separate operational rights over property from its ownership, and thereafter proceeding to separate enterprise corporate ownership from property rights and operational rights. Only then can enterprises genuinely become market mainstays engaged in independent management and assuming sole responsibility for profits and losses, while at the same time meeting the requirements for the development of the market.

(5) A knotty problem in transforming government functions centres on properly handling of excessive organizations and surplus administrative and managerial personnel.

A planned economy is responsible for everything under the sky, thus establishing the most formidable management structure in history. Of all the countries, China takes the lead in this respect. How big then is China's management structure, including those other than government organizations? Different statistical methods have resulted in two figures: one said about 10 million and the other said about 40 million. According to a news report carried in the *Heilongjiang Daily* on October 29, 1992, Hulan County with a population of about 650,000 had 100 section-level organizations with nearly 3,000 employees on the government pay roll. Calculated on this basis, by the end of 1990, the country had a total of 2,182 counties and county-level cities, with a total of over 6.5 million government personnel. If these figures are combined with those government employees working at the prefectural, cities, provincial, autonomous regional and central levels, the figure will total well over 10 million. Reportedly, the figure is rising at an annual rate of over 10 percent, reaching soon a warning point that the common people could scarcely afford to support them.

The market economy relies mainly on the operation of market mechanisms requiring only small but vigorous government organizations to play their macro-control role. Therefore, we can say that the size of government organizations is inversely proportional to the level of development of the market economy. Retaining the unwieldy management organization and continuing to indulge in empty rhetoric about transforming government functions will be to no avail. How can the existing *yamen* (government offices) and officials at every level refrain from what they see as their responsibility to taking charge of enterprises? It is thus crystal clear that we must adopt a method of "removing the firewood from under the caldron." This means dissolving management organizations unsuited to the needs of the market economy is the only way possible to transform government functions and provide enterprises with an environment enabling them to engage in independent management.

We can adopt the transitional method used in some cities and counties, merging the Party and government organizations of the same category by putting up two signboards, with same working staff. For example, the organizational departments of city Party committees can be merged with the personnel and labor bureaus of the city government under the same name. The organizational department of a city Party committee and a city government will have one economic bureau to exercise unified management over all economic work. The relationship between the city government (party B) and enterprises (party A) will be as follows: party B welcomes party A's investment; when party A makes profits, party B collects taxes; when party A violates the law, party B investigates and punishes party A; and party B sympathizes with party A when it goes bankrupt. This is, in fact, the relationship between taxpayers and tax collectors, a general rule governing the market economy in all countries.

In terms of the macrocosm, the approach would be similar to demobilizing a million military personnel and transferring them to the civilian sectors in a planned manner. A good experience in this respect has been recorded by some provinces which have transformed some of their subordinate departments and bureaus, including those in charge of commerce, grain, supply and marketing, materials and petroleum into industrial companies. Under the planned economic system, many capable people were concentrated in higher-level management organizations. As a result they have accomplished nothing. But when they are given an opportunity they will display fully their remarkable abilities during the surging tide of the market economy. This vast capital of human resources should be effectively used for the development of the market economy. This is a matter of great significance, we must not adopt radical measures to cut numerous management organizations at one stroke without making proper arrangements for the numerous management personnel just dismissed, because it might cause social instability which will in turn hinder the smooth transition to the market economy.

(6) When transforming functions and streamlining structures, we must avoid the appearance of companies operating under new names, but retaining old products and techniques.

During the reform of government organizations and the transformation of their functions, various specialized economic departments have attempted, or are attempting, to streamline their structures and rearrange personnel by becoming various types of economic entities, or organizing group companies under the placard of enterprise groups. One survey revealed that the former specialized economic departments that have changed into new economic entities can be roughly divided into the following three categories:

1) Those which have dissolved original specialized economic departments, turning them into group companies. Two prominent situations have surfaced in regard to this particular type of group companies: Firstly, a small number of group companies have played a certain role in organizing the production and management of their member enterprises through unified contracts, linking wages with enterprise performance, personnel rights, preserving and increasing the value of state assets, and examining and approving major investment projects. However, since the responsibilities of the government and enterprises have not as yet been separated, group companies temporarily retain some trade management and administration functions, including trade statistics, the collection of financial statements and reports, the transmission of documents and the work for Party and mass organizations. Secondly, most group companies have not yet been actually formed. For example, the bureaus of a city in charge of chemical, machine-building, electronics, textiles, building materials, materials have been transformed into group companies. Nonetheless, they can not play the role in organizing the production and management over their subordinated enterprises nor can they truly function as key enterprises. They simply act as independent enterprises engaged in market competition, and to a great extent their relationship with their subordinated enterprises is one of partnership. They only take charge of appointing and dismissing Party and government heads of enterprises and statistical work of different trade sectors.

2) Some will retain original specialized economic depart-

ments with a limited number of personnel to undertake government functions, while most people will be reassigned to run group companies. For example, the commercial department, grain bureau, and supply and marketing cooperative of Guangdong Province retained a small staff to take care of trade management and the work for retired cadres of the department and bureau, with most of their personnel reassigned to organize group companies.

3) Some will retain the original specialized economic departments and will at the same time rename themselves as group companies. In the process of transforming itself into an economic entity, the commercial department of one particular province temporarily adopted the form of one organization with two names. This transitional form is trying to cope with the needs of both the upper and lower levels, because the dissolved commercial department is still required to fulfill its legal procedures. An investigation showed that there was no instance of one organization with two names in its true sense, but the investigation did reveal the existence of two sets of organizations under two names with same staff assuming concurrently both government and enterprise responsibilities.

The results of a fact-finding survey indicate that the transformation of specialized economic departments into economic entities has recorded achievements, while at the same time experiencing problems. The structure of specialized economic departments has been simplified and there has been a reduction in the number of personnel, while enterprises generally experienced a dramatic reduction in the number of meetings and inspections arranged by higher authorities.

Simultaneously, the following problems have emerged. Firstly, group companies operated by specialized economic departments are often unworthy of the name. Prior to the establishment of group companies, departments and bureaus did not conduct any conscientious research and feasibility studies together with enterprises concerned. Many group companies were not established on the basis of market competition and voluntary union, but instead were created by relying on administrative power. Enterprises witnessed no noticeable changes following the establishment of group companies, compared to when they were under government control. They generally agreed that such group companies represented government interests in terms of their relationship with enterprises, while they represented enterprises in their relationship with the government, a change in name only. Secondly, the phenomenon surfaced whereby enterprises were asked to keep government organizations provided in everything, while the government reassumed power, withheld profits and shifted difficulties to enterprises. A typical case in point involved a provincial forestry department. While preparing to establish a forestry industrial and commercial enterprise group company, the department found it lacked necessary funding, and requested its subordinate enterprises to raise 1 million yuan to fund the effort. In addition, the department, which had no operational base, moved into a building belonging to a timber company. The department, which also lacked an operational staff, transferred the general manager and key members of the timber company. For the convenience in management, the positions of the general manager and deputy general managers of the group company were filled concurrently by the deputy directors of the provincial forestry department. Moreover, the group company retained an extra 13 percent income tax levied on the subordinate enterprises. The added tax increased total tax levies on the subordinate enterprises from 33 percent to 46 percent, thereby increasing the already heavy burden they shouldered. Another case in point involved a provincial supply and marketing group company which violated related provincial regulations by collecting a 33 percent income tax from its subordinate enterprises which, in addition, had to hand in after-tax contracted profits to higher authorities. It not only collected a 30 percent fixed assets depreciation fee, but also charged the enterprises both public welfare fund and public accumulation funds.

By way of summarizing, the cases mentioned above show that the transformation of certain specialized economic departments of the government into economic entities involves a complicated situation, and hence they cannot be generalized as "companies which have changed their names, but have retained their old products and techniques." Companies which have been transformed from administrative departments but use original administrative powers as the means for production and operations feature the following four characteristics: a) They use their original management powers in planning, including fund-raising and materials allocation, the power to examine and approve capital construction and investment projects, and coordination and certificate issuance rights over trades as the means for organizing production and operations. b) When preparing to establish such companies they rely on the transfer of enterprises' production conditions, withdraw the powers already delegated to enterprises, withhold profits, and shift difficulties onto the enterprises. c) They remain connected to the original administrative organizations in terms of funding, personnel and functions, while at the same time failing to undertake independent accounting or assume sole responsibility for profits and losses. d) They abuse administrative power to organize groups arbitrarily.

A point well worth noting is that during the process of exploring ways for structural reform in various localities, the establishment of companies by dissolving specialized economic departments and reducing staff are an inevitable result of transition from the planned to the market economy and an effective way out to reassign the redundant personnel. So long as these companies are making efforts to separate the government from enterprises, engaging in independent management and assuming sole responsibility for profits and losses they should be encouraged and supported. It should also be noted that the emergence of new problems is inevitable since the transformation of specialized economic departments to economic entities is still in the exploratory stage, and with no experience to go by. Enterprises on the one hand and specialized economic departments on the other hand are contradictory to each other as an economic phenomenon, and how to properly handle the relationship between them has always been an issue requiring a solution during the reform. Enterprises and special economic departments often hold diametrically opposed views towards the transformation of management departments into economic entities. While enterprises might say "it changes only the liquid, but not the drugs," a change in form only, the specialized economic departments might contend that the transformation represents a change in both the liquid and the drugs, because they are no longer on the government pay roll and have to make a living for themselves. Objectively speaking, however, transformation of a management department to an economic entity and from administrative management to market operation requires a process of gradual advance from a change in quantity to a change in quality. Hence, problems arising in the transitional process should be realistically studied and solved.

Streamlining the structure and transforming functions are the general trend. How then can a specialized economic department avoid changing in form only as it attempts to transform itself into an economic entity? It should strictly adhere to the following points: a) The newly-established economic entity should be completely dissociated from the original economic department. There should first be a separation of functions, followed by the separation of personnel and eventually the separation of accounting. b) The new economic entity should engage in equal competition with the original enterprises, and maintain operations by relying on available skills in production and operation, rather than taking advantage of the convenient conditions available previously in controlling funds and materials, to seek for unjust benefits or place undue pressure on enterprises in regard to funds and materials. c) The new economic entity must not rely on its previous administrative influence to control the original enterprises, nor should it indulge in arbitrary transfers, withdrawing power, withholding profits or shifting difficulties onto enterprises. d) The new economic entity attempting to establish a group must act in compliance with the objective needs of market competition, and respect the opinions of enterprises. It must not use administrative means to style itself as the nucleus and force enterprises into submission by cancelling the corporate status of the original enterprises.

In terms of structural reform, the transformation of some specialized economic departments into economic entities is an important way to streamline the structure and reassign personnel. However, this type of reform involves many difficulties since it represents a readjustment in the pattern of power and interests. Therefore, we must conduct conscientious studies and proceed with prudence.

1) It is necessary to study methods and effective ways for distributing the functions of the specialized economic departments. Under the old conditions of the planned economy, specialized economic departments served as the funnel for planned management and as a tool used by the state to directly manage enterprises. Today, while attempting to introduce a market economy, we should effect a fundamental change in the functions of specialized economic departments, with some being dissolved or merged. Economic entities transformed from such departments can no longer be allowed to exercise and control their previous administrative functions on behalf of enterprises. At present, some substantive companies have no desire to have such administrative functions, but due to the lack of coordination and synchronous steps of reform and burdened by the need to satisfy both the upper and the lower levels, they are compelled to continue to serve as the funnel of administrative management. There is an urgent need to provide guidance in these aspects. Related State Council departments should organize investigations and studies, accelerate efforts to draft related policies, adopt measures to liquidate companies unworthy of the name, study and adopt methods and effective ways for distributing the functions of specialized economic departments, and thoroughly separate administrative functions dependent on economic entities. This in turn will transform them into genuine economic entities.

2) When establishing economic entities, specialized economic departments should devote great efforts to qualitative change, and "earn a living" by relying on their actual ability. Economic

entities established by specialized economic departments are usually congenitally determined to have an undesirable base and will thus unavoidably be viewed in a different light. In addition, such companies often inherit certain past practices and the old habit of many years which have made them the topic theme of discussion among the people. Therefore, such companies should thoroughly discard traditional concepts, overcome the long-standing inertial thinking in placing enterprises under their direct management, establish market concept and sense of section and make an earnest effort in the transformation of mechanism. They should be determined to cut off the tail by themselves and make a thorough transformation. They should turn themselves into genuine economic entities, establish partnership with other enterprises, engage in equal competition, make a living on their own genuine ability of production and management, instead of on withdrawing power and withholding interests belonging to enterprises.

3) We should discard administrative means and develop enterprise groups in accordance with the market economic principle. In establishing economic entities, specialized economic departments should not simply put together their subordinate enterprises under the new name of so-called "group companies" without considering the availability of objective conditions. To organize enterprise groups is a kind of market behavior, and it won't do to go by administrative orders and set up companies in name only. Economic entities currently run by specialized economic departments are operating under the name of enterprise groups, because some people are not clear about the meaning of groups and the conditions necessary for organizing groups. Based on their traditional concepts, they have turned enterprise groups into a form to manage enterprises by administrative means. Therefore, we should step up efforts to formulate and promulgate Regulations on the Organization and Management of Enterprise Groups, so as to lead them onto the road of healthy development.

4) Integrated departments in charge of macro-control are not allowed to run companies. In the course of running entities

by administrative institutions, some comprehensive departments, such as banking, financial and taxation departments, have also run some companies. Attention must be paid to this situation. It should be clarified that comprehensive economic management departments are not allowed to set up companies themselves, nor should they set up under them various types of affiliated companies, otherwise they will cause adverse effect on macro-management and bring chaos to the economic order. Therefore, comprehensive departments which have already set up companies should dissolve them if possible, companies which cannot be dissolved must be completely severed from the original units.

Chapter IV
Issues Concerning the Socialist Market System and Market Mechanisms

1. The Establishment and Perfection of a Unified Socialist Market System

(1) The establishment of a unified socialist market accelerates China's reform and modernization process.

Prerequisites for a unified market.

Some economists contend that a unified socialist market means a thriving and vigorous competitive market linked with the international market to ensure commercialization and free circulation of domestic resources, free from regional and trade restrictions, and restrictions from different forms of ownership. The eventual realization of such a market mode will indeed be advantageous for all China's localities, industries and enterprises to exhibit their unique strong points and initiatives in economic development, promote extensive communications and cooperation between China and countries throughout the world, accelerate China's modernization process and achieve higher production efficiency through the mutual absorption of advanced science and technology and management expertise, as well as take full advantage of available resources.

Realizing such a market mode requires the emancipation of people's thinking, renewal of ideology and deepening the reform so as to prepare various conditions required for the establishment of a unified market.

1) Both subjective and objective factors of the market should be established in line with the demands of the market economy. The factors will in fact be enterprises and individuals operating

with their own interests in mind, and which will have autonomy in terms of decision-making and operations, as well as sole responsibility for profits and losses and self-development. The determination of the various factors is designed to ensure all economic actions of enterprises and individuals are transformed into market resources. Therefore, all the enterprises and individuals must act as either subjective or objective factors in order to ensure the establishment of a unified market. Since the question was originally raised under the product economy, initial construction of the market will begin with reforms in aspects such as the form of ownership and decision-making system, as well as organizational structure, and the generating and operational mechanisms of enterprises. Emerging enterprises will be liberated from the bondage of the so-called "one big workshop" of social production, and they will become commodity producers and business entities operating with self-interest and independent management power, creating necessary conditions to enable them to automatically and conscientiously enter both the domestic and international markets. With regard to the labor market, the labor force will enjoy a free-flowing in the market according to the demands of enterprises and individual preferences. This means that the labor force will also become subjective and objective factors in the market.

2) The status and functions of the government and enterprises must be reasonably defined. An enterprise must be a commodity producer and business entity with its own interests, while enjoying independent rights in terms of employment, finance and property management. Its basic function will be to earn a profit from supplying products and services to society. State-owned assets will be represented by state assets companies. The government will serve as a management body overseeing the microeconomy. The government's basic rights and responsibilities will be to adopt overall plans and coordinate national economic development, rationally regulate the distribution and redistribution of national income, and ensure the basic balance of the economic aggregate, structure and ratios, as well as the rational arrangement of the economic structure. The comprehensive and direct adjustment and control by the government over enterprises will

be transformed into indirect adjustment and control through the market and relying on its industrial, technical, financial and monetary, and credit policies, as well as economic levers. Indirect adjustments and controls of this type will be a multi-layered system shared both vertically and horizontally by the central and local governments. Administrative powers and financial rights must be redistributed, and the common and respective scope, content, methods and measures for adjustments and controls must be well defined.

3) Pricing mechanisms should be cultivated based on the prices determined by the market. China's existing commodity price system must undergo two basic transformations, one of which is from state and enterprise to domestic market price-setting, and the other is from domestic market to international market price-setting. The realization of these transformations will require that due respect be paid to the legitimate rights of the commodity producers, business operators and consumers, the adoption of market economic orders and the removal of barriers hindering the free flow of commodities. Great effort should also be made to oppose trade protectionism and the monopoly of highly profitable commodities, while at the same time opening all commodity markets. Prices will be determined in accordance with market competition.

4) An open commodity circulation system should be established. Developing a market economy and establishing a unified market require all China's localities and departments to develop an open circulation network with multi-layered channels in various forms, while at the same time helping to create a simplified, flexible new commodity circulation system. To achieve this goal it is necessary to establish a totally new market structure with enterprises as the main body. Various existing domestic wholesale and retail sales markets will be further developed, and specialized and comprehensive markets, futures markets and border trade markets will be opened. In addition, import and export trading companies and specialized export-oriented factories will be developed to promote the expansion of both domestic and international trade. Market planning and regulations will be implemented to

eliminate interference from monopolistic organizations, as well as to curb market domination and extortive prices, and eliminate counterfeit and shoddy products so as to ensure the market for equal competition and fair trade.

5) A complete market system should be established. The market system can be separated into two major categories, one as a visible commodity market, including a wide variety of consumer goods and capital goods, and objects of labour and the labour force. The other category is an invisible commodity market, including technology, information, capital, transportation and various other tertiary services. The goal of establishing a complete market system is to commercialize all resources, processed goods and services, and link to the various systems of the international market in order to form a truly market economy with competitiveness in the world market.

6) An active effort should be made to the development of imports and exports, and Sino-foreign economic and technological exchanges. China will proceed on the basis of mutual benefit to regulate its commodity surpluses and shortages with all countries and regions in the world. China will import and export advanced science and technology and resources so as to achieve a balance of supply and demand for the production element market and the market of elements for daily use, and to accelerate the four modernization drive.

7) A new unified flexible financial and taxation system should be established. One of the key aspects will center on creating a taxation system based essentially on the central tax, value-added and resource taxes, while at the same time establishing, in accordance with the reality, the tax rate, taxpayer categories, payment channels, and commendation and punishment regulations. Tax burden shared rationally by all enterprises represents the fair distribution of tax revenues and payment. This will help to stimulate the enthusiasm of the state, localities and enterprises, as well as individuals and foreign businessmen. A multi-step financial structure based on tax distribution system will be established to achieve a respective balance in both the central and regional finance.

8) Enterprises should develop horizontal economic cooperation and establish shareholding enterprise groups. Market economic relations are in essence the horizontal economic connections, and the establishment of a unified market itself is designed to maximize the development of horizontal economic links, enabling the free flow of production elements and the elements for daily use, and creating the necessary conditions for accelerating economic development. Fractions and blocks formed under the planned product economic system, which are in fact artificial obstacles hindering the free flow of production elements and elements for daily use, will be eliminated. Different levels of shareholding enterprise groups, with varying scopes, forms and contents, will be developed to enhance horizontal economic cooperation. In line with the law of the scale efficiency in market competition, a considerable number of relatively large shareholding enterprise groups must be organized, including joint ventures between transnational corporations and Chinese enterprises. Groups of this type are needed to expand professional cooperation, optimize the organizational structure of enterprises, expand the market scope for production elements and daily-use elements, strengthen the competitiveness of enterprises and give play to the advantages of Chinese economy in certain areas.

Problems occurred in forming a unified market.

China has scored remarkable achievements over the past 10-odd years in its efforts to establish a unified market. Notwithstanding, there are a number of lingering problems:

1) The subjective factors of the market are not as yet fully in place and the operational mechanisms of enterprises require more thorough transformation. a) Mechanisms to inspire production and stimulate enterprises have not been properly established. Consequently, non-state enterprises account for only a small proportion of the business results, with the lion's share going to the state. The interest sharing pattern between the enterprises and the state have not been properly readjusted. The so-called practice of "eating from the same big pot" still exists to various extent for employees of a number of enterprises. b) Enterprises have exces-

sive departments overstaffed with nonproductive personnel and, in some cases, also with productive forces. Enterprise structures and labour organizations have not yet optimized. The problem of waste of resources, high production costs and low economic efficiency has not yet been fundamentally solved. c) The irrational organizational structures of enterprises have not been fundamentally improved, with most small enterprises still retaining a complete set of departments. As a result of the control of administrative forces and the clear-cut restrictions set by cities and provinces, horizontal economic links and enterprise groups can not develop rapidly. The optimized use of the existing capital and production elements is still much desired, this situation has in turn led to an overall low socioeconomic efficiency. d) The fact that enterprises have been forced to undertake too many social functions has prevented them from concentrating their strength on production and business operations. e) Mechanisms to ensure the technological progress of enterprises are not strong enough, serious shortages in funds for scientific research as well as in scientific research staff and a low capacity for scientific development have prevented enterprises from upgrading the quality of their products and developing new products. As a result, enterprises remain relatively low in their competitiveness and flexibility to cope with the changeable market. f) Most large and medium-sized state-owned enterprises lack the savvy to compete in the world market, instead confining themselves to the limited domestic market and partial interests. g) The self-regulating mechanisms of enterprises have not yet established due to the absence of a property rights system for publicly-owned enterprises based on independent legal entities. As a result, many enterprises care only about their immediate interests in terms of technical renovations and expansion of reproduction. Short-term actions are rampant, with some enterprises going so far as to deplete their profits and capital.

2) The functions of the government have not as yet been completely transformed. Although reform enabled people to be aware of the necessity and the basic approaches needed to transform the functions of the government, the original highly central-

ized structure of planned economy has not as yet been dismantled. This in turn has to a certain extent dissected the unified market, limited the functions of market mechanisms and harmed the interests of enterprises. In addition, the administrative power and financial rights of the central government and localities have not been reasonably defined. The new double-tiered system for macroeconomic control has not operated coherently, thereby resulting in low efficiency and overstaffed structures. The industrial structure lacks rationalization, and the passive situation of overlapping in production and low social efficiency has not been reversed.

3) A complete market pricing system is not yet in place, and the contrast between planned and market prices is quite obvious in different parts of the country. For example, in a few southern provinces, the prices of commodities determined by the market account for 90 percent of the total value of commodities. However, the figure drops to only 40 percent in several northern provinces which have long been bases for heavy industry. The double-track pricing system, based on both government planning and the market, is still adopted for certain capital goods which are in short supply, as well as items requiring long-term construction and high investments and, in some cases, daily-use items. These factors clearly reveal that the market pricing system is far from complete.

4) Market institutions and the market system are not well developed. The outmoded structure of vertical circulation has not been completely uprooted. For example, some capital goods and commodities are still controlled by state materials departments and special stores responsible for planned distribution. A national futures market has not been established and the capital market has not matured. As a result, enterprises have far too few fund-raising channels. The first-class stock market has not been popularized in large and medium-sized cities and there are even fewer second-class stock markets. A comparatively high-level human resource market has not been established.

5) Irrational elements continue to exist in the taxation and financial systems. A rational interest-sharing structure between

the state, localities, enterprises, individuals and various modes of ownership has not been formed, and state-owned enterprises continue to shoulder an unfair burden in terms of interests and taxation. The practice of repaying loans prior to the payment of taxes is not conducive to controlling the business activities of enterprises, nor to controlling the investment scale. The present income taxes are divided into tax items according to different economic components, with progressive taxes applied in some cases, and proportional taxes in others. Different tax policies and taxation rates are disadvantageous to the competition amongst different economic elements. The existing turnover tax system, which dislinks the product tax with the value-added tax, fails to adequately meet the needs for readjusting the industrial structure, and the structure of supply and demand. The value-added tax has not been implemented throughout all industrial links, the tax itself is imperfect and not standardized, in addition to the existence of unfair tax burdens. Local tax income is too little in scale, affecting the implementation of tax distribution system. Under the financial contract system the central and local governments at various levels strengthened their interference in the finances of their subordinate enterprises. They use their financial rights to initiate small but nonetheless comprehensive investment projects. In protection of their own enterprises, they disrupted the unified market and sharpened contradictions between various regions and also contradictions between partial and overall interests.

6) The effort to deepen the reform of foreign trade system is not as yet complete, with the right to engage in foreign trade independently granted only to local governments and specialized foreign trade companies. Some large and medium-sized state-owned industrial enterprises which already have conditions required for engaging in foreign trade activities have not been granted independent rights to do so. Currently, there is no overall arrangement for absorbing, digesting the advanced foreign technology projects imported, and nor any plan to transfer them to inland areas. Some of imported foreign technology projects are duplicates. High customs duties are collected on imports in order

to protect the market for domestic products. Such practices are disadvantageous to Chinese enterprises in improving their business operations and developing new technology.

7) The structure and pattern of cities remain irrational. While the scale of large and medium-sized cities continues to expand, small cities and towns are not adequately developed. Most of them are small in scale, lack necessary functions, and remain backward. The urban and rural structural pattern is also far from rational. Large and medium-sized cities have made only a minimal effort in entrusting township enterprises for processing their products and spare parts. The current level of many township enterprises are very low and it is very difficult for the large number of the surplus rural labour force to find new jobs, thereby hindering the expansion of the Chinese market and the overall marketization of the economy. Inland cities are not active enough to invest and establish enterprises in coastal open cities. Most advanced technology projects imported by coastal cities have not as yet found their ways to inland areas. Coastal cities have failed to adequately play the role as windows for China's opening to the outside world.

Regional blockades become major obstacles hindering the development of a unified market.

Regional blockades and local protectionism have become major obstacles hindering the establishment and formation of a unified national market. This question was in fact raised in the early stages of reform. The Provisional Regulations Regarding the Development and Protection of Socialist Competition issued by the State Council in 1980 explicitly stipulated that "regional and departmental blockades must be eliminated" to ensure fair and legal competition. However, local protectionism has existed since the 1980s and unfair competition continues.

So-called regional blockades refer the actions taken by departments in certain administrative divisions to protect their own regional economic interests, hinder the flow of products of other areas to the local market, and vice versa. They relied on local rules and regulations or other improper methods, including arbitrarily raising and lowering prices. Strictly speaking, regional blockades are an administrative act rather than an enterprise act. In fact, such actions are totally unrelated to enterprise competition, nor are they to be found in the related legislations of other countries of the world.

However, the situation in China is different. For a long time in the past, China's economy was subject to administrative interference. Governmental administrative and management departments, which were usually overstaffed, directly controlled enterprises and interfered in the operations of enterprises. For instance, new projects required the approval of planning departments; capital needed depended on bank loans; prices were set by price-control departments; employment was controlled by labor departments, and accounts were supervised by financial and auditing departments. Enterprises had no rights in terms of labor, finance and materials, and assumed no independent responsibility for production, supply and sales. In a word, the government exerted an excessive control over enterprises with numerous restrictions. Consequently, even today there are a large number of enterprises whose success or failure is still under the direct control of governmental departments. Faced with such conditions, how can enterprises enter the market and independently carry out production and business activities under the guidance of the market, and how can they engage in fair competition? On the other hand, viewed from a more profound perspective, the formation and existence of regional blockades and local protectionism result in numerous complicated factors related to the system structure, ideology and economic reform, as well as adjustment measures and managerial methods. Nonetheless, economic interests are behind all such factors. Under the responsibility system of the local governments and local financial contract system, local governments are responsible for the development of local politics, economy and social development. Therefore, it is quite difficult for them to be free from the limitation of taking their regional interests as the centre in considering the production and construction of their own regions. As a result, numerous contradictions have emerged in economic activities. When local governments found it impossible to fulfill their tasks economically, they have no alternative but to transfer their burdens to enterprises. Enterprises are thus ordered to purchase low quality local products at high price in order to protect the local market, taxes and financial revenue. In such cases, the government forcibly interferes in the operations of enterprises which are forced to accept the administrative actions of their respective local government. In this way, regional blockades and local protectionism have forced local production and business activities to operate on a low level, while at the same time disrupting the market and adversely affecting commodity circulation, thereby violating the objective economic law, and in some cases depressing and even suppressing fair competition. This is especially true at the present time as the entire nation is joining in a effort to develop the market economy. Regional blockades and local protectionism are totally contradictory to the reform and opening effort, and to the effort to establish the socialist market economic structure at the earliest possible date.

Under the current situation, it is absolutely necessary to eliminate all barriers and blockades, and to establish a unified socialist market linking both urban and rural areas as well as different regions. How then can problems related to regional blockades and local protectionism be solved? On the one hand, it is necessary to further deepen structural reform, especially the reform of the financial structure to enable local governments to be liberated from the grips of regional economic interests. On the other hand, laws must be established to regulate the various types of behaviors related to local protectionism. For example, local governments responsible for instituting regional blockades will be instructed to rescind their related decisions and orders otherwise their decisions and orders will be declared invalid. They will also be ordered to compensate the losses. Officials responsible for such actions will be subject to administrative censure and fines, and in some cases, will be subject to legal proceedings. Law enforcement agencies with responsibility for supervision and management will be established at high government levels, preferably at the central and provincial levels.

Strategies and measures for establishing a unified market.

China's economic operational mechanisms and resource allocations must be guided by the market, and must function on the basis of market mechanisms. In the interim, various measures for the planned management and planned regulation should be improved. Based on the current tendency of national economic development, the state should at the earliest possible date discard mandatory regulatory forms and measures characteristic of a planned economy, which depress the functions of market mechanisms in all fields, as well as the supply-production-marketing activities of almost all enterprises. The future state socioeconomic development planning must by no means be a simple operational process of distributing funds, materials and human resources, but rather be a guidance plan based on market analysis, reflecting the demands of the law of value, the balance between supply and demand, and conditions resulting from shortages of resources. The intermingling of guidance plan and market mechanisms will represent the true unification of the plan and the market. The priority of planned regulation should be placed on macro total demand, and long-term structural readjustments should emphasize basic industries and the construction of infrastructure. However, while granting enterprises a freehand in business activities, under exceptional circumstances, the state can only issue limited mandatory plans in capital construction, production and circulation. At the same time, however, certain mandatory plans should be limited to only a small number of enterprises. Most enterprises will be permitted to treat the state macro regulatory plan as a reference and not as a required directive. Enterprises enjoy the right to regulate or adjust their own development plans, production and business plans according to market demand and the fluctuation of prices as well as their own economic interests. Once freed from the interference of planning departments, enterprises will automatically enter the track of a standardized market, and will engage in competition with rivals in order to promote the formation of a vigorous and active socialist unified market.

Continued effort should be made to transform the functions of the government and simplify governmental departments. What then is the objective in the transformation of the functions of the government? In our opinion, the government is the coordinator of the macroeconomy. Its chief function is to formulate strategies for national economic development and the overall plan for socioeconomic development, while at the same time, exercising indirect regulation and control over the national economy. On the one hand, in order to meet the changes and demand of the market, the government should appropriately balance the major ratios between national economic aggregate and structure by using various markets, various flexible policies, economic levers and indicators, as well as the financial might of the government. In order to achieve a relatively balanced ratio between the supply and demand structures of market commodities, it should ensure that increased consumption conforms to the development of production and promote the sustained and rapid development of the national economy. On the other hand, the government should act in accordance with the targets for socioeconomic development to standardize and guide the economic activities of enterprises. At the same time, it should further complete a set of legal measures for scientific management, while evaluating and correcting various economic activities of the society and enterprises in accordance with related laws and regulations.

Continued effort should be made to accelerate price reform and promote the complete formation of price mechanisms, ensuring prices to be determined by the market. The practice of price reform has proved that no matter how serious the shortage is in supply, information based on the prices set by the market will help to guide and regulate the allocation of social resources, and gradually improve the supply of commodities in high demand. Notwithstanding, when the price of commodities in demand rises to a certain level, it will fall naturally. When the supply of specific commodities exceeds market demand, price signals will lead to the reallocation of resources according to the principle of optimized combinations. This will lead to the abandonment of low quality commodities and promote those of high quality. This will result in a relative rise in the social productivity level and as a consequence the production costs for certain commodities will be reduced. From the standpoint of consumers, they will initially suffer from inflation pressure and their consumption psychology will reach new laws. However, following several production cycles, the increasing supply of commodities will enable consumers to enjoy the relatively lower prices for higher quality commodities. Their consumption psychology will improve and they will acquire a new understanding of freed prices. China's reform over the past dozen years has resulted in a dramatic increase of various consumer and capital goods, not only satisfying the basic necessities of the people, but also enabling the society to march towards a better standard of living. Most enterprises can now purchase raw materials needed in production from the markets. Based on such material conditions, except for prices of public products and services which remain to be set or regulated by the state temporarily, prices for all other commodities should be open. Prices for a few rare raw materials can also be open by increasing import volumes.

Continued efforts should be made to strengthen the market organizationally and promote the cultivation of the market system. The most difficult part in the construction of the market system is how to establish a market of capital. We believe that the practice of distributing the capital vertically by national banks according to specialized banks in a planned way has many disadvantages which are apt to create the irrational allocation and flow of the capital. This is indeed an urgent problem to be solved. At present, however, under the current condition of independent operations, some enterprises might be unable to obtain funds for capital construction, and in some cases, it might even be difficult for them to get circulation funds for production, thus leading to a deformation in the national economic structure. There is an urgent need to increase channels available for fund-raising. Therefore, while temporarily maintaining the proportion of the capital to be distributed by the national bank according to mandatory plans, the funds by market regulations must be increased accordingly in proportion. The funds for bank loans mainly come from the deposits of enterprises and individuals, as well as loans and interest recovered. Based on the prerequisite that the volume of currency issued is strictly controlled by the central bank, the amount of bonds and stocks issued by enterprises through banks should be expanded. Surplus state revenue after satisfying the state budget can be used by the Ministry of Finance to issue mid- and short-term financial credit loans in order to provide emergency funds for the production and construction activities of enterprises. The circulation of funds should be allowed between finance departments of provinces and municipalities directly under the central government and banks. On the other hand, the policy of opening to the outside world should also apply to the development of the capital market to solve the shortage of funds. Apart from the introduction of capital and allocations by state financial departments from United Nations International Monetary Fund and the World Bank, foreign banks should be encouraged to directly establish financial institutions in China. With guarantee from city level financial departments or banks, foreign banks should be permitted to offer direct credit loans to China's state- and collectively-owned enterprises.

(2) Perfection of the socialist market system should emphasize the cultivation of various market factors and promote the development of financial, labor, technology, information and real estate markets.

The construction of a socialist market structure is the basic task for creating a new socialist market economic system. In 1992, China witnessed a remarkable acceleration in the rate of market growth, and began to break the limitations of the traditional commodity market and developed a market based on the productive factors. Comparatively speaking, major progress has been achieved in strengthening links between domestic and overseas markets, reaching a new stage of development.

However, China's market reform is far from satisfactory in depth and in breadth. At present, markets of various factors are still in their initial stages and unable to meet the demands of a socialist market economy. Therefore, it is necessary to emphasize the cultivation of various factors markets and promote the sustained development of the financial, labor, technology, information and real estate markets.

Active cultivation of financial and stock markets.

More than ten years' efforts have enabled China's financial market to take shape. The year 1992 witnessed an accelerated development of the market of capital, especially the market involving various bonds and stocks. Bonds valued well over 100 billion yuan were issued during the year, while the volume of stocks issued surpassed dramatically the statistical figures at the beginning of the year. An integrated, multi-layered and multi-functional securities market has basically formed with the Shanghai Stock Exchange, the Shenzhen Stock Exchange, the National NET system and the STAQ system as concentrated stock exchange centers. All of these will have a great impact on the development of China's long-term funds market and the formation of the financial structure.

At the same time, the state has established a securities committee and a securities supervision and management committee to strengthen the organization and leadership of the stock market. Generally speaking, however, much work remains to be down with regard to forming a financial market suited to the socialist market economy.

A national unified loan market should be formed at the earliest possible date. Specific measures include: a) Establishing a number of inter-regional and trans-industry funds loaning markets on the basis of existing regional and the inter-regional financial networks in order to lay a solid foundation for the establishment of a national unified funds loaning market. b) Accelerating the construction of a satellite banking network to ensure the transformation of the existing national market price reporting and transaction information system into a national funds loaning center. c) All funds loaning markets are required to conduct transactions through fund circulation institutions and should be linked to the price reporting and transaction information system in order to finalize the formation of a national unified funds loaning market.

Active efforts should be made to develop the bond market, and perfect and finalize the bond issuance and transfer system.

It is essential to gradually discard the administrative distribution of bonds and replace it with contracted sales by financial institutions. At the same time, a system of open auctions and bidding should be adopted gradually.

Efforts should be made to steadily promote the stock market. a) Along with the effort to perfect the management of the stock markets in Shanghai and Shenzhen, it is also necessary to continually expand the scope of open issuance of stocks in the two cities and increase the number of listed companies. b) Securities institutions specialized in investment funding business and funds management organizations should be established to collect individual investment capital to ensure the unified trading of stocks so as to reduce risks and stabilize the stock market.

The securities markets should be expanded. Proceeding on the basis of a strengthened unified management of the securities market, experiments related to new securities items, such as investment funds, transferable and trust interest securities, will be organized to activate the securities market. It is also necessary to further open and activate the secondary securities market and continue with the experiment in special Renminbi stocks (B-Shares). Satellite communications facilities and computer networks should be used to gradually connect securities-related activities in various localities directly with the Shanghai and Shenzhen stock exchanges, and the national financial market price reporting, transaction and information centers, so as to accelerate the information exchange and the settlement of accounts.

Accelerate the development of the technology market.

Operating under the principle of "lifting restrictions and giving active support and guidance," China's technology market has witnessed brisk transactions and a rapid increase in the application rate of scientific and technological achievements. The situation has resulted directly from the accelerated pace of reform in China's technological and scientific structure, and further improvement in the overall economic situation. In the first half of 1992, 27 provinces, autonomous regions and municipalities directly under the central government signed 98,400 technological contracts valued at 5.78 billion yuan, increasing 17.71 percent and 54.15 percent respectively over the figures of the same period of the previous year. The total value of technological contracts for the year was expected to surpass 10 billion yuan. At present, somewhere between 60-70 percent of all industrial scientific achievements in the country are being applied and popularized. The technology market is rapidly becoming an important channel for combining the economy with science and technology, and is an indispensable bridge leading the scientific and technological innovations into production.

It is essential to strengthen the comprehensive management of the technology market and promote the process of transforming scientific and technological results into productive forces. Acting in accordance with state industrial policy and as well as technological policies, scientific and technological plans and economic plans, and the existing situation of the technological market itself, management departments in the technology market should regularly publicize projects for technology development and exchange of commodities. In addition, they should regulate and rationalize the development, transactions and flow of technological commodities by implementing policies related to credit loans, risk investment funding and the prices of new technological products.

Due importance should be attached to intermediate technological service institutions, bringing their role into full play. The major tasks of intermediate institutions include: gathering, sorting and delivering information; locating and selecting trade partners for both sellers and buyers; fulfilling commissions entrusted by governments at various levels and enterprises by sponsoring public bidding for the development and promotion of key technological development projects; allocating funds for technological transactions; participating in risk investment; organizing feasibility studies and secondary development of key application projects; gathering feedback on market information; and sponsoring various trade fairs.

Technological operational mechanism at grass-roots levels should be perfected and the circulation of technological commodities should be accelerated. The mainstay in the circulation of the technological market include suppliers of technological projects and their consumers at grass-roots levels. Specifically, those engaged in selling include scientific and technological research units, schools of higher education, factories and mines, enterprises, social organizations and non-governmental scientific enterprises, as well as individual inventors. Grass-roots units involved in various trades and industries, industrial enterprises in particular, are the consumers in the technological market. Such institutions must gradually conform with the development of the technological market along with the deepening of reform. Scientific and technological research units engaged mainly in technological development must accelerate steps towards industrialization. Technological trade departments of enterprises should expand all business activities. Scientific research institutions in schools of higher education should make every effort to ensure the industrialization of the scientific research departments.

Simultaneously, it is necessary to perfect the legal system of the technological market, as well as to stabilize and develop policies to support and guide the market, strengthen coordination and ability for macro-control and regulation.

Breaking away from the theoretical barrier of "labour is not a commodity," speeding up the formation of labour market and placing wage distribution under market regulation.

The traditional system resulted in the rigid allocation of labour resources. Therefore, one of the most important targets for market economy and the cultivation and development of the market structure is to ensure that economic entities seeking for maximum efficiency are able to determine labour resource allocations according to market signals. At the same time, suppliers and users of labour resources are free to make choices and implement voluntarily on the basis of evaluating and calculating their own interests.

The development of China's labour market is faced with an important theoretical obstacle—the theory that under the socialist system labour is not a commodity. In practice, however, the theory has proved groundless. At present, the public ownership of the means of production takes the form of state ownership. Although the state is the representative of the people, it is inaccurate to conclude that labourers are the owners of the means of production. However, it is obvious that the power of labour is owned by individual labourers. Therefore, it is essential to place the labour power at the disposal of the state in the form of commodity transactions so as to combine state-owned capital resources with individually owned labour power. The necessity for such a relationship becomes even clearer when the government and enterprises are clearly separated and enterprises become chief sectors in the ownership of the means of production.

During the reform we dare not to face the issue of labour market, and it was referred to as the human services market and the professionals (talents) market. However, the so-called human services market and the professionals market are only part of the labour market. The assumption of taking these markets for the whole of the labor market has resulted in the abnormal growth of China's labour market. At present, though the labour services market and the professionals market are relatively active, the labour market as a whole has not yet matured. The labour resources, being the chief component of the national resources, has only partially entered the path of market regulation due to the theoretical obsticale. The next step of reform should clearly define the concept of the labour market so as to promote its cultivation and development.

The key to the formation of a mature labour market is for the state to give up its special position as the major user and distributor of the labour force so as to create conditions letting enterprises and laborers make their own choices. Of course, granting it needs a transitional period to realize complete autonomy in this regard and it can not be achieved by a mass movement, nor should there be any hesitation in this matter.

Like many other countries undergoing reform, China's economic reform was sparked by the introduction of interest incentive mechanisms, including adjustments in the wages of workers and staff members, restoration of the bonus system and the wage reform in 1985. A structural wage system was carried out at that time in government departments and institutions, while a different system in which the total wage volume was directly linked to economic efficiency was adopted in the enterprises. Despite the fact that this represented progress compared with the traditional systems, these reform experiments did not change the existing wage system under which the state served as the main distributor of income, and wage standards and levels were determined by administrative means. The efficiency-based wage system adopted by enterprises was still partially coordinated by administrative means. One of the fundamental reasons for this was the lack of suitable standards to evaluate the value of labour. The ownership of the labour force remains in the hands of the state, and individual labourer is simply a productive factor belonging to the state, negating the commodity quality of labour power. As a result, the state has to assume overall responsibility for the daily needs of the labourers, thus placing an additional burden on the state and dampening the initiative of the labourers. To change this situation, it requires the formation of a multi-layered labour market under which labourers can choose jobs and earn living. It is also essential to establish a comprehensive social insurance system to liberate labourers from single mode employment insurance and establish mechanisms to ensure the free flow of labour power.

The state should gradually abandon its function as the chief distributor of wages, so as to better play its role in macro regulation and supervision. As long as the level of wage distribution and the amount of wages accruing to individuals remain under unified state management, the practice of egalitarianism will linger and the existing double-track individual income will not vanish. The adoption of the market regulation in real wage distribution requires the state to withdraw from its control of income distribution. In this way, wage distribution would not be paid directly from state revenue; instead the total wages, increased levels and the volume of individual income will all be determined by enterprises. The state should use income taxes to regulate the total volume of wages and individual wage level and control the annual increase rate of wages in accordance with the level of economic development. It should protect the interests of the labourers by adopting relevant laws guaranteeing a minimum wage level. From a long-term point of view the wage system based on efficiency now adopted by enterprises should also be placed under the market regulation, because it is still a wage system determined partly by administrative means. Wages paid from state revenue should be appropriately readjusted in line with the wage level of enterprises and economic development, rather than being determined by the need to balance revenue, so as to form a positive wage increase mechanism.

An effort must be made to visualize the invisible wages. At present, the true function of wages are diminishing, while the proportion of invisible wages, such as bonuses and welfare benefits, are expanding. A major prerequisite of reform is to transform all welfare and subsidiary income into currency-based wages and to properly visualize the total wage amounts. However, the visualization of the currently invisible income means that the wage earner has to pay more income tax. Such an effort should be combined with the promotion of the wage, housing and taxation reforms. Therefore, various other supporting reform measurers are required to ensure the visualization of the wage income.

Promoting and standardizing the real estate market.

China's present real estate market has reached a considerable scale, and the market principle has palyed and continues to play a guiding role in the process of land allocations. Nonetheless, a standardized market has not yet formally established. Hence, it is of utmost urgency to strengthen planning, formulate relevant policies and measures, perfect market laws and regulations, and ensure the real estate market to develop in good order.

It is thus necessary to further deepen the reform of the system of land use and the housing system, as well as to clarify ownership relationships concerning land and housing. Greater efforts should be made to work out scientific and rational plans for land use and in accordance with these plans implement a comprehensive system of compensated use of land at the earliest possible date. Administrative allocations should be continued in terms of land used for office buildings of the Party, government, military and other institutions, and the advantages of market mechanisms should be fully employed to create an environment based on fair competition. The key of housing reform lies in the explicit determination of the property rights of publicly owned housing, so as to facilitate the transactional operations of the real estate market in good order.

The real estate market system should be established, developed and perfected. Appropriate policies should be adopted to promote the real estate in reserve to enter market circulation. On condition that the state's profits are guaranteed, preferential polices related to taxes and pricing, including land prices and land use fees, should be enacted to protect the reasonable interests of real estate brokers and lenders. The initial real estate market based on land use right and transferals will be monopolized by the government. However, secondary markets and other emerging markets, i.e. the development and management of real estate on marketed land and transactions related to real estate in reserve, should be open and promoted under the macro management of the state. The pace of such activities should be accelerated to form a complete real estate market, including the circulation of land use rights and the ownership of housing.

Great efforts should be made to strengthen price management and establish a price system for real estate conforming to the commodity economic law. Land prices will be reasonably determined in accordance with comprehensive factors, including the socioeconomic development level, different types of land use, differentiated interests, development costs, and supply and demand. The prices of commercial housing should also fluctuate in accordance with different categories of buyers. With regard to residential housing three-level-price system—welfare, low interest and market—should be established to meet the demands of consumers at various levels. A legal system for real estate should be established and perfected according to the existing situation in China, with due consideration for generally accepted international practices. Emphasis will be placed on drafting and implementing the Housing Law and the Real Estate Law, as well as other subsidiary laws and regulations.

According to the principle of streamlining the management, marketing and the operation of real estate, a real estate management system should be established which conforms with the requirements of the socialist market economy and facilitates the macro guidance and unified leadership.

Experts point out that any attempt to cultivate the real estate market should be conducted from the central to the local level due to the fact that the real estate market in China is currently at a low level and characterized by serious problems resulting from departmental and regional partitions and blockades. This is one of the characteristics in establishing a market economic system in China. Since the introduction of the reform and opening policy, China has gradually evolved from its old planned economic structure based on searching commodities for the market to a new structure of commodities looking for markets. The most urgent task under the new situation is that governments at all levels should operate under the guidance of the state macro plan to adopt various legal, economic and administrative measures to eliminate departmental dissection and regional blockades in order to enhance the formation of a national unified market.

2. Perfecting Socialist Market Mechanisms

(1) Legitimate competition is an effective means to promote development of the market economy and should be perfected gradually in practice.

Competition mechanisms represent the nucleus of the socialist market economy.

Competition mechanisms are the nucleus of the socialist market economy, and a socialist market economy would be out of the question without competition, or with competition immature.

Some experts have noted that the competition being discussed refers to market competition in the economic arena, and it means the efficiency competition between numerous economic entities, including both suppliers and consumers, rather than the competition described by some economists as chickens fighting for food. Efficiency competition means mainly price competition, and non-price competition as secondary, including competition in products in terms of quality, design and new models, competition in conditions such as discounts, goods supply, payment and services, as well as marketing competition in terms of advertising, packaging and promotions.

Competition, as a concept of the commodity economy, refers to contentions and struggles between different producers and managers of commodities to gain a favourable position on the commodity market in terms of production and marketing. The stronger survive while the weaker perish. Just as the law of value is bound to play an objective role in the commodity economy, competition will also play its role as a compulsory law, as long as such commodity economy exists.

Competition in the socialist market economy is an indispensable external force which promotes the development of socialist productive forces. Firstly, it encourages enterprises to constantly upgrade their technology and management and raise their labour productivity, thereby facilitating the development of social productive forces. Competition, which is linked directly to the material interests and fate of enterprises, compels each enterprise to constantly improve the technology of its production and management, adopt new production methods, tap potential, reduce consumption, lower costs, and raise work efficiency, in order to realize best economic returns. Secondly, competition helps achieve a balance between social supply and demand. Since competition concerns the material interests of enterprises, each enterprise must pay attention to market trends, investigate social demand, gather information and carry out market forecasting in order to produce large quantity of new high-quality low-cost products of all varieties and designs. The problem of producing same kind of products for decades will be fundamentally solved. Thus, production will be organized according to consumption demand, the improvement of the living standards of the people, and the constant changes in the consumption structure, the balance between social supply and demand will be achieved through competition and the role of market prices. Thirdly, competition will promote the implementation of the principle of material interests. The fact that competition has a direct bearing on the material interests of enterprises and their employees will encourage enterprises to better their management, increase profits and pay more taxes which in turn will bring them more profits. As a result, their employees will enjoy more material interests, and which will again arouse the enthusiasm of the labourers for more cultural and scientific knowledge, so as to improve their professional proficiency and skills. Thereby the cultural and scientific level of society as a whole will be upgraded. As a matter of fact, competition may also possibly bring about various types of negative phenomena, and in some cases might even induce illegal behaviors. This is an aspect unavoidable in a commodity economy.

In short, while perfecting the competitive mechanisms of socialism, great efforts should be made to improve both of their stimulant and restrictive roles, as well as to perfect an environment for equal competition, while at the same time preventing monopolies. Given these facts, it is necessary to formulate rules for competition under the socialist market economy.

An environment for equal competition is the primary condition for market competition.

At present, the Chinese economy is in the midst of a transition from the traditional planned economic system to a socialist market economy, and there is much to be desired in the standardization of the market. Although changes of some factors can be predicted, such as changes in population and the natural and technical environment, various other factors, particularly those related to the economic environment, are fraught with problems and will make it more difficult to succeed in the competition even if they can manage to adapt to the market economy. This, in fact, involves the question of creating a rational and normal market economic environment. In other words, it is necessary to realign the distorted market economic environment and create an environment for equal competition. These represent the basic external conditions required for enterprises to participate in market competition. Such conditions will make it possible for enterprises to adapt themselves to the changes of the economic environment and gain success in competition through their own efforts.

Equal opportunity for competition does not stress eventual results, but instead the procedures of competition, which implies an opportunity for everyone to engage in competition. It not only allows collectives to select individuals but also, perhaps more importantly, enables individuals to choose collectives. In short, a complete description of an equal opportunity for competition should include participation in competitive activities, fair rules for competition, transparent procedures, and the validity of competition results, on the premise of acknowledging possible inequality from the starting point of competition, i.e. the natural inequality of individuals, and the different strengths and scales of enterprises.

Participation in competitive activities means that every micro-entity has the right to choose independently to participate in competition. They may choose to relinquish this right, but they must first of all possess the right. The decision on the use of the right to participate or relinquish in competition must be made by micro-entities themselves. The fairness of competition rules refers to the fact that the rules governing the competition process apply to all participants. Transparent competition procedures refer to the publicity of the rules for competition, open competition and the prohibition of back door deals and manipulations behind the scenes. The validity of competition results means that the participants of the competion must recognize and accept the final results of the competition. Both winners and losers must bear the obligations once they participated in the competition, and accept the results based on their recognized logic of competition. No one can rely on prerogatives to acquire additional power for profits, or "immunities" for losses.

What influences will equal opportunities for competition exert on efficiency?

Firstly, unequal competition opportunities mean that individuals are deprived of equal opportunities to participate in competition. If higher authorities are to determine who can or cannot participate in the competition, it will inevitably lead to the so-called "rent seeking" behaviours. "Rent seekers" strive to obtain their opportunity to participate in competition by engaging in rent seeking activities, while "rent setters" acquire extra profits from their ability to set rents. Such behaviours will undoubtedly lead to corruption and a decline in social values, and damage economic returns.

Secondly, unequal competition opportunities may result in assigning mediocre people to posts which should be filled by more capable people. Rent seeking behaviours will exist in the absence of equal competition and openly advertising for employees, thus keeping off people who are very competitive and capable but have no relations or "back doors." Therefore, it is quite common for a position which needs only one person to be filled by three people. Though the number of employees has increased, the quality has declined. This is known as "exclusive inefficiency," or in other words, inefficiency caused by the exclusion of the most qualified people as a result of unequal competition opportunities.

Thirdly, unequal competition opportunities aggravate the natural inequality between people. If one falls behind others only one step in the beginning, he/she is likely to remain behind permanently. Once people are excluded from good occupations, they lose the motivation and opportunity to raise their technical level, which may prove that they are actually qualified for the job. Such circumstances may produce a type of centrifugal force and widen the gap between social interest groups and members, thereby resulting in inefficiency caused by internal strife.

Under conditions of the market economy, and owing to the functions of the law of value, the pursuance of efficiency is bound to create inequality in income. Attempts to forcefully even up incomes as it was under the old system will inevitably dampened labourers' enthusiasm in production, impede the implementation of the principle of efficiency, and restrict the growth of economic returns. This shows that the pursuit of equality of result will end up with neither equality nor efficiency. The principle of equal competition opportunities, however, embodies equality. Generally speeking, equal competition opportunities go simultaneously with efficiency. Unequal opportunities lead to inefficiency, which grows at a doubled speed. On the other hand, equal opportunities will produce efficiency, and a higher level of equal opportunities will yield higher efficiency.

At present, China's market lacks an environment conducive to equal competition, which is manifested as follows:

1) Unequal tax burden

Paying taxes is a social responsibility borne by all enterprises, irrespective of the type of ownership they belong to. This in fact is the only way to achieve equal competition. As a matter of course, in order to achieve certain policy targets it is necessary to adopt preferential policies on tax exemptions and reductions for particular tax rate or tax categories. However, excessive preferential treatment will not only reduce financial revenue, but also lead to unequal competition and harm the healthy development of the market economy. Currently China's township enterprises, foreign-funded enterprises and enterprises in special economic zones and development zones enjoy more favourable policies than state-owned enterprises, especially the large and medium-sized enterprises. Some foreign-funded enterprises are actually funded by domestic capital remitted from abroad, yet they enjoy preferential treatment. These problems must be solved in order to create an environment for equal competition.

2) Unequal promotion methods

Sales promotion is an important marketing activity enabling enterprises to participate in market competition. Such activities call for certain means and funding. For sales promotion, enterprises abroad must allocate huge sums not only on publicity, but also on business entertainment expenses. According to statistics in 1990, the dividends all Japanese enterprises paid to the shareholders totalled 4,000 billion Japanese yen, but their business entertainment expenses reached 5,000 billion yen. Albeit a massive amount, the funds were expended in accordance with the law. In China, although enterprises expend funds on business entertainment everyday, there are no clearly defined rules regulating such expenditures. Some township and private enterprises act wilfully in their business entertainment expenses, with some adopting competitive methods prohibited even in capitalist countries. Comparatively speaking, state-owned enterprises enjoy less flexibility in allocating funds for business entertainment. Moreover, there lacks a clear understanding of what is legal and what is not. This is actually another form of unequal competition.

3) Inequality resulting from local protectionism

Some localities, in order to protect their own interests, rely on the administrative power of local governments to protect backwardness, and have provided local enterprises with many favourable conditions. For example, some localities have adopted stipulations that raw materials and spare parts needed by local enterprises must be purchased from local enterprises, and daily necessities needed by local residents must be local products, and no products from outside are allowed to enter the local market. As a result, advanced enterprises and high-quality products from other areas can not enter local markets. This is of course an unequal competition.

4) Inequality resulting from ineffective market management

Equal competition must be guaranteed by perfected laws, regulations and rules, as well as market management and strict enforcement of the law. Flooding the market with counterfeit and shoddy commodities, and an excessive degree of competition caused by blind development of low-grade products, will combine to create unequal competition. Without strict management, famous brand products produced by advanced enterprises, which have dedicated years of effort, will be buffeted, and famous trademarks will lose their reputation overnight.

Some of the aforementioned factors of inequality must be overcome by using legal means, with others eliminated by readjusting related policies, and still others by strengthening macro-management. All these are beyond the control of enterprises, but this in no way implies they can do nothing. Enterprises must comprehensively strengthen their marketing management and operations. They must be good at formulating competitive strategies and bypassing disadvantageous factors, bringing their strong points into full play and making active moves to strive for victory in the market competition.

The practice of reform has proved that energetic development of non-state economic sectors, in conjunction with actively and steadily advancing the reform of the state-owned economic sector, is the key to shortening the process of establishing a market economic structure and developing equal opportunities for competition. The development of non-state economic sectors has been a catalyst for the establishment of mechanisms of equal competition opportunities in the following two aspects:

First, the demonstrative effect. Under ordinary circumstances, the process of the development of non-state economic sectors should be one of equal competition. The establishment of such enterprises, the recruitment of employees, the distribution of wages, the formation and modification of management policies, and the development or bankruptcy of enterprises are all conducted according to the law of value, the law governing demand and supply, the law of competition and the law of equal profits characteristic of the market economy. Under such a situation, everyone equally participates in competitive activities, the rules for competition are basically fair, for everyone must obey the authority of the market, the procedures of competition are essentially transparent, no one is permitted to conduct surreptitious deals by applying prerogative rights, the results of competition are basically valid, and there is no leeway for "bargain" or "recourse" if an employee is dismissed or an enterprise declares bankruptcy. Such a mechanism has not only provided non-state economic sectors with enough motivation, but also set a good example for the transformation of the state-owned economy.

Second, the pressure of being "overwhelmed." Prior to the development of non-state economic sectors, the state-owned economic sector relied on its monopolistic status to reap exorbitant profits. However, the situation has changed drastically since the development of non-state economic sectors. If the state-owned economic sector remains unchanged, it faces the growing danger of being "overwhelmed" by non-state economic sectors. To ensure its existence, the state-owned economic sector must thoroughly alter its management mechanisms and rely on its financial, technical and intellectual advantages to compete with non-state economic sectors. This will undoubtedly force the state-owned economic sector to adopt the mechanisms of competition for equal opportunities.

To sum up , the establishment of a socialist market economic system represents a process. Mechanisms of equal competition, such as equal participation, fair rules for competition, transparent competitive procedures and validity of competition results should be our goals, and based on these goals we should formulate plans and measures for reform. By doing so, the market economic structure to be established in China is expectedly to be an economic system of high efficiency.

Laws should be adopted to prohibit illegitimate competition.

With regard to economic legislation, previous legislation concerning market rules enacted during the past 10-odd years of reform was relatively weak and incomplete. Not enough attention has been attached to the establishment of a good market economic order and to the formulation of a unified law on legal and equal competition, nor any effective measures and unified rules have been adopted to curb illegitimate competition and protect legal, equal and open competition. In the recent years media has made great efforts to expose market domination and extortive prices, counterfeit and shoddy products, and other illegitimate competition behaviours. All these have revealed the fact that China's market is faced with incomplete legislation and the lack of strict enforcement of laws. Government organizations often resort to "campaigns" to disseminate policies within a fixed period of time to limit and crack down on various illegitimate competitive behaviours. To fundamentally solve these problems, it is imperative to accelerate the formulation of legislation and rules on legal, equal and open competition and standardize competition activities, while at the same time punishing illegitimate competition behaviours such as manufacturing and selling counterfeit and shoddy commodities. Only by so doing can the interests of consumers, the order of normal market competition and healthy development of economy be effectively protected.

At present, there are no unified worldwide definitions delineating illegitimate competition. Some countries define it in broad sense, while others explain the term in narrow sense. In a broad sense, illegitimate competition refers to all illegal behaviours related to commodity production and management, as well as actions contrary to business ethics and social morality, including monopolistic behaviours, as well as behaviours which limit competition, and the use of illegitimate means to create competition. In a narrow sense, with the exception of monopolies and behaviours which otherwise limit competition, illegitimate competition refers to behaviours which are against the law or habits, including actions such as using deception, compulsion, blockades, stealing, dirty tricks and slander to seek exorbitant profits.

China's legislation contains a clear definition of illegitimate competition which is manifested as follows: First, the means adopted to determine legal and illegitimate competition are quite different. The means used for legal competition are in line with stipulations of laws and policies, including mobilizing the enthusiasm of employees to improve quality and technology, lower costs and enhance credit. But illegitimate competition relies on behaviors and means which are incompatible with stipulations of relevant laws and policies, and contradict to legal business exchanges. Second, the legal results and social effects of the two kinds of competitions are completely different. Legal competition is encouraged and protected by the law, because it effectively promotes productivity, increases economic and social benefits, accelerates scientific and technological progress and facilitates the healthy and vigorous development of the socialist market economy. Illegitimate competition is prohibited by law and must be resolutely curbed, because it not only harms the interests of consumers, but also adversely affects the accumulation of social wealth, seriously disrupts the order of the socialist market economy and impedes the growth of productive forces.

In accordance with the international legal practice as well as concrete conditions in China the following illegitimate competition behaviours should be curbed.

Behaviours of bribery or bribery in disguised forms in competition, such as directly offering cash or valuable goods under various pretexts, irrational commissions or other benefits, using packaging materials irrelevant to the property, quality and safety of commodities, offering additional gifts and other benefits in purchasing and marketing.

Behaviours of deception in competition, such as using fake trademarks, packaging, decorations and business names; lying about or withholding the location, source and producer's name of commodities or otherwise providing misleading information; using fraudulent methods to obtain titles of honor such as famous quality products or quality service; collecting prepayments for advance sales but without the ability to supply goods; and promoting sales of over-stocked, damaged or defective goods under the name of clearance sales or discount sales.

Behaviours which not only violate the product law and the law on standardization of products, but also bring serious harms to the interests of consumers, such as producing sub-standard products or making false publicity of the quality, properties, composition of raw materials, manufacturing methods, usages and price of products.

Behaviours in direct or indirect deals, such as market domination, forced purchases and sales, irrational sales requirements, marketing with additional conditions, hoarding and cornering the market, and selling commodities at high prices by controlling or withholding the supply of goods.

Behaviours of changing prices inappropriately, such as forcing prices up to compete purchasing or forcing prices down to dump commodities in order to damage the interests of rivals or other concerned parties.

Behaviours of signing irrational agreements, including the ganging up of a number of managers to damage the interests of their rivals, or dirty tricks such as rigging bids.

Behaviours unrelated to commodity transactions, such as defaming or depreciating the commercial prestige of their rivals or reputation of their commodities and services, stealing or revealing the commercial secrets of others, and using illegitimate means to buy over the staff of their rivals.

The aforementioned behaviours have led to serious consequences in China's economic life, with many having aroused great popular indignation, and laws must be formulated to stop such behaviors. It is imperative to proceed in line with China's reality to formulate as early as possible the Law of Anti-Illegitimate Competition to correct behaviours of illegitimate competition in a narrow sense and bahaviours to limit competition partially. The Anti-Monopoly Law and the Law of Suppressing Behaviours Which Limit Competition should also be adopted when the market economy is further developed and legislative conditions are ready.

(2) Perfecting pricing mechanisms to meet the needs of a socialist market economy.

Chinese prices remained stable under the traditional system. The introduction of the market economic structure has broken the old pattern, the irrational prices for some commodities set in the past must be realigned to allow the market to determine prices of commodities. As a matter of course, the application of pricing mechanisms involves a series of coordinated reforms. On September 1, 1992, the State Price Administration decided to grant enterprises the right to set prices for 571 types of capital goods, and delegate the price-setting right for 22 types of products to provincial price administrative departments, while the state retaining the price-setting right for only 89 kinds of products. In addition, the decision also cancelled the unified ceiling producer price or purchasing and marketing prices for capital goods outside the plan, including crude oil, iron and steel. This is a step forward in employing pricing mechanisms suited to the needs of a socialist market economy.

Major problems facing current price reform.

The current price reform faces problems in the following aspects:

1) Imperfection in the government's macro-regulation system of the market price.

The state has decontrolled the prices of most commodities along the on-going effort to deepen price reform. Therefore, price fluctuations to a certain extent are unavoidable. This is in fact a normal phenomenon when the law of value and the law governing supply and demand play their true roles. To a certain extent, price fluctuations are advantageous to the rational readjustment of the economic ratio and the optimized distribution of resources. However, in recent years, after the control over prices was relaxed, drastic price fluctuations of some major products, including farm produce and industrial goods, have stifled channels of circulation and resulted in national economic instability. The major reasons for the aforementioned phenomenon rest with underdevelopment of the market and the lack of effective means by the government for macro-control of the open market, particularly the failure to use economic means to maintain a balance between supply and demand of some strategic products.

2) The double-track price system for capital goods is detrimental to the normal development of the capital goods market.

The introduction of the double-track price system for capital goods has produced numerous drawbacks. However, the system did play a positive role in the early stage. Some capital goods, outside of the state plan, were placed under market regulation, and this proved to be more flexible than unitary planned distribution. The move helped to enliven the economy and created important conditions for the establishment and development of the capital goods market. However, the existence of one product with dual prices at the same time fostered illegal practices such as bribery and the acceptance of bribes and exchanging power for money, which corrupted the minds of some cadres and became the catalyst for the emergence of certain corrupt dealings. Meanwhile, the system led to unequal competition in the market and impeded the healthy growth of the capital goods market.

Same problems emerged in the pricing of land, an essential factor in production. Most often government prices for the transfer of use rights of the state-owned land were relatively low. Some people reaped exorbitant profits by immediately transferring land-use rights they have just obtained, and this is detrimental to the healthy development of the land market.

3) The widening of the price scissors between industrial and agricultural products.

The successive good agricultural harvests in recent years

have led to a decline in prices for farm produce, and changes unfavourable to agriculture appeared in the price parities between industrial and agricultural products. Compared with the previous year, the volume of agricultural products exchanged for industrial goods dropped by 3.1 percent in 1989, 6.9 percent in 1990, 4.9 percent in 1991 and still further to 1 percent in 1992. The rate decreased 15 percent over the four years, averaging 4 percent annually. However, in the decade between 1979 and 1988, the volume rose by an annual average of 5.8 percent. The price scissors, which had narrowed in the previous 10 years, expanded again. The government contracted purchase price for grain is lower than the market price, and failed to narrow the price scissors. The government has adopted a rewarding policy based on providing chemical fertilizers at the listed price for the volume of grain and cotton purchased by contract, in addition to introducing protected prices for grain sold on the market. Nonetheless, these measures have encountered many problems in practice. A considerable number of farmers could not receive benefits or have just gained partial benefits. Moreover, in recent years, the practices of refusing to pay cash for farm produce purchased by state-owned shops and supply and marketing cooperatives, and the collection of fees and fines of all kinds arbitrarily have aroused strong indignation of farmers. Such practices are indeed harmful to the development of agriculture.

4) The relatively low prices in "bottlenecked" sectors hindering the rational readjustment of the industrial structure

The fact that state-set prices of energy and railway freight have remained too low while costs of these sectors have soared during the process of reform calls for prices to be raised by a big margin. However, price hikes will undoubtedly have a great impact on other economic sectors and the daily life of people. During the course of the progressive reform, the only method to minimize such influences is to raise prices gradually and by a small margin. This method will require a fairly long period, and prices have still not been realigned today. Problems related to prices remain a major obstacle impeding the development of these sectors. Increases in costs in these sectors can be attributed mainly to the following factors: First, the development of large numbers of lean ore mines have resulted in lower productivity and high costs. Second, the marketization of productive factors has increased expenditures and the rate of depreciation. Third, the growth rate of productivity of these sectors in general is lower than the national average, while their payrolls have increased on a par with the average growth rate, thereby leading to increased wage costs. Fourth, rising prices for energy and raw materials have led to increased costs being passed on to consumers. The aforementioned phenomena have seriously curtailed the development of the so-called "bottlenecked" sectors.

Tentative plans for price reform—further developing and perfecting the socialist market price system.

1) Further relaxing price controls, and establishing and perfecting price mechanisms based mainly on market competition

The market economy calls for the determination of prices for most commodities through market competition. At present, the government sets prices for only a few commodities under monopolized management and also those must be strictly controlled by the government. Hence, further decontrolling prices is still a major task for future price reform. Although the government decontrolled prices for a large number of heavy industrial products in 1992, the prices of a great number of such products remain under control. Many of the products, which could in fact be distributed through the market, are still distributed administratively with prices set by the government. As conditions gradually mature, the control over the prices for heavy industrial products should be further relaxed. In addition, the control over the prices for some farm produce can be further relaxed or introducing better managerial methods. Prices for the productive factors must be decontrolled to a greater extent.

2) Establishing a normal operational order for market prices

China's reform experiences clearly show that decontrolling prices does not necessarily mean the completion of the change of price formation mechanisms, to say nothing of the automatic formation of normal market order. Certain conditions must be ready and a great deal of work must be done.

A qualified main market body must be established. The normal operation of market price mechanisms require enterprises to become independent commodity producers and managers responsible for their own profits and losses. This is necessary because such enterprises are more sensitive to price changes and can proceed in their own interests to decide acceptable prices by bargaining on the market. Following the price changes in the market, they can make timely policy decisions concerning product mix, production output and management strategy. These represent the micro-foundation necessary for the normal operation of market price mechanisms. The on-going efforts to change the operational mechanisms of state-owned enterprises and the functions of the government have undoubtedly provided preconditions for the normal operation of market price mechanisms.

It is necessary to establish complete laws, regulations and rules. The normal operation of price formation mechanisms needs laws, regulations and rules to protect legal competition and curtail blockades, monopoly, and unequal and illegitimate competitions. Currently efforts are devoted to the formulation and improvement of the legal system in this regard. The completion of this work and the implementation of the relevant laws and regulations governing market activities will guarantee the orderly progress of market competition and the normal operation of market price mechanisms.

An efficient, accurate, complete and open market information network must be established. It is an important condition for ensuring the normal operation of market price formation mechanisms. The accurate and systematic transmission of market information will help to link market prices in various localities and will prevent sharp fluctuations in prices.

3) Improving the system under which the government indirectly regulates and controls market prices

The macro-control system must be improved. Between 1989 and 1991, China established a national economic macro-control system in an effort to rectify the economic order and improve economic results, including the regulation and control of prices. During the process to further decontrol prices and form a socialist market economy, it is necessary to improve and perfect this system, perfect various economic means, and establish a system which will effectively coordinate the operations of such economic means. The government must use financial, taxation and monetary policies to regulate the operation of the national economy and ensure the continuation of fairly rapid growth of the national economy and the basic stability of market prices. In the previous stage, China focused efforts on opposing inflation. In the future, while continuing to prevent new inflations, the government must also prevent the plummeting of prices. Excessive increases or decreases in market prices are equally disadvantageous to the smooth development of the national economy and social stability, as well as to the prevention of chaotic market order.

A certain amount of price subsidies should be maintained. However, the distribution method of subsidies must be improved. Since China introduced reform, subsidies provided by the state for prices have played an important role in ensuring the smooth transition of the price system. In the future, when operating under the market economic system, a certain amount of price subsidies must be retained. The objectives and methods of subsidization, however, should be improved. The priority of price subsidies should focus on providing assistance to agricultural production in order to stabilize the agricultural economy, enabling the major farm produce to keep up with the market demand. Most price subsidies provided for consumers should be abolished, with only a limited amount for the country's poor. Effective results should also be stressed with regard to price subsidies, and meaningless price subsidies should be abandoned.

The market preservation and price regulation fund system for important commodities should be improved. The system which was initially established during the three years of economic rectification should be perfected. When acute fluctuations in the price of certain strategic commodities occur, either reserves or the price regulation fund should be used to regulate the supply and demand and mitigate further price fluctuations. Capital for the price regulation fund and the fund against agricultural risks mainly come from reductions in price subsidies granted to consumers. Meanwhile, in accordance with the principle of he who benefits bears the burden, part of the funds should be collected mainly from producers and managers.

The system of direct government interference in market prices requires transformation. Direct government interference in market prices is needed under special circumstances, but this should be limited to a specified time period. For example, when market prices fluctuate drastically, in addition to economic means to regulate and control the situation, the government may, within a certain period of time, use administrative measures to implement direct interference, including placing controls on the rate of price differentiation, setting ceiling prices, freezing prices and rationing supply. The goal of setting time limits is to adopt diversified emergency measures within a specified time period, measures including the use of state reserves and the emergency imported goods to increase supply so as to ease the pressure of the market. However, administrative interference should be abandoned once the goal has been accomplished.

4) Establishing a relatively flexible pricing system under the government

In order to avoid serious distortions it is necessary to establish a system to examine, set and readjust prices for all commodities under the management of the government within a fixed period of time, for example, one year. Prices may be readjusted at any time under special circumstances. Some trade sectors may establish a system to automatically readjust their prices following the changes in the prices of items such as coal and petroleum, and in turn report to responsible government departments for the record. Price changes will automatically go into force if responsible government departments offer no different opinion within a stipulated time limit. Such a system will both simplify procedures for price readjustments in these sectors and prevent runaway prices.

The examination and setting of prices for commodities under the management of the government should include the participation of representatives of producers, major clients and theoreticians to ensure the decision is made through democratic discussion.

5) Actively realigning prices to facilitate the establishment of a socialist market economy

Distorted prices should be realigned by continued effort in readjusting and decontrolling prices.

In realigning the prices of capital goods, the price of coal should be subject to market regulation through a gradual reduction and final abolition of the portion subject to unified government distribution. However, prior to accomplishing this goal, the price of coal subject to unified government distribution should be raised. The moderate price of crude oil subject to planned allocation will gradually be replaced by the high price for planned distribution, with the latter being set in line with world market prices. Prices for electricity and railway freight may be readjusted by relevant departments acting on their own in response to price changes for coal and crude oil, with all changes being reported to responsible government departments for the record. The readjusted prices may go into force if there is no objections from responsible departments. Prices for refined oil, airline tickets and highway and sea transport will be gradually decontrolled. Prior to the freeing of such prices, a method similar to that used for electricity and railway freight may be introduced. Prices for capital goods still controlled by the government should all be freed. As a result, the double-track price system for capital goods will be eliminated, and the long-standing situation in which the prices of capital goods remained low will be reversed.

It is necessary to realigning residential housing rents. Rental costs for government-owned housing should be managed effectively, with rents being gradually raised to cover the eight items, i.e. maintenance, management, depreciation, investment interest, property taxes, land-use fees, insurance premiums and profits. Low-income families will be provided with low-rent housing. Rents for housing owned by enterprises should be determined by the enterprises themselves, with rents for privately-owned housing subject to market regulation.

It is also necessary to realigning prices for the productive factors. While transferring the land-use rights of state-owned land, the land can be divided into land to be used for business and non-business purposes. Prices for land dedicated to business purposes will mainly be decided through public bidding and auctions, while prices for land transferred between users and the secondary market will be subject to market regulation to ensure that land value will play a role of regulating land resources and attaining the objective of optimized allocation. The government will levy value-added land taxes on the secondary market. The price of foreign exchange will be opened under appropriate conditions, and will be determined by the market. Before it is relaxed, the price of foreign exchange should be readjusted in a timely manner to reflect as much as possible the supply and demand on the foreign exchange market. Interest rates charged by commercial banks should gradually be determined by the market. Before they are opened, interest rates should be readjusted in a timely manner to reflect the situation of currency supply. Once the rise in commodity prices surpass the interest rate, the value preservation interest rate should be adopted to avoid the emergence of a negative interest rate for savings deposits. Various fringe benefits and subsidies should be incorporated into wages in order to transform incomplete wages into complete wages. The wages enterprises pay employees should be decided through discussions between enterprises and employees, with the government setting the minimum wage levels. Salaries of the employees in government departments and state cultural, educational and public health departments are determined by financial allocations. The salary level of employees in such departments should be set according to the average wages of the employees of enterprises in similar positions. Growth in the average wage level of employees nationwide should be lower than that of social labour productivity, and should be readjusted in line with changes in the living cost index of urban employees.

In short, readjustments and the decontrol of prices will effectively change price formation and operational mechanisms, solve the problem of seriously distorted prices, and perfect the socialist market price system. Moreover, a unified market price system which links domestic and international markets and operates in a flexible and orderly manner will take shape, and the role of price regulation will be brought into full play.

The focus of price reform centers on promoting reform of the prices of the productive factors.

Many experts have pointed out that China's price reform in the 1980s achieved great results by focusing on prices for material products and labour services through combining readjustment with decontrol. In the 1990s, and particularly after the clarification that the goal of economic structural reform is to establish a socialist market economic structure, in order to display the role of market mechanisms, optimize the distribution of resources and improve the efficiency of national economic activities, efforts are called for to further deepen and expand the perspective of the price reform. Future emphasis will be placed on the reform of prices for the productive factors, while advancing the price reform in other fields.

Prices for the productive factors mainly include prices for capital interest, salaries for the labour force, rental costs and land prices, and the rates of exchanges between Renminbi and foreign currencies. In accordance with the requirements for the development of a socialist market economy, they all call for market regulation in order to prevent the distortion of important market information and the adverse affects hindering increased efficiency in the allocation of resources.

The price of capital interest is perhaps the most important of prices for the productive factors. This is due to the fact that capital is the most important and insufficient economic resources in every market economic society. When attempting to achieve the marketization of prices for the productive factors, it is imperative to first achieve the marketization of interest rates.

In a market economy, interest rates are the most important lever enabling the state to regulate the operations of the macroeconomy. Therefore, socialist countries must regulate interest rates in order to ensure steady, coordinated and effective economic growth. For example, if the economy is overheated, it is necessary for the government to increase the central bank's rediscount rates and re-lending interest rates, sell large quantities of bonds, chiefly short-term state treasury bonds, on the open market so as to exert influence on the increase of market interest rates, keep inflation under control and tighten the economy. On the other hand, during economic slumps, the government should lower the Central Bank's rediscount rates and re-lending interest rates, purchase bonds on the open market, lower market interest rates so as to stimulate investment and consumption, and strive to invigorate and expand the national economy. However, the government or Central Bank regulate mainly the basic interest rates so as to exert influence on market interest rates, instead of directly stipulating such rates and making changes. The government should not interfere with interest rates of savings deposits and loans granted by commercial banks and other financial institutions, which should, instead, be subject to market regulation. Likewise, the interest rates of loans granted to various enterprises and companies should be determined by the loaners, and there should be no government interference. At the same time, it is necessary to differentiate commercial banking from policy-oriented banking. While providing preferential loans for infrastructure construction and pillar industries in accordance with the state's industrial policies, the method of paying interest in the form of deductions when selling bills of exchange may be adopted in order to differentiate the practice from ordinary financial banking.

The marketization of interest rate is a process which is inseparable from the development and maturity of the financial market (including monetary and capital markets). The formation of a unified and open financial market is the only way to ensure fairly standard market regulation of interest rates. And market interest rates can truly reflect the situation regarding the supply and demand of capital and indicate the degree of fund shortages.

Wages represent the price of labor. Reform of the wage system should be geared to the market, meaning that wages should be formed through a competitive labour market.

Marketization of labourers' price wages is also a precondition for transforming enterprises into genuine independent commodity producers and managers responsible for their own profits and losses, in addition to being a precondition for making enterprises the main body of market activities. How can enterprises effectively compete on the market if labour force cannot flow freely and employees are tied to life-long jobs and are treated the same no matter how they perform? Market mechanisms cannot play their true role if the principle of the survival of the fittest is not applied to both enterprises and their employees. Hence, marketization of the labour price wages and the establishment and development of the labour market must be closely coordinated with the establishment and gradual perfection of the social security system, a fact which will help stabilize public perception and society as a whole.

In the past, land in China, particularly land in urban areas, was used free of compensation. As a result, the country's land, a limited and non-renewable resource, was neither appropriately nor effectively used, causing a serious waste. Since the reform began in China, however, market mechanisms have been introduced to land management, and the role of prices has come to the surface. Nonetheless, the process continues to face numerous problems. Along with the accelerated economic development, the demand for land in urban areas grows rapidly, resulting in skyrocketing prices for urban land, chiefly because of black market deals, in addition to the practice of a growing number of people to resell land for exorbitant profits. Owing to the expansiveness of Chinese territory, land prices vary in different cities and even in different sections of the same city, ranging from several yuan per square metre to several ten thousand yuan per square metre. Formation of land prices is far from standard. In order to raise the utilization rate of land, it is imperative to gradually push the deal of land to the market, including both the primary and secondary markets, thereby gradually clearify land as a commodity and its price, forming a comparatively standard market regulate price, and improving the overall efficiency of national economic activities.

The development of a socialist market economy calls for China to continue all-round opening to the outside world, actively participate in world market competition, link the domestic market with the international market, strive to act in accordance with generally accepted international practices for economic exchanges, and gradually ensure the marketability of the exchange rate of the Renminbi. Although many countries relegate the opening of the exchange rate of their currencies to the later stages of the transformation of economic mechanisms, opening exchange rates is in fact the major demand for the transformation of economic mechanisms, and for its part the government should mainly rely on economic means to interfere in and regulate the process. In order to complete the transition, the government should on the one hand rationally readjust the official interest rate to a level close to the market exchange rate, with the price difference around 10 percent between the two. On the other hand, it is necessary to develop the foreign exchange regulation market to ensure that foreign exchange needed by the government will be chiefly purchased from the foreign exchange regulation market, and either limited or no administrative means will be used to obtain foreign exchange. Simultaneously, limitations on trading at the foreign exchange regulation market will be gradually eliminated so that every enterprise or company and citizen can enter the market and trade foreign currencies freely. Once success is achieved in these two fields, together with the development of foreign economic relations and an increase in foreign exchange reserves, it will not be long before the Renminbi becomes a freely convertible currency.

In a word, the focus of China's price reform will be gradually shifted to the reform of the productive factors. The pioneering areas in the reform, such as special economic zones, have actually focused on the reform of prices for the productive factors.

Meanwhile, we should not slacken the reform of prices of material products and labour services, and should continue to solve remaining problems related to distorted prices, particularly prices for commodities and labour which have entered competitive markets. Prices for other commodities, including products subject to double-track prices and products currently in short supply but in high demand should be decontrolled quickly and be subject to market regulation, thereby giving full play to the role of market mechanisms in automatically linking supply with demand.

During price reform the general level of commodity prices must be kept under control.

Some experts have pointed out that excessive rises in the general level of commodity prices will not only adversely affect the normal operation of the national economy and the daily life of the people, but will also create difficulties for price reform itself. Soaring commodity prices constitute quite naturally a prominent problem in the process of price reform. However, this problem will continue to exist even after price reform has reached the set objectives. This holds true, because the fluctuation in the general level of commodity prices is an inevitable phenomenon accompanying the market economy. The key to the problem lies in how to effectively place it under control.

The following measures should be adopted to regulate and control the general level of commodity prices at present and for the long-term as well.

1) Establishing a commodity price stabilization reserve fund to control prices

In order to stabilize the prices of commodities and materials for which there is a stable or high demand, or which are closely linked to production and the lives of the people, the state may establish a commodity price stabilization reserve fund similar to the foreign exchange stabilization reserve fund established in countries with market economies. The state will establish a commodities and materials reserve system to directly participate in the purchases and sales on the market. In cases where supply exceeds demands, the state will increase purchases and storage, or will strive to organize exports, while in cases when supply falls short of demand, the state will sell large quantities of the goods in question, or organize imports in order to stabilize commodity prices. The commodity price stabilization reserve fund may be funded with the former state treasury expenditure on commodity price subsidies, and also part of the penalties and confiscated funds handed over to the financial departments by the administration of industrial and commercial prices. In order to give full play to the initiative of both central and local authorities, commodity price stabilizing reserve funds may be established at different levels. Progress of the reform will not only help stabilize commodity prices, but will also play an active role in eliminating financial deficits. This is because, first, in terms of the variety and quantity of commodities, the scope of regulations applying to the commodity price stabilization reserve fund is much smaller than that of state subsidies. In addition, this fund is not a long-term expenditure, and will not increase on an annual basis. Instead, it will only be used when relatively serious fluctuations occur in the market price for some commodities. This in turn will greatly reduce the burden on the state treasury. Second, with regard to the source of funding, funds can be obtained from annual financial subsidies immediately after establishment of the fund, and deficits can be appropriately supplemented on an annual basis. Such an approach is indeed practical.

2) Developing market organization and rationalizing market prices

The establishment of a price system in conformity with a socialist market economic structure is indispensable for the construction of a market organization and system. In modern economic life, decontrolling prices alone will not necessarily lead to the formation of good market mechanisms. Severe fluctuations in commodity prices which surfaced in the previous two stages of price reform were partially related to the low stage of organization and the backward transaction methods in the market. With regard to the development of market organization itself, it generally evolves from a scattered and sub-standard low stage to a relatively concentrated and standardized high stage. Man-made obstacles and other negative factors such as deals accompanied by briberies block the circulation of commodities and market transparency is low, thereby making it difficult to form rational prices reflecting the true relationship between supply and demand. However, the situation improves noticeably during the high stage of the market organization. The Shenzhen Nonferrous Metals Exchange and the Zhengzhou Grain Wholesale Market, established with the approval and guidance of the State Council and the State Commission for Restructuring the Economy, represent exploratory efforts in the establishment of a market organization with a high degree of order. Both markets operate in line with special laws and regulations characteristic of a high-level market organization, as well as contractual and standardized spot transactions. They have introduced part of the mechanisms for futures trading, such as the membership system, guaranteed funds and transfers of long-term contracts. They have also endeavoured to develop long- and medium-term transactions and gradually expand futures trading. The practice of open transactions, equal competition, and all business transactions conducted according to fixed procedures has enabled prices to truly reflect the relationship between the value of goods and supply and demand. Prices on the high-grade market are highly representative, because prices for certain commodities are determined by commodities which account for a larger proportion in the total market transaction volume. This approach clarifies and rationalizes prices for commodities transacted on a large scale. Precisely because commodities transactions in developed countries are usually in large quantities and in a concentrated way, their commodity prices not only play a representative and regulatory role in their own countries, but often represent the price level on the international market. In fact, this type of high-grade modern markets are found also in less developed countries. For example, some newly-industrialized countries and even some economically backward countries have scored great achievements in this regard. Successful examples include the rubber exchange in Singapore and the cotton exchange in Bombay, India. However, China is a late comer in the development of high-grade markets compared with other countries. Hence, while striving to make economic progress, China should actively develop all types of modern market organizations. The first step for such organizations is to develop a fairly large regional (provincial) influence and then become representative large domestic markets. As a second step it is necessary to strive to link the domestic market of some commodities, particularly commodities with strong competitiveness and monopoly commodities on the international market, with the world market, while striving to develop an export-oriented economy. Without a mature market organization it is impossible for the macro-economic management body and microeconomic entities to obtain initial market signals. And it will be extremely difficult for market prices to play their true role in rationalizing the allocation of natural resources, and for the state to carry out indirect regulation and control over market prices.

3) Deepening the reform of the banking system, strengthening the independent position of banks

Banks form the supply system of capital and the most important macro-regulation system in the national economy. During the first stage of reform of the banking system the Central Bank was separated from specialized banks and their functions were clearly defined. The effort has played an initial role in promoting economic development and the establishment of a macro-control system. In conformity with the perfection of a market system and price reform, the second stage of reform of the banking system should make the banking system independent of the administrative system. On the one hand, the Central Bank should be independent of the government, while at the same time coordinating with the government in its business principles, credit policies and currency flow. However, the Central Bank should be responsible to and report its work to the National People's Congress, regarding the formulation and implementation of credit plans, currency supply and the control of the overall credit scale. On the other hand, specialized banks must be independent of the Central Bank and government departments, and must be put under enterprise management. In order to achieve the goal, the ownership of such banks should be transferred from the government to the State Assets Administrative Bureau or its subordinate investment companies.

4) Readjusting industrial structures to create conditions for fundamentally rationalizing the relationship between supply and demand

The most direct factor affecting the price structure and changes in the general level of commodity prices is the relationship between supply and demand which in turn is restrained by the industrial structure. To rationalize the relationship between supply and demand as well as the price structure, and to maintain the relative stability of the general level of commodity prices, a basic measure is to readjust and optimize the industrial structure. Under conditions of a market economy, it is very difficult to use a subjectively set ideal price structure to achieve the rationalization of industrial structure, because the objectiveness of prices will increase daily. Given the present situation, while making continuous effort to control overall demand, it is also necessary to shift the focus of macroeconomic policy from the control of demand to the control of supply, comprehensively readjust the structure of the manufacturing sector, increase efficiency, and eliminate the hidden obstacles resulting from structural contradictions threatening the price reform. While formulating industrial policies, the government must first distinguish key industries for national economic development from ordinary industries and industries which should be limited or eliminated. Secondly, clear-cut measures should be adopted for products whose prices have not yet been decontrolled. The prices of products which should be raised in accordance with the industrial policy must be appropriately raised, while those which should be cut down must either be appropriately lowered or cut to such a low level that the producers have to either suspend production or shift to produce other products. Thirdly, with regard to the products whose prices have already been decontrolled, coordinated efforts in areas such as taxation and credits should be made to let the indirect macro-regulation system play its role. Fourthly, the central government should establish an industrial development leading body to oversee the implementation of various industrial policies, and coordinate and solve problems emerged during the readjustment of the industrial structure. This must be done due to the fact that local protectionism is a major obstacle hampering the readjustment of the industrial structure. From an overall point of view, some industries should be limited or even eliminated, regardless of the fact that they may be the major source of financial income of certain localities. Hence, it calls for an authoritative organization to coordinate the contradictions arising between overall and partial interests in the development of various industries. It is thus quite obvious that optimizing industrial structures, though very difficult at the beginning, will make fundamental contributions to realigning the relationship between supply and demand and the price structure, as well as to stabilizing the general level of commodity prices.

3. Standardization and Legalization of the Socialist Market

(1) The market economy calls for standardization and legalization.

There is an urgent need to ensure that the market economy operates according to law.

Experts stress that a market economy is in fact an economy governed by law, and that the establishment of a socialist market economic structure urgently calls for the strengthening and improvement of the legal system.

The autonomy of the main operational body of the market economy calls for rule by law. The main body of the modern market economy has long been changed from individuals holding a certain amount of capital to legal entities composed chiefly of enterprises. The legal entities system is a basic condition the legal system grants to the market economy. The autonomy of legal entities first calls for the autonomy of their properties, meaning that legal entities should have the power to possess, utilize and dispose their own properties, as well as to assume sole responsibility for their profits and losses resulting from the independent operation of such properties. This calls for the perfection of the legal system related to property rights during the process of constructing a legal system. Based on the separation of the government administration from enterprise management and the separation of the proprietary rights from management rights, it is absolutely necessary to define the scope of proprietary rights, management rights and other property rights, while at the same time intensifying restraints on property rights and interest relationships. It is also necessary to use the power of the state to guarantee that proprietors are free to normally exercise their rights and enjoy their interests.

Another requirement for the autonomy of legal entities is to ensure their independence in management, operation and in making decisions related to production and operations. This calls for the perfection of an enterprise legal system during the construction of a legal system, the transformation of the operational mechanisms of enterprises, and the application of legal means to guarantee the autonomy of enterprise management. In this way, enterprises can free themselves from being dependent on government departments, and develop independently under the market economy. The main body of the market economy also faces questions of entering and withdrawing from the market. Questions related to what kind of entity is qualified to enter the market and what kind of entity can or must withdraw from the market can only be answered with the establishment and improvement of the legal entity registration system and the bankruptcy system, both of which depend on the perfection of a legal system. The number of registered companies in China had reached 480,000 by the end of 1992. Nonetheless, the country still lacks a corporation law. A considerable number of enterprises in the country are ready with conditions to declare bankruptcy. However, few have actually done so in accordance with the Enterprise Bankruptcy Law. This shows that it is an arduous task to build a legal system governing the major body of the market.

Contracts related to market economic activities calls for rule by law. Commodity exchanges and economic transactions between the main bodies of the market economy are conducted mainly in the form of contracts. The development from transactions to first preliminary contracts and then written contracts protected by law reflects the inherent demand of the market economy and the result of constant improvement of the market economic system. In China's market-oriented reform in recent years, more and more economic activities are conducted in the form of contracts. According to statistics released by relevant government departments, more than 3 billion economic contracts and 230,000 technological contracts were signed in 1992 alone, with the total transaction volume soaring to over 15 billion yuan. In China contracts will be used on an expanded scale along with the establishment and development of a market economic structure, and the legal system based on contracts will be further improved, especially laws concerning new contractual form and economic sectors such as futures trading, mortgage and pawn need to be perfected quickly.

The credibility of market economic exchanges calls for rule by law. Credibility is the inevitable result of the development of commodity exchange, a question which exists as long as there are market economic exchanges. Credibility exists in credit sales, bank credit loans, the issuance and transactions of stocks and bonds, and contracts. All forms of credit, including state, bank, commercial and consumption credit, relies on law to ensure the normal credit order and the realization of the principle of honesty and credibility. In recent years, numerous factors have resulted in some serious problems such as the chain debt, with lax enforcement of credit law and discipline as the main reason.

The competitiveness of the market economy calls for the rule by law. The establishment of a market economy is based on full competition, and only through competition can the rational allocation of social resources be realized and can the economy enjoy sustained vitality. However, competition should follow certain rules and should be standardized and readjusted by law. On the one hand, we should formulate and implement the rule of the equality of competitive parties, granting the main bodies of the market economy equal status and opportunities. On the other hand, we should formulate and implement rules on fair competition and rely on the power of law to limit monopolies, ban illegitimate competition behaviours, and crack down on activities of producing and marketing counterfeit and shoddy products.

Unification of the market economy calls for rule by law. It will be impossible for a market economy to exist without a highly developed market system. The market system in China has witnessed significant development in recent years. By the end of June 1992, the country had more than 70,000 pedlars' markets, 13,000 specialized and wholesale markets, and 3,000 capital goods markets. In addition, preparations are currently under way for the establishment of a number of large futures markets. Under such circumstances, the demand for the unification of the market is high. On the one hand, there is an urgent need for a unified domestic market system, enabling a nationwide free circulation of commodities and all productive factors. There is also an urgent need to eliminate any form of monopoly, blockades and local protectionism, and to oppose closed markets controlled by administrative departments or particular trades; different regions and trades should open to each other so as to form a unified national market system. On the other hand, there is a genuine need for the unification of market rules. With regard to the basic rules of market operation, we must on no account stress local or departmental characteristics, nor must we allow the practice of each going his own way. Local policies enforced by some localities and departments impede the establishment of a large-scale unified national market and are disadvantageous to economic development; all such policies must be banned resolutely. Obviously, we can only rely on the power of law for establishing a unified market system and guaranteeing its normal operation, instead of relying on a single locality or department.

A market economy with an international orientation calls for rule by law. The market economy is an all-round open economy. Along with the ever increasing mutual economic reliance and infiltration of all countries throughout the world, no country can be separated from the world economic system and develop independently. The on-going development of a market economy will definitely break through economically the boundary line between countries and form a world market and diversified international economic links. In line with the trend, a series of relatively unified and universally-accepted international economic and trade treaties, practices and rules have already been or are being formed. Along with implementation of the reform and open policies over the past dozen of years, the Chinese economy has already been closely linked with the world economy. In 1992, China's total import and export value exceeded US$160 billion, ranking 11th in the world. Thus far, the country has established economic and trade relations with more than 200 countries and regions, and the influx of foreign capital has increased annually. Statistics show that the country had established more than 90,000 foreign-funded enterprises by the end of 1992. The establishment and development of a market economic structure will facilitate China's effort to open its doors wider to the outside world and expand its links with other countries. This calls for China to attach great importance to the international features of the market economy, while at the same time striving to rapidly gear its legal system with international economic and trade rules and regulations.

The necessity for exercising macro-control over the market economy calls for rule by law. Markets in themselves are in no way omnipotent, and they too have weaknesses and passive aspects. Hence, government macro-control is necessary. At present, China is in transition from a planned economic system to a market economic structure. We should attach great importance to the legalization of the macro-control means in order to prevent the restoration of the old system, and the possible of chaos following the birth of the new system. On the one hand, it is necessary to rely on legal means in defining the scope of the state macro-control and the limit for government activities. On the other hand, it is necessary to use legal means to define the methods of government macro-control, thereby making the planning method, financial and monetary policies, and the application of various economic levers in line with the legal system.

The necessity for judgement and arbitration activities in the market economy calls for rule by law. Market economic activities involve acute competition, and the market as a whole is actually a competitive arena for economic returns. Hence, there will be an increasing number of cases requiring judgements and arbitration and judicial judgements and civil arbitration will be widely used. Relevant judgement and arbitration activities should be substantially strengthened within the scope of the legal system. This will help create a sound external environment for the main body of the market, ensure the legitimate rights and interests of the main body of the market and its managers, solve commercial disputes in the private sector, and establish the operational order of the market economy. For this reason, judicial and arbitration organizations have reformed and strengthened their functional organizations, forms of activities and procedures for hearing cases. The effort has thus achieved rule by law in judgement and arbitration activities.

The principle of "first establishing market rules and regulations, and then developing the market" should be followed in establishing the market economy.

Experts contend that it is impossible for a market economy to exist without rules and regulations. Only by following the principle of "first establishing market rules and regulations, and then developing the market" can we realize the cultivation, development and fair competition of the market as well as its connection with the world economy.

At present, acting in accordance with the principle of "first establishing market rules and regulations, and then developing the market" has six benefits:

—It will facilitate the cultivation and development of the market and the formation of market order at the earliest possible date. Under the market economy, the subordination of enterprises to the government will be eliminated, and the traditional administration of the government over enterprises will be replaced by government administration over the market.

—It will help maintain a fair competition amongst the main bodies of interest. In China today, state-owned, collective, private and foreign-funded enterprises each have a distinct property relationship with the state, with said relationship fostering different main bodies of interest. With regards to the market economy, different main bodies have different interests, they nonetheless begin from the same starting line and compete under the same standards.

—It will help attract foreign investment and accelerate our efforts to link with the world economy. The market economy is in essence an open economy, which will eventually gear to the world economy. In a sense, a market economy has no national boundaries. The detailed and perfected of our market rules and regulations, and the closer they are to the universally-accepted standards and practice in the development of world economy, the more attractive they are to foreign investors, and more effective in promoting the restoration of China's signatory status in the General Agreement on Tariffs and Trade (GATT) and the development of the country's foreign trade and economic relations.

—It will also help to avoid and reduce instable factors and maintain good social order. Influenced by historical and cultural tradition and the social system, Chinese people have for generations pursued moral precepts based on "no pains, no gains" and "getting rich in accordance with the law." Chinese are very sensitive to behaviors of some "upstarts" who rely on illegal means to gaining wealth or take advantage of imperfect rules and regulations, as well as polarization between the rich and poor. Establishment of the market economy requires people to alter their traditional concepts concerning money. However, this is in no way a recommendation of the prevalent tendency that "money is above all else." The functions of market rules and regulations have the mandatory backing of the state which offers clear stipulations as to what it advocates, encourages and protects, as well as what it limits, bans and imposes sanction upon. Therefore, the key to placing great importance to and solving the aforementioned problems lies in the establishment of strict rules and regulations, as well as effective operational market mechanisms. Otherwise, over a certain period of time negative influences to the social stability and social order will inevitably arise.

—It will ensure that government officials honestly perform their duties and minimize actions of taking advantage of their positions and power for personal gains. Even under the market economy, the government and not enterprises will play the main role. Although the traditional administrative functions and "dominant" role of the government no longer exist, it nonetheless retains the right to grant licenses, carry out examinations and determine restrictions and compulsory requirements for enterprises and individuals who have entered or wish to participate in market competition. The construction of a clean and honest government is an important aspect throughout the process of economic development. One of the major components for market rules and regulations is to prohibit Party and government officials from concurrently engaging in trade and accepting gifts.

—It will facilitate the on-going effort to reform the governmental structure. In order to ensure the establishment of market mechanisms and alter government functions, it is necessary to "emaciate" the existing government apparatus. Structural reform represent readjustments in government interests, which must be completed in accordance with the premise of standardization. Changes in the operational mechanisms of enterprises must be planned and adjusted in accordance with the "Regulations on Changing the Operational Mechanisms of Enterprises Owned by the Whole People." In a sense, it is even more necessary to ensure that changes in government functions are standardized and controlled by laws governing the reform of government apparatus.

Market rules and regulations in China fall into two categories, with the first being policy rules and regulations. The government organizes and regulates the market economy by stipulating and implementing policies. Simple procedures are needed to formulate such policies in the shortest possible period of time. However, they are subject to change and less authoritative, particularly when they are used to solve disputes resulted from market competition and exchanges between interested parties. Another category includes market rules and regulations stipulated through legal procedures. The government has finalized in a legal form of the standards for market conduct governing all interest parties. The government in fact organizes and regulates the market according to these standards, which are characterized by such advantages as publicity, authoritativeness and unity. They can also be used by judicial organs or administrative judicial departments in handling cases involving disputes. Their shortcomings, such as the complicated procedures for stipulation, can be overcome by government legislation.

Quite obviously, the characteristics of the market economy, such as its competitiveness and openness, as well as its operational procedures must be based on legalized market rules and regulations. Legalization of market rules and regulations have to be realized step by step due to the historical segments of the traditional economy and the complexity involved in establishing market mechanisms.

While implementing the principle of "first establishing market rules and regulations, and then developing the market," it is necessary to solve problems in the following three areas:

1) The basic content of the market rules and regulations should be determined on the basis of scientific argumentation.

2) Different attitudes should be adopted according to concrete conditions when implementing the principle of "first establishing market rules and regulations, and then developing the market." For example, the principle should be followed strictly when introducing successful Chinese or foreign examples. The market economy can be tried in pilot areas prior to the establishment of market rules and regulations, or experiments and the formulation of market rules and regulations can be carried out at the same time. On the other hand, major reform measures which have a significant bearing on the overall situation or which may spark a chain reaction, must follow the principle of "first establishing market rules and regulations, and then developing the market." In terms of exploratory reform measures, principal rules can be stipulated first, with detailed rules being formulated after a certain scale of development has been reached and experience has been attained. Policy rules and regulations for the market can be set for encouraging and programming measures, but prohibitive market rules and regulations measures must be defined in legal terms.

3) Reliance must be placed on the government, society and various other sectors in establishing market rules and regulations. With regard to basic market rules and regulations, and those with established precedents to follow, we can entrust to experts, scholars and related entities who will be responsible for drafting and solicitating opinions from others before submitting drafts to relevant authorities for examination and approval.

(2) Accelerating the reform of the legal system and establishing a socialist market economic legal system.

It is necessary to accelerate the reform of the legal system in order to establish a system which is compatible with and reflects the socialist market economy.

Experts point out that an urgent aspect of implementing the socialist market economy is to improve and perfect a legal system compatible with the socialist market economy. Therefore, it is essential to reform the legal system established under the planned economic system.

The tasks for the reform of the legal system are as follows:

1) Solving problems concerning the role of the legal system

This particular problem is in fact related to the relationship between "rule by man" and "rule by law." The problem has been discussed on several occasions, and the basic consensus reached unanimously is that economy should be ruled by law, and not by the will of individuals, and the practice of "rule by man" must be replaced by "rule by law."

2) Solving problems related to the relationship between the legal system and economic reform

The relationship between the legal system and economic reform is in fact a problem concerning the form of economic restructuring. China has achieved great progress in the reform of its economic structure in the wake of the Third Plenary Session of the 11th Party Central Committee. Nonetheless, conflicts, frictions, and in some cases chaos, arose from time to time, due to the fact that the legal means have not applied to all aspects of the reform. All efforts to reform economic structure should be carried out in accordance with the law, and should include the perfection of relevant rules and regulations. In reality, the reform has been promoted by direct administrative means, and law itself has simply played a role of confirming and consolidating the achievements in the reform. This in turn has weakened the authoritativeness of the law, placing the law in a vulnerable and passive position inappropriate for strengthening the legal system. In addition, the limitations by administrative means often create disorder, incompleteness and even restoration in some cases. Therefore, in transforming the old structure, we should also pay great attention to the method we use, and carry out the reform in accordance with the law. Administrative means must be brought into the orbit of the legal system, and must be implemented in conformity with the law. The legal system should take an active move to adapt itself to these demands and play its due role of guidance and protection. Reform as a whole, including its content and procedures should all be guided by the law.

3) Solving problems concerning perfection of the legal system and completion of rules and regulations

Over the past few years China has stipulated a series of laws and regulations and has changed to a great extent the situation in which there were no laws to go by. However, the legislative effort has lagged behind the practice of the reform. Hence, the legal system has proved more and more imperfect as the reform continues to develop.

The perfection of China's legal system first of all requires the establishment of a socialist commercial law. Commercial law, an outcome of the market economy, is the general term for legalized standards governing profit-making and business activities of the main economic sectors of the market. Hence, the commercial law is a law most closely related to the market economy. The system of commercial law is quite different from that of civil law and hence has its own regulatory limits and high degree of independence. Therefore, the establishment of the socialist market economy requires the adoption of the socialist commercial law to fill the gap in our legal system.

4) Solving problems related to eliminating old laws and introducing new laws

China's effort to introduce generally-accepted international practices in conjunction with building and perfecting the socialist market economy should include drawing on the successful experiences of developed countries.

Once the target of the socialist market economy has been set, China will be confronted with a situation in which many laws and decrees stipulated under the old system cannot suit to the new system. It is thus necessary to conscientiously sort out laws and regulations which are incompatible with the socialist market economy, some of them should be eliminated. Generally-accepted international practices should be considered when formulating new laws.

In addition, the outdated method of relying on government departments to draft laws and regulations should be abandoned.

5) Acting according to law in administration and changing government functions

An important feature of modern administration is to act according to law. Under the influence of the traditional economic system and habits, China is far from having a complete legal system guiding its administration. This problem has become more acute and prominent under the new economic system. To a large extent, the establishment of the socialist market economy depends on the completion of concepts of administration guided by law and the legalization of administrative structures. If administrative interference in the market, enterprises and the concrete economic activities is let go unchecked, it will be quite difficult to establish the new system and to realize the transformation of the operational mechanisms of enterprises.

China's current legal system does not suit to the needs of the market economy.

Some experts emphasize that China's original economic structure is a highly-concentrated mandatory planned economy which relies on administrative orders in the allocation of resources. By nature, such a system is suited to the practice of rule by man and it neglects rule by law. As a result, such an economic system hinders the formation of laws and regulations and their implementation, and it has become the root cause for China's imperfect legal system and inadequate implementation of law. However, since China has entered a new historical stage, the original economic system has been reformed step by step, and greater attention has been paid to law. The past dozen years have witnessed the initial shaping of the socialist legal system. Statistics by the end of October 1992 show that China has its Constitution, 204 laws, including 19 decisions on revisions and supplements to laws, and 62 decisions concerning legal problems, as well as 617 administrative laws and regulations, 2,360 local laws and regulations, and 13,000 regulations. Nonetheless, the legal system still cannot suit to the needs of the socialist market economy. The reasons for this are as follows:

1) The majority of China's current laws and regulations have been stipulated since China's implementation of the reform and opening policies. They were in fact promulgated to adapt to the planned economic system, which was supplemented by market regulations, a system proposed by the 12th National Congress of the Party, or suit to the planned commodity economic system adopted at the Third Plenary Session of the 12th Party Central Committee, or to the unified system under which planned economy was integrated with the market, a system adopted during the Party's 13th National Congress. In short, all the systems were adopted prior to the 14th National Congress of the Party, which decided to establish the socialist market economic system in China. There is little doubt that all the systems mentioned above represent improvement and progress compared with the previous system, marking a new starting point and demonstrating the deep-going development of the reform of the economic structure. The existing legal system formed during the process has laid a solid foundation for the further consolidation of the legal system. However, the current legal system lags far behind the urgent need of the market economy. It is confronted with new contradictions and a heavy burden brought about by fundamental changes already taken place in the economic structure.

2) It is true that the existing legal system was formed in the wake of rapid development of the commodity economy and along with the progress of the market. However, the influence of the regional system is deep-rooted and legislation is always lagging behind. As a result, it is highly inadequate in providing new, clear and positive stipulations on the legal status, rights and duties of various economic sectors already in existence. According to authoritative state departments China has divided its economy into nine sectors in line with the new economic standards. They include state-owned, collective, private, individual, integrated, stock, foreign-funded economies, economy funded with investments from Hong Kong, Macao and Taiwan, as well as other types of economies. All are considered as main sectors of the market

economy and enjoy an equal position, as well as common rights and duties. However, the existing legal system has stipulated the activities of some sectors and ignored others, while some articles have stipulated unequal terms. At present, it is quite difficult to ensure wide-spread fair competition due to the influence of long-held concepts and behaviors of the people and their concepts of value.

3) The existing legal system is noticeably deficient in standardizing macroeconomic management. Objectively speaking, this is directly connected with the fact that the property right relationship is not yet rationalized, the functions of administration and enterprises are not yet separated, and the government has not completely changed its functions. Subjectively, however, it is due to the inadequate understanding of the state that the macroeconomic management and government interference must go by law. The government still follows the habitual practice of issuing an instruction today and a decree tomorrow. It has drawn no lessons from past overheated economic development or from the research into better modes a macroeconomic management should take.

4) In terms of China's existing legal system, standards for microeconomic behaviours are numerous and complicated, compared with those for macroeconomic management.

Laws and regulations thus represent power to competent government departments, but to the market sectors, especially the private and individual sectors, laws and regulations represent duties they should fulfil. On the one hand, the decisions of powerful administrators and leaders are always considered correct, while the rights of market sectors are often neglected, and more often than not they are unwilling to or dare not to defend themselves. This situation is not only incompatible with the relationship under the market economy, but is also in opposition to the key functions of the government determined during the Party's 14th National Congress.

This particular series of laws and regulations, which are meant to govern microeconomic behaviors. During the past decade new stipulations, revisions and supplements were added to govern microeconomic behaviors under the product and commodity economies, as well as the market and natural economies. The force of inertial of the product economy finds its way into various types of microeconomic behaviors, and the influence of the natural economy also must not be underestimated. The coexistence of foreign trade directly linked to the international market, modern urban trade and rural pedlars' fairs, and the target of building a socialist market economic system make the task of unifying the standards of microeconomic behaviors all the more difficult and complicated.

It is unavoidable to have confusions in the process of standardizing microeconomic behaviors due to the multiple objectives and detailed items involved, in addition to the fact that we are in a transitional period from the old to the new system. This confused situation demonstrated by the more than 10,000 rules and regulations, in addition to the numerous administrative documents on standardization. Before and after the promulgation of the Administrative Procedure Law, ministries and commissions and local governments made an effort to sort out the existing laws and regulations. In order to meet the demands of the market economy it is necessary for them to make another effort to sort out once again all laws and regulations as well as related documents.

The main task now is to provide the main sectors of the market with a set of unified rules and regulations to standardize market behaviors and normalize market order. At present, however, the extant laws are ineffective in accomplishing the task. In fact, the labour service, capital goods, technology, finance, securities, and futures markets all have their own unique characteristics, in addition to certain common features. Some of the existing laws and regulations are incomplete and others are at the initial level, inappropriate for the country as a whole, with many remaining inoperable until just recently.

The overall conception for the legal system of the socialist market economy.

Some experts have proposed the following conception for the legal system of the socialist market economy.

In terms of the overall framework, this legal system is considered as a branch of the socialist legal system. First of all, the new system must be commanded by the Constitution and in conformity with the laws of other sectors. Nonetheless, it should be equally relevant to laws in several sectors, taking the market economy as a unified objective for readjustment. In order to accelerate the establishment and perfection of the market economic system, it is necessary and beneficial to make a breakthrough in the division of the law categories and give prominence to this branch legal system.

With regard to the form of expression, the new law, just as laws in other areas, should be expressed according to the Constitution, related laws, administrative laws and regulations, local laws and provisions and other valid legal documents. The division of departmental laws only has a relative significance in the statute laws of a country, in drafting legislative plans, making up lopeholes of the law for a comprehensive coordination and the application of legal branches, legal education and studies. In fact, the legal expressional forms, the legal standards and the departmental laws are often overlapped. This is indeed the case in China, just as it is in all countries which have adopted the division of public laws and private laws according to Roman Law. The division of public and private laws should be very strict in the eyes of some scholars, but this is opposed by others.

The market economic legal system covers two major areas, i.e. macroeconomy and microeconomy. There are three main laws governing market operational procedures—the law of the main market sectors, the law of market behaviors and law of social protection. In accordance with concrete conditions in China, the law of main market sectors should emphasize self-independence and equality, while the law of market behaviors should emphasize freedom and fairness, with the law of social protection focusing on fairness and effectiveness. In formulating the standard regulations, different conditions should be allowed to have difference emphases, focusing on the effectiveness not only in correcting existing shortcomings but also in facilitating a sustained stability of the regulations in the long run.

Legal and economic experts have put forward many constructive suggestions concerning the requirements of the market economic legal system. The suggestions can be divided into three major categories: First, laws and regulations needed but not yet available should be stipulated forthwith. Secondly, existing laws and regulations should be combined, revised, supplemented or abolished in accordance with the demands of the market economy. Finally, laws of other sectors should be stipulated, revised or abolished in order to suit to the needs of the market economy and its accompanying legal system. As a result, the entire socialist legal system should be harmonious in content, perfect in form, and coordinative and unified as a whole. The three tasks are arduous and should be accomplished under a unified plan. They should be carried out timely so as to advance simultaneously with the construction of the socialist market economy. The market economy is a legal economy and the market economic structure itself embraces the legal system. Therefore the establishment and perfection of the market economic legal system is an inseparable part of the general task of establishing and perfecting the market economic structure.

The formation of the legal system of the socialist market economy.

Some experts point out that the legal system of the socialist market economy is constituted by civil and economic laws, as well as commercial laws such as company law, bill law, insurance law, maritime commercial law, securities law and other types of laws.

1) The law of the main market sectors covers the organizational forms and positions of various main sectors of the market. The main task of this particular law is to define the different forms of the main market sectors and their respective legal status. The government is the main economic sector under the overly concentrated planned economic structure. However, as the planned economy is transforming into the market economy, the government as the main market sector or business

entity is replaced by enterprises and individuals who engage in business activities. They operate under various forms, including companies (limited stock companies, limited liability companies and foreign companies), cooperatives, partnership enterprises, state-owned and collectively-owned enterprises, private or solely-owned enterprises, and business households, including individual industrial and commercial households, as well as rural contracted households. Partnership enterprises and business households represent newly emerged forms among the main market sectors, even though they are not yet considered as main market sectors. In line with the aforementioned forms, the law of the main market sectors should include company law, cooperative law and partnership enterprise law, with each being stipulated according to the different legal forms, as well as state-owned enterprise law, collectively-owned enterprise law, private or solely-owned enterprise law, business household law and bankruptcy law which are stipulated according to different economic forms. The company law, cooperative law, partnership enterprise law, private (solely-owned) enterprise law and bankruptcy law are basic legal forms governing the main market sectors adopted by all countries with the market economy. If enterprise laws stipulated according to the economic forms should contradict those stipulated according to legal forms, the former should obey the latter so as to maintain the consistency of the law of main market sectors.

2) The task of the law governing the behaviors of the main market sectors in carrying out transactions is to provide standards for the main market sectors to carry out comprehensive business activities. One of the progresses made in legislation during the transition from the planned economy to the market economy is to publicize the originally covert standards for enterprise behaviours. These highly transparent legal standards should take the definition and protection of the rights and interests of the main sectors of market business as the main content, thereby enabling the main bodies of the market to clearly understand the range of accepted behaviors and enter the market without interference. Since the behaviours of the

market main sectors cover a wide scope, the law governing such behaviors should certainly include standards covering the law of right in rem (including general rules on right in rem, law of proprietary right, law of business right, law of right of use of property, law of mining right, law of pawn right, law of mortgage right, and lien law), the law of obligation (including the contract law and the law on infringement act), the bill law, and the insurance and maritime commercial laws. Among them the law on right in rem and the law of obligation are important components of the civil law, and have already listed stipulations for the general rules of the civil law. However, these stipulations still cannot fully meet the needs of the main market sectors, and thus it is necessary to develop the stipulations into a civil code. Commercial laws and statutes, excluding the maritime commercial law, are all but nonexistent in China. Obviously, the situation is far lagging behind, the needs of the development of the market economy.

3) The market management law includes universal legal standards governing fair market competition and maintaining good order for competition. Its main task is to ensure that public social welfare is free from any infringements and maintain the unity of the market. Its main content should include the banning of all unfair business practices of the main market sectors, and enable them to have a clear understanding of the scope of their duties. During the process of developing the market economy, the market management should focus on the management of the overall market and the society under market competition. Therefore the market management law should include the anti-illegitimate competition law, the anti-monopoly law, the law on the protection of the rights and interests of consumers and the producers' responsibility law. Without these basic laws and regulations the main business bodies may possibly at any time violate public interests by engaging in illegal activities, actions which would encroach on the legal rights and interests of other business entities and consumers alike. Practice has proved that the development of the market economy has common laws. Illegitimate competition may exist side by side

with legal competition and it is unavoidable for free competition to develop into monopoly. Therefore, the aforementioned laws and regulations are not only indispensable but also in urgent need.

4) The law of market system recognizes the difference between markets and sets standards for some particular market laws. This law is based on the law governing the behaviors of the main market sectors and the market management law. The major task is to standardize the behaviors of business entities in transactions and the management of concrete markets. In order to promote the development of the market economy, it is necessary to establish and perfect the socialist market system, including the establishment and perfection of the consumer goods market, capital goods market, financial and securities markets, labor market, technology market, information market, real estate market, construction projects market and futures market. Since the market takes various forms, the stipulations which constitute the market system law vary accordingly. They should at the least include the goods trading law, credit law, securities transaction law, labor market management law, technology trading law, information law, construction projects bidding law and futures transaction law. These laws should include stipulations of the rights and duties of business entities, as well as special rules and regulations for the maintenance of the market order.

5) The market macro-control law refers to laws and regulations of the government in exercising macro-control of the market. China's socialist market is by no means a laissez-faire market economy, but instead is a modern market economy operating under government macro-control, and making full use of experiences from abroad. The main task of the macro-control law is to guarantee the steady and coordinated development of the national economy on the premise of respecting the legal status of business entities. It mainly includes the following contents: the budget law, banking law, pricing law, taxation law, investment law and industrial policy law or planning law. These laws and regulations should clarify the scope of the

government control and the legal forms the government uses for macro-control, thus clearly defining the government's status and role in the development of the market economy. Proceeding in line with the market economic system, the government is impossible to interfere directly in the internal affairs of enterprises, or to take over the management as it did under the planned economic system. However, this in no way implies that the government has nothing to do now. On the contrary it can adopt control measures according to the law and conduct effective and legal interferences from outside. Interference of this nature is carried out mainly not by administrative orders, but by interest mechanisms, and it is in fact scientific. The existing problem now is to establish and perfect the aforementioned laws at the earliest possible date so as to standardize the managerial actions of the governmental organizations.

6) The market protection law is to safeguarding social stability under the condition of the market economy. The experience from abroad regarding the development of the market economy has proved that the normal operation of the market economy depends on the precondition of social stability, in addition to the perfection of the aforementioned laws and regulations governing the behaviors of the main market economic sectors and public orders. In order to maintain social stability, in addition to continue with the effort in the reform of the political system, it is also necessary to perfect laws and regulations governing social security. Social security laws include mainly the labour law and the social security law. The labour law should include the employment law and wage law to guarantee a stable life for labourers and full employment of the labourers on the premise of steadily increasing economic returns. At the same time, the government should set in a legal form the minimum wage standard in accordance with concrete conditions in China to ensure the minimum material need for the lives of the labourers. In the development of modern economy, no country can avoid economic fluctuations and enterprise bankruptcies completely. Even in situations free of economic fluctuations and bankruptcies, workers still have to

face possible illness, retirement and disabilities. Under such circumstances, the stability of workers relies on the social insurance law. In other words, the government should, through the establishment of a social insurance law, arouse the enthusiasm of the state, enterprises and individual workers, and raise social insurance funds so as to do away with the practice of "eating from the same big pot" in regard to social welfare, and guarantee the livelihood of labourers under the aforementioned special conditions.

Chapter V
Economic Development and Inflation

1. Realizing Rapid Economic Development at a Minimum Cost

Experts point out that it is impossible for a country to easily achieve rapid economic growth free of cost. While this is true, we should nonetheless extend the greatest possible effort to reduce costs. Perhaps the best way to go about reducing costs is to learn from other countries. The experiences of developed countries can serve as a mirror which can be used by newly emerging developed countries as they undertake economic development, with the experiences of the latter being a valuable tool for developing countries. During the transition from poverty to wealth, the behavior of people in developing countries and regions is largely identical, with only minor differences in certain respects. Socio-economic phenomena in the United States during the 1960s were quite similar to those Japan experienced in the 1970s, as well as those in Taiwan and the Republic of Korea in the 1980s. Had Taiwan been able to draw lessons from the United States and Japan regarding development, the region would most likely have been able to avoid many problems arising in the 1980s such as social instability, political chaos and financial speculation which had cropped up in many other developed countries.

Since the end of World War II, almost all independent countries have extended great effort to boost their economies. Upon reaching the stage of expanded economic development, countries will begin to employ all policy tools available to accelerate economic growth. Many countries have paid heavy costs in achieving rapid economic growth. This has led numerous experts to stress caution when selecting the road of rapid economic growth.

(1) Economic growth is not a goal, but simply a means.

Experts have pointed out that economic growth in itself is not a goal, but simply a means. In other words, economic development helps raise the living standards of the people, while at the same time improving their overall quality of life. Raising the living standards of the people is an overriding task for any country in the early stages of development. How best can a country improve the living standards of its people? The most effective way is to maintain sustained economic development. Raising the living standards of the people would be out of the question without economic development. Hence questions related to having enough to eat, enough clothing to wear, living quarters, necessary vehicles, a primary education and recreational facilities would be mute. However, once basic living demands are satisfied, the next goal for economic development will center on improving the quality of life. Sustained economic growth is a prerequisite for improving the quality of life. In reality, the quality of life would most likely deteriorate in the absence of economic growth.

(2) No perfect methods and measures exist for accelerating economic growth.

While there are many methods a country can call on to boost its economy, none are considered flawless or perfect. Economic results mainly depend on what policies and measures the country introduces.

The Gross National Product (GNP) of a country is composed of:

$$Y = C + G + I + V + (E\text{-}M) \tag{1}$$

Here, Y refers to GNP; C, civil consumption expenditures; G, government consumption expenditures; I, the formation of fixed assets; V, the increased volume in stock; E, the volume of exports and labor services; and M, the volume of imports and labor services.

At the point of equilibrium, a country's total supply $(Y + M)$

equals total demand $(C + G + I + V + E)$, that is,

$$Y + M = C + G + I + V + E \tag{2}$$

Prices will fluctuate if total supply fails to balance with total demand. When viewed from the standpoint of production, GNP includes the gross agricultural product (Ya), gross industrial product (Yi) and gross service production (Ys), that is,

$$Y = Ya + Yi + Ys \tag{3}$$

The growth rate in GNP represents the economic growth rate. A country hoping to raise the growth rate of its GNP must increase consumption expenditures C, government expenditures G, fixed assets I, volume in stock V and exports E. However, certain restrictions exist in terms of domestic supply Y and foreign supply M.

If consumption expenditures (C) expand too rapidly, savings (S) are certain to fall correspondingly. The decline of savings will in turn adversely affect the growth of investment $(I + V)$. In cases when government expenditures (G) rise too quickly and government revenues fail to rise accordingly, the government can issue bonds to increase financial income. Should the growth of exports exceed that of imports, the resulting favorable balance of trade will lead to revaluation of the domestic currency. With regard to an economy oriented to foreign trade, the most important approach to accelerating economic growth is expanding exports. Supporting the expansion of export requires a country to accelerate industrial production, with the latter depending on increased investment, as well as corresponding increases in the accumulation of materials, equipment and money. Excessive investments may become the source of inflation, while overly strict economy may lead to economic stagnation.

(3) Drawing on experiences and lessons from Taiwan, and preventing inflation while accelerating economic development

Over the past 40-odd years, many developing countries and regions have attempted to employ every means possible to realize rapid economic growth, with only a few countries and regions having gained success. A good example is Taiwan, a region which has succeeded in realizing both rapid economic growth and a high per-capita income. The region has also experienced a medium-level inflation and a low rate of unemployment. The region has maintained an appropriate level of public finance, with public debt remaining low, while the level of personal savings and that of foreign exchange savings have remained high. However, this does not mean that there have been no shortcomings in Taiwan's economic development. In fact, Taiwan offers many lessons from which others can learn:

1) Excessive investment led to inflation.

On the one hand, excessive investment can spark a booming economy, and on the other hand, it can lead to runaway inflation. Interest rates rise when investments exceed savings, thereby increasing production costs, a fact which is not conductive to enhancing competitiveness. Excessive investment will result in an inadequate supply of raw materials needed to support production. Correspondingly, prices for raw materials, machines and equipment will climb.

2) Taiwan was far from selective in its choice of methods used to accelerate economic growth.

Once Taiwan set a goal of rapid economic growth, the region was far less than selective in policies implemented for encouraging investment. Some investments in various projects known to involve serious pollution were encouraged by the government because they would increase exports and create job opportunities. Such a case was true for the following examples:

a) Non-selective industrial development.

As one Chinese saying goes: "A hungry person is not choosy about food." This could in fact be analogous to the fact that Taiwan was less than selective about the development of its industrial sector. In fact, industry was welcomed and encouraged as long as industry created job opportunities. A case in point rests with development of shipbreaking industry, an industry known as a notorious polluter. Taiwan, which has long been known for its shipbreaking industry, paid dearly in terms air and water pollution as it developed the industry.

b) Improper selection of the factory's location.

The choice of factory areas is closely related to environmental protection and the living environment. The lack of long-term city planning led to sites for many factories being within the city proper. While the factories in question have indeed manufactured products, they have at the same time created air and water pollution in surrounding areas.

c) Unlimited use of farmland.

The priority of economic development centered on trade related industries. Over the years, a large number of factories in urban areas have polluted vast expanses of farmland. Many of Taiwan's rivers have seriously been polluted and previously fertile land has deteriorated. Perhaps one of the most serious consequences was the fact that the transformation of farmland into aquatic hatcheries resulted in the excessive depletion of underground water reserves. As a result, the water table has dropped to a point below sea level and salt now encroaches on the stratum. Another case involves the fact that demobilized soldiers planted fruit trees on mountain slopes. While they earned a large amount of money in the early stages, the continued dumping the residue from fruit trees into rivers and reservoirs has not only led to serious pollution, but has also posed a threat to the continued use of reservoirs.

3) Protecting immature industries.

The country's locomotive industry, including the automobile industry, has provided the greatest momentum to the national economy. Taiwan has protected its automobile industry in the past 35 years, a fact which has resulted in the small island having eight automobile manufacturing companies. While the companies produce many models of motor vehicles, none have attained an appropriate economy of scale, thereby resulting in high costs, low quality and the inability to compete on the international market.

4) Neglecting the long-term effect of subsidy policies.

The Taiwan authorities adopted a number of encouraging measures to stimulate investment and accelerate economic growth, including adopting reduced or exempted taxes and low-interest loans. While such policies and measures provided positive short-term benefits, they nonetheless had an adverse impacts in the long-term. Many factories and businessmen who enjoyed the subsidy policies offered by the Taiwan authorities failed to contribute to economic growth. For example, various factories and businessmen took advantage of the regulations on rewarding investments by offering faulty exports, a fact which led to government losses.

5) Side effects resulting from rapid economic development.

High-speed economic growth spawns many opportunities for speculative activities, with some low income people with no concept of proper behavior gaining wealth by engaging in speculation. While a certain portion of this group of people hope that society recognizes their new found wealth, they nonetheless continue to engage in unacceptable behavior, with their actions exerting an adverse influence on the outlook of the younger generation towards work. The younger generation tends to seek ease and comfort, and hopes to gain extra advantages such as "free lunches." When faced with a shortage of funds needed for enjoyment, they might possible resort to robbery, murder, violence, and other acts which disrupt social orders. Taiwan, in fact, witnessed the emergence of such phenomena in the 1980s.

(4) The government's main responsibilities for high-speed economic growth center on providing improved public facilities, maintaining a desirable investment environment and ensuring convenient operating conditions for the economic market.

No matter which a country is, economic development depends on both the government and people, with the former being more important. The role of government in developing countries, in particular, is even more prominent. The aforementioned analysis leads people to ask why government policy-makers make so many mistakes. Are such mistakes the result of negligence or are they planned? The simple fact is that such mistakes are the result of both reasons.

a) A government sometimes places undue stress on short-term economic returns, while neglecting long-term influences.

The government often behaves much like a fire break when instituting stop-gap measures. Policy-makers quite often consider only urgent needs which fail to include long-term planning.

b) Governments more often than not neglect the sequence of policies and preconditions in the application of policies, with the eventual consequences of the policies hampering further economic development.

c) Governments quite often fail to assess policies prior to their application. It is all but impossible for policy-makers to make experiments with policies prior to implementation. Therefore, policy-makers should proceed with caution prior to formulating policies. While there are numerous ways to the Roman Empire, there is inevitably one method that is most effective. Policy-makers should choose the most efficient policies to avoid the waste of material resources.

d) Incomplete information will create a phenomenon revolving around people acting in a confused manner.

Ignorance arises from an unawareness of the situation involving supply and demand. In particular, future policy-makers should stay abreast of the latest trends involving various situations.

e) The success rate of policies will rise if policy-makers review all choices and suggestions prior to making decisions. However, the success rate will be very low in cases where policy-makers consider themselves as supermen or Gods. One unfortunate fact is that when rising to a position as a policy-maker, some people often believe in their own observations and judgments. Misconceptions such as these lead to errors in policy.

Regardless of the situation, the major responsibilities of a government during each stage of economic development are to provide complete public facilities, maintain a good investment environment and ensure convenient operating conditions for the market economy. If the main parts of the population are not well educated, the government should take the responsibility to educate them. Such compulsory education is the base of industrialization. Meanwhile the government should help businesspeople set up the rules of games to enable them to participate in fair competitions under the frame of law.

2. How to Judge China's Current Economic Situation

Since 1992, China has entered a new stage of high-speed economic growth and comprehensive transformation of the economic system. While much progress has been made under the new situation, a number of deep-seated contradictions and problems have come to surface. For example, in terms of macro-economic control, the scale of investment has been excessive and the general social supply and demand has increased much too rapidly, which provide evidence of the over-heated economy in some sectors. In addition, inflationary pressure has gained prominence.

The emerging circumstances led to the appearance of divergent views on how to judge China's economic situation, with some views being of a contradictory nature. How then should China's economic situation be valued and judged?

(1) China's overheated economy is mainly manifested by an excessive scale of investment which has led to the expansion of supply and demand and an increase of unstable social factors.

Experts' and scholars' various views concerning the current economic situation not only demonstrate their different understanding of social problems, but also reflect the inevitable outcome because of their different ideals and experiences.

Some contend that the current economic situation in China is good. The 1993 growth rate in GDP was 8 percent, but many expected that it would rise to 10 percent. Estimates for the first five months of 1993 cited the difficulty in maintaining the growth rate at 8 percent, but were optimistic about keeping the figure below 12 percent. An analysis revealed that keeping the economic growth rate between 10 and 12 percent would prevent so-called "bottleneck" factors from expanding to a point where they adversely affected economic returns in various sectors, thereby ensuring smooth development during the year. The targeted inflation rate was originally 6 percent. However, a survey conducted according to the conditions in the first five months in 1993 indicated that the set inflation rate would most likely be broken through. Nonetheless, the government maintained hope of controling the rate at around 10 percent. Realizing the goal of "two 10 percents" called for the adoption of micro-control measures. Between January and May 1993, retail sales jumped by 10.2 percent over the same period of the previous year; the cost of living index rose by 12 percent; and the average living expenditure index in 35 large and medium-sized cities, by 16.7 percent. Such figures were indeed a source of concern. However, it was estimated that the 1993 retail sales price index would possibly be controlled around 12 percent. Even with major rises in service fees, it was nonetheless feasible to control the residential living expenditure index at around 15 percent, and living expenditure index in 35 large and medium-sized cities near 20 percent. In any case, the living expenditure index should not exceed 20 percent, a figure which some felt was dangerously high.

Further analysis revealed that the existing economic growth rate stood at 12 percent. Between January and May 1993, the rate of price hikes (or inflation rate) was 10 percent; residential expenditures rose by 12 percent; and prices in 35 large and medium-sized cities by 15 percent. The situation in turn led to a sharp rise in prices in the real estate sector. When judging from internationally accepted indices, China's economic situation could be classified as being "overheated." However, an important factor revolves around problems related to inaccurate data. Using prices as an example, price sampling is far less than an easy task, and the sampling method we adopted far from comprehensive. If we continue to take samples in line with the traditional weight method, various newly developed commodities such as certain electrical appliances and imports with the highest price growth rates will be excluded. Therefore, conclusions calling for price increases to range between 12 and 15 percent were quite possibly on the low side. In addition, if calculated on the basis of the old sample structure, which is quite different from the new structure used today, calculated prices will certainly be on the low side under conditions where certain proportions rise, but there are not enough weight varieties. In fact wages do not include all remunerations for labor, non-labor remunerations, such as education fees, housing costs and pensions, not included. All such items should be calculated as a part of wages. The growth rate of these items set a record high of 30 percent. As these items are not included in wages, a true picture of the overall situation can not be given. As to the financial sector, government deficits remain unknown because of incomplete data. Someone said that taxes and interest handed to the state by the country's more wealthy provinces, including Guangdong Province, were decreasing successively. However, available data revealed a quite different situation. In reality, there was in fact a wide gap between actual tax and interest payments, and surface tax and interest payments.

Some experts held that the failure to effectively enforce some macro-control measures in the second half of 1992 has added to the severity of existing problems, particularly excessive investment, expanded issuance of currency, large increases in prices, an overheated "foaming economy," and chaotic financial order; and such problems have led to a certain level of fluctuations in terms of economic life, with same being manifest in soaring inflation and the psychological discontent of the masses. The emergence of increasing problems has reached a serious level. The situation, in fact, is rather rigorous in some aspects. To be more concise, the excessive issuance of currency was a major factor in the abnormal financial situation. In 1992, the nationwide issuance of currency jumped by 120 billion yuan, with more than 110 billion yuan in additional currency being issued during the Spring Festival period of 1993 alone. According to the old pattern, currency issued in early in the year can be fundamentally withdrawn from circulation at the end of June that same year. However, the pattern changed in 1993, and the withdrawal of currency from circulation each month, except February, led to a slump. By June 1993, a total of 60 billion yuan had remained in circulation, a fact which quite obviously led to a currency expansion.

The second aspect involved the excessive expansion of investments in fixed assets. The growth rate of investments in fixed assets of state-owned enterprises during the first six months of

1993 hovered at an unprecedented 70 percent, a figure which remained in place for several successive months. In particular, there was a sharp increase in new projects, a factor which spurred a new round of the nationwide construction craze. Hence, it seems we will continue to follow the beaten track of relying on new projects while carrying out economic construction.

The third factor was that overheated "foaming economy" has continued to rise, with the trends going from bad to worse. The craze for the real estate sector, development zones, stocks and raising capital has gained a momentum since the second half of 1992. The craze exhibited no signs of decline in the first several months of 1993, but instead continued to expand. The most serious factor was that the "craze" was supported by capital provided by financial institutions. Capital was accumulated by the introduction of high interest rates and various illegal activities, with such factors leading to the further deterioration of the phenomena centering on corruption.

The fourth factor was the failure to effectively control price rises after the control over prices was lifted. Freeing price control means that price levels are determined by the market, a major aspect of price reform. However, the formation of market mechanisms whereby the determination of prices calls for certain environmental conditions, and fair competitive regulations and laws. Moreover, it also calls for necessary macroeconomic control. Freeing prices is by no means allowing prices to drift. Since 1992, major achievements have been recorded in the effort to free prices. However, problems have arisen due to the fact that macrocontrol has failed to keep pace, resulting in an abnormal phenomenon in which prices continue to climb, and trade monopolies continue to emerge. The price index for means of production has increased by between 30 and 40 percent, while the nation's total index of retail sales prices has hit the double-digit level.

The fifth factor was the slow rise of exports, the expansion of an adverse balance of international payments and radical fluctuations in the foreign market. The growth rate of exports dropped down sharply to 7-8 percent in the first six months of 1993, with that of imports rising to over 20 percent. At the same time, trade payment deficits expanded considerably. Foreign exchange rates changed on a monthly basis, and appeared to be out of control. Following the introduction of administrative controls in March 1993, transactions on foreign exchange markets cooled somewhat, but the black market flourished. Since decontrol of the foreign exchange rate in May, foreign exchange rates have jumped sharply, almost to a level considered out of control.

The sixth and final factor was that state revenues failed to take a turn for the better along with rapid national economic development. In fact, difficulties related to the state financial situation were even more spectacular. While the national economy has developed at a high rate since 1993, state revenues have increased by only a small margin, thereby failing to coincide with overall economic development. On the other hand, however, financial expenditures have kept pace with economic development with a growth rate between of 15 and 18 percent. As a result, various localities and departments have faced difficulty in making payments.

The aforementioned situation concerning the six aspects fully demonstrates that China's macroeconomy is out of control, and that both economic growth and construction speed have exceeded the state's comprehensive bearing capacity.

Those who espouse the opinion of an "overheated" economy maintain that China's economy is at a crucial stage. The key problem during this stage is how to ensure a stable and coordinated macroeconomy.

In 1993, China's economy continued to grow at high rate based on the high-speed development in 1992. Various localities must exhibit a fervent spirit geared to rapid development. However, higher authorities and local governments held different views concerning the economic situation in the first half of 1993, as did the macro and microsectors. Higher authorities considered the economy was overheated, while various localities expressed discontent with the situation, all the while hoping to be granted additional power to promote their economies. Due to the lack of a unified recognition of the situation, the economic principles for 1993 set by the Party Central Committee and the State Council have not been effectively implemented. As a result, various problems arising in 1992 were more outstanding and tended to be more serious, thereby greatly accelerating current economic fluctuations.

In short, many say that China's present economy is indeed overheated, a fact which is proved by the excessive scale of investment which in itself leads to a rapid expansion in supply and demand, and by rapid rise in prices, factors which create unstable factors adversely affecting society. The real estate and stock crazes have been the major culprits leading to the "foaming economy."

(2) Views of the "overheated economy" lack clarity. Rapid economic growth has led to phenomena which should be regarded as normal.

Other economists held a quite different view concerning the "overheated economy" mentioned above. In their opinion, economic development is a process of solving economic problems and improving the living standards of the people. Over the past 40 years, the Chinese economy has experienced rapid growth which has helped solve many problems. Nonetheless, new problems have surfaced. The fact is, however, that such problems are due less to the "overheated economy" than to an imbalance in supply and demand. So long as there is an adherence to the market economic system, such an imbalance will be subject to automatic regulation which will restore balance. Price fluctuations are difficult to avoid in the process of regulation. Inflation should not be feared so long as economic growth is maintained at a normal rate and the living standards of the people continue to be improved.

Some experts pointed out that many people have reached a common understanding concerning the current situation of economic reform. Simply stated, the symptoms of an overheated economy in certain sectors have appeared, and microregulatory measures have been introduced to solve related problems. New arguments emerged concerning "economic overheating," with some predicting that "the phenomenon of 1988 would resurface." Why were such arguments misguided? Problems we actually face lie in sustained price rises. Therefore, prejudice against the current situation is justifiable when considering the adverse results of inflation. Actually, the state has initiated austerity measures. For instance, the real estate craze has resided somewhat. What led to the noticeable decline in the real estate sector when the trend in rising prices remained? This particular phenomenon resulted from acceleration of market process after 1992. China decontrolled the prices of numerous commodities between 1992 and the first half of 1993. In addition, the markets of key elements appeared, including the real estate and capital markets. Prices were bound to rise under such circumstances. In the interim, still other questions have surfaced concerning how to prevent overly restrictive measures, with measures adopted in 1988 being inappropriate for the present situation. Since tightening measures will most likely lead to a slump, we will closely monitor the effects of the present austerity measure over the next eight to 12 months. The adoption of overly tight measures would most likely lead to even more difficulties in the following year. Microregulatory measures are necessary during the process of developing the market economy. When viewing the emergence of some abnormal phenomena, one immediately has the idea that "the situation is getting worse." Therefore, due consideration should be given to the prevention of unnecessary tightening. This in fact means that a growth rate ranging between 8 and 10 percent is indeed possible. Even though the economy is cyclic, the economy should not witness major fluctuations in the coming year. If we subjectively use the austerity policies to slow the economy, we will undoubtedly face even greater difficulties.

Some economists disagree the argument that the economy is "overheated," and consider the argument as unscientific. They insist the word "overheated" belongs to the realm of physics. However, the term has now entered the realm of economics. Therefore, what is the criteria for "overheated"? How can it be measured? At this point, the answers to such questions remain unclear. No matter what approach or appreciation of the Chinese economy, one must first understand the actual conditions in China now. China is a large country with a big population, and unequal nationwide economic development. China is still a poor country. Furthermore, it has long been subject to a planned economy. Based on these circumstances, it is definitely unscientific to use the term of "overheated" when summarizing China's economic craze. Are there Chinese citizens, enterprises and local governments against rapid development? The fact is that enthusiasm has been analogous to the eruption of a volcano. Receiving encouragement from Deng Xiaoping's speeches during his tour of south China in 1992, China's outlook has been subject to monumental changes in a short period of time. Deng Xiaoping pointed out that it was unnecessary to argue over the meaning of "socialism" and "capitalism." At the same time, the central government has promoted the market economy. These two factors alone have had brought the enthusiasm of the people into full play. We must refrain from suppressing the enthusiasm displayed by the people. The fact is that the economies of various localities are far from overheated, with many being rather cool. This in no way implies that we should ignore the various aspects of serious problems. We should treat serious problems in certain areas, or certain projects, individually and, as the saying goes, refrain from allowing "a mouse to spoil a pot of soup." We should carry out an in-depth analysis of concrete conditions. At present, however, many figures lack proper analysis.

Another problem rests with the fact that some people are alarmed at perfectly normal phenomena, such as inflation, financial deficits and an imbalance in foreign trade. A market economy would not exist if everything were in an ideal state, a situation which was in fact the goal of the planned economy. We of course oppose serious inflation, a problem which has not as yet reached a serious level in China, even though some people become quite disturbed when hearing the word. While the United States has a financial deficit several hundred times greater than ours, it nonetheless proceeds along the same course. Therefore, we should not be surprised at the phenomena if they remain in desirable limits. The absence of such phenomena would not be indicative of the market economy, but instead for the planned economy.

Some economists express confusion over the dispute as to

whether or not economic development is "overheated." The prevailing thought is that the key problem in economic development does not rest with the moniker "overheated," but instead with the ability to carry out "reform." If we fail to deepen reform, but instead revert to adopting administrative methods to suppress the phenomena of overheating, the phenomena will be worsen over a period of time. Conversely, reinforcing reform will make it possible to release factors that should be allowed to develop, and prevent unnecessary overheating of other factors.

If we continue to dispute the volume of investment and number of projects instead of touching on the old system, we will never escape the "rapid-to-sluggish" cycle, or the "cooling-to-heated" cycle. We must attempt to cool the overheated economy, and spur growth once the cooling process is no longer desirable. In the past, we often acted unwisely by allowing the economy to grow too rapidly, and fall too sharply. We must make every effort to avoid such fluctuations and proceed with national economic development. A good example of this is the attempt to cool the craze for establishing "development zones." Administrative orders make it easy to indiscriminately halt the construction of zones. While it is appropriate to halt the construction of zones that should not be established, we must refrain from taking indiscriminate action.

The hot topic in the not too distant past centered on whether or not the economy was overheated, while the topic of how to carry out the reform remained on the back burner. However, since the second half of 1992, various units have been content to simply state their opinions on how to accelerate reform and adopt general directives. They failed to adopt specific directives or take concrete measures, let alone introduce important reform measures. During the on-going upsurge of reform, we should advocate less empty talk, with emphasis instead being placed on an earnest working spirit, and achieving significant advancement in reform.

Foreign experts have attributed China's high-speed economic growth to the following three factors: First, China has adopted correct policies for economic development; second, China's economic growth began at a relatively low level, so it is highly possible for China to reach the growth rate of Japan in the 1960s; third, China is a vast country with a potentially large market. China is not only a highly productive country, but also a major consuming country capable of attracting a large volume of foreign investment. China has in fact been highly successful in the use of foreign investment. All these factors make it possible for China to maintain a 10 percent growth rate in the next three to five years.

Some foreign experts have also pointed out that the Chinese economy is on the high-speed track. Continued high-speed growth has also led to the emergence of problems related to the Chinese economy, including the excessive issuance of currency, skyrocketing prices, financial deficits and the mounting pressure for better infrastructure, all factors which pose a certain threat to the economy.

Various foreign experts disagreed with the view that the Chinese economy was overheated in 1988 alone. They contended that the overheated economy in 1988 resulted from the lack of government attention over several years leading up to 1988. They also disagreed with the view that as the present growth rate is equivalent to the average growth rate of 11.5 percent in 1984, China should maintain the present growth level for the foreseeable future. The high-speed growth in 1992 resulted from certain beneficial conditions. While such conditions might possibly continue, they will most likely be subject to change. Therefore, many experts contend that the growth rate is not necessarily the key problem. The key they say is how to maintain a normal growth rate. The growth rate should be determined in line with concrete conditions both at home and abroad. Based on differing conditions, a growth rate of 9 percent is not necessarily inferior to a rate of 12 percent, and in some cases a growth rate of 5-6 percent is ideal.

Still other experts hold the view that China's economic situation cannot be measured by standards used for developed countries. The economic growth rate in developed countries stands at 3 percent or less, an annual growth rate with which they are satisfied. However, many developing countries, China in particular, would find it difficult to meet necessary financial expenditures with only a 3 percent annual increase. Therefore, China's economic growth rate cannot be measured by the standards for Western countries. At the same time, in view of China's current situation it would be unwise to consider the economic growth rate for only one or two years. The growth rate in 1992 stood at 12.8 percent, with estimates calling for the same rate in 1993. We must refrain from considering the growth rate for only one or two years, but instead consider same for a much longer period of time. Judging from the period between 1987 and 1992, the average annual growth rate for the five years stood at only 8.7 percent, a figure much lower than the average growth rate in the four years following the initiation of the reform drive in 1979. The figure was also lower than the average growth rates of Taiwan, Hong Kong, Singapore and the Republic of Korea during their respective economic boom periods. Secondly, China's economic development is cyclical, with a cycle extending about six to seven years. Cycle can however be divided into two stages—the first stage featuring a rising economy and the other stage, regulation. During the rise, the growth rate will increase more rapidly, while it will be quite low during the regulatory stage. China entered a new economic cycle in the second half of 1991, with the present cycle encompassing the rising stage, a stage expected to last from 1992 to 1994. Third, high speed growth does not necessarily equate to an overheated economy. What then are the standards for an overheated economy? Apart from growth rate, we must also consider whether or not economic returns and the technical levels fall, whether or not there is a major increase in the inefficiency of the means of production, whether or not there is an imbalance in the industrial structure, whether or not financial deficits increase sharply, and whether or not the living standards of the people fall by a wide margin. Judging in terms of these standards, such items have not declined, but instead have improved in China. A case in point is the actual quality of life of the Chinese people. Even though living standards have not yet improved to the ideal level, they have nonetheless improved significantly. Another example rests with economic returns. Although economic returns have not improved greatly, no further deterioration has been recorded. Such circumstances are truly indicative of the fact that the problem of overheating is nonexistent in modern day China.

Some experts maintain that the Chinese economy has experienced three relatively spectacular microeconomic cyclic fluctuations since the initiation of reform and opening to the outside world in 1978. The periods in question refer to 1978-1983, 1984-1987 and 1988-1992. In terms of the causes for the cycles, fluctuations between 1978 and 1983 were mainly caused by mistakes of planners under the traditionally "centralized system." Fluctuations during the two other cycles resulted from competition between pluralistic main bodies under the "decentralized system," and conditions resulting from "soft budgetary restraints." Since the implementation of reform of the state ownership economy focusing on "granting additional autonomy to enterprises and allowing them to retain a greater proportion of profits," the behavior of state-owned enterprises and local governments in terms of investments and consumption spurred the overheated economy. The previous aspects were the basic characteristics of the last two cycles. The degree of inflation constituted the major difference between the first two cyclic fluctuations and the latter. Inflation was in fact a direct result of changes in the price system. Planned prices played a leading role during the first two periods. Excessive total demand was manifested by "supply shortages," while during the last period the fact that the market economy gained a considerable foothold led to the manifestations of excessive total demand in the form of evident inflation, which itself was further accelerated by "the signals of price relationships." Even more new changes have emerged under the present economic structure than did in the structure prevalent between 1988 and 1989. They include the increasing role of the nongovernmental ownership economy, the development of the securities, bonds and real estate markets, and the expansion of channels for individual investment which has helped ease the pressure of inflation, as well as the basic formation of market regulated prices for consumer commodities. All of these factors have proved beneficial to maintaining the stability of macro-economy.

However, we must pay due attention to some basic elements in China's economic system. When compared with the economic systems between 1984-1987 and 1988-1992, the existing economic system has not experienced radical changes, with the state ownership economy system continuing to play a leading role in all sectors and soft budgetary restraints for enterprises and local governments remaining stagnant. On the other hand, however, certain aspects have been accelerated; and no decisive progress has been made in the reform of the financial system. This shows that China's current economy has entered a new round of fluctuations following the same mode prevalent during the previous two periods of economic fluctuations. Meanwhile, the thorough implementation of the policy for "granting more autonomy and allowing the retention a greater proportion of profits" has further complicated the financial market, reduced the efficiency of the central monetary policy and created even more difficulties in an effort to stabilize the macroeconomy.

When proceeding from a long-term viewpoint of stabilizing macroeconomy and considering the root causes of economic fluctuations arising in the years of reform, we should first concentrate efforts on deepening reform. We should immediately consider the following measures in earnest: Accelerating efforts to clarify state-owned property rights for assets, transforming state-owned enterprises into "corporate entities," more actively developing the non-governmental economy, allowing the development of non-governmental financial institutions, and deepening the reform of the financial system.

Some experts have pointed out that China's current economy is not yet a true market economy. Therefore, in China prosperity resulting from circulation is quite different from that in capitalist countries. Since the largest majority of assets in China belong to the state, investment policy-makers do not have to accept the consequences of their behavior. Soft restraints on the budget may in fact lead to an overheated economy, yet another factor different from the efficient boom circulation in capitalist countries. The expenditure of a capitalist company is the final responsibility of the owners of the company. Therefore, such expenditures will not exceed set limits due to the rigid budgetary constraints determined by private property rights. Take the enterprise groups' consumption particular to China as an example. The expenditures and investment of state-owned enterprise groups in China may expand without limitation. Because even though their investments fail, investment decision-makers don't have to take the responsibilities. This big-pot system may picture real economic crisis. Without the restraints of private property rights, imposing effective administrative and disciplinary restraints on such behaviors is the prerequisite for the normal operation of this economic system. The problem rests with the fact that disciplinary sanctions imposed by the Chinese government on state-owned enterprises remains the only effective administrative restraints. Without administrative restraints, macrocontrol measures on state-owned enterprise are basically invalid.

In reality, the problem of an overheated economy does in fact exist in China. Inflation is not only a problem arising from the increasing issue of currency and normal prosperity of circulation, but also a problem related to reducing the effects of investment resulting from the shortage of soft budgetary restraints which come to the surface under the state ownership system, especially during periods of prosperity.

Some experts pointed out that the so-called overheated economy should be judged in terms of the speed and scale of capital construction, with the former having been quite rapid since 1992, and the latter being quite extensive. However, actual figures indicate that the rapid rate is a result of the nature of restoration. The economic growth rate in 1992 stood at 12.8 percent, a significant rise of the projected low target which had diminished during the previous three years. When calculated on an average annual basis, the growth rate was in fact only about 7 percent. At the same time, the scale of capital construction in 1992 increased by 37.6 percent. However, when allowing for price factors and the growth in foreign capital, the actual scale leveled off at the 1988 level. In addition, the actual nationwide scale of capital construction in 1991 was 10 percent less than that of 1988. This was a direct result of the cutbacks of the several year earlier. The 1992 price level rose by 5.4 percent in 1992, some 70 percent of which was a direct result of price reform. Between 1992 and 1993, decontrolled prices accounted for 80 percent of the total, a fact which led to inevitability of price hikes. The very factor was prominent in the first half of 1993. Some experts point to the fact that price indices rose by 11.2 percent in the first five months of 1993, with some 50 percent of the total being directly attributable to price reform. Another factor centered on the fact that the business tax was raised from 3 percent to 5 percent on April 1, 1993. The tax rise and the resulting chain reaction promoted price hikes of some 3 percent, a figure which was reflected in the 11.2 percent increase in price indices. Price factors accounted for between 5 and 6 percent, with the turnover factor standing at between 2 and 3 percent. As a result, the actual percentage in the price rise was somewhat less than 11.2 percent. In addition, the price indices for major consumer goods in 35 medium-sized and large cities actually soared to as high as 35 percent. Housing costs in various cities in fact doubled, and in some cases tripled. For example, housing costs in Beijing tripled, with prices for running water and gas doubling, with significant increase in prices for items which had remained unchanged for several decades. Price reform has obviously raised the indices for living expenditure to a record level. Therefore, the current situation indicates the major problem is not simply a matter of an overheated economy, nor is it inflation, but instead it revolves around what measures should be taken.

(3) The current economic situation resulted from the stagnation of reform of the macrocontrol system during the transition from the planned to the market economy. Prices should be stabilized as quickly as possible to provide an appropriate environment for deepening reform.

An almost identical view held that the current economic situation resulted from serious stagnation of reform of the macro-control system during China's effort to shift to a market economic system. In terms of the financial, fiscal levying, investment and foreign exchange control systems, reform of macrocontrol lagged far behind that of microreform. Consequently the economic development has expanded abnormally on the premise of unreasonable government's behaviors, thus forming the present difficult situation.

Experts have expressed a number of differing opinions as to the detailed reasons for the current situation.

Some contend that the current overheated economy stemmed from the excessive scale of investment in fixed assets, a situation which emerged mainly because since early 1993 various local governments have stressed rapid economic development and have blindly developed various economic development zones. This has in turn led to excessively high growth and has created a tense relationship between supply and demand.

Most experts agree that the root cause of the current intense economic situation centered on the fact that monetary policy was out of control. An overheated economy had emerged by the end of 1992 following two successive years' currency issue which exceeded the corresponding economic growth, with the excessive amount of basic currency issued by the central bank leading to a substantial rise in total demand.

Some contend that the stock and real estate crazes which absorbed large amounts of capital for a period of time sparked the rising market interest rates and led to economic entities facing capital shortages. In addition, price rises for items such as rolled steel, basic raw materials and labor services enlarged the costs of economic entities. The nature of current inflation centers on what is known as cost push. Therefore, one cannot summarize the current situation as being simply the result of the excessive issuance of currency.

In consideration of the aforementioned views, experts suggested the adoption of macrocontrol measures with well-defined objectives in mind. Proceeding on the basis of a unified understanding, we should persist in following correct regulatory policies suited to lessening friction and promoting the development. China's current economic problems have resulted from the process of advancement. The emergence of problems was unavoidable during the transition from the old to the new system. Nonetheless, if we consider reform as the principal method and handle the effort appropriately, negative effects can be transformed into favorable factors, and the further emergence of adverse effects can be reduced to a minimum. At present, we should persist in three principles: First, persevering in reform and strengthening the construction of operating mechanism as guides to promote healthy economic development; second, refraining from dampening the enthusiasm of the locales, while at the same time lessening friction and adopting drastic measures to deal with the economic cycle; third, persisting in the use of economic means to properly deal with the economy. In terms of points of contention resulting from the administrative push, we must adopt necessary administrative measures to solve them, and adopt necessary administrative measures to guarantee the implementation of economic means.

We should properly control the flexibility and dynamics of macrocontrol policies. China's market mechanism and monetary system have been greatly strengthened, and thus macrocontrol policies must suite the changes. Particular consideration should focus on the flexibility and dynamics of macrocontrol policies. In addition, we must strengthen the timeliness and purpose of macrocontrol measures. Due to repeated delays and missed opportunities, the current regulation on interest rates has raised costs, but has provided fewer results. Introducing the regulation stipulating an interest rate of 2.18 percentage points several months earlier would have not only given "signals," but also produced great momentum with the use of only "limited power." The prolonged adherence to the low-interest rate system has caused distorted prices for capital, a rise in multi-tracked interest rates and chaos in the capital market. Enterprises have been unable to obtain loans from normal channels, high interest on capital has run rampant and serious corruption has emerged in the financial sector. Therefore, it is quite improper to say the overheated economy has had nothing to do with the delayed regulation of interest rates. The current interest rate level plays a weak role which is far too inadequate to control expanded demand.

It is imperative to control friction arising from investment expansion, especially those related to the many existing economic hot spots. The source of the existing overheated economy lies in the investment-push expansion. However, the existing investment expansion is somewhat different from that in 1988. The fact is that indirect financing has expanded rapidly, while the expansion of direct financing has reached greater extremes. Although various types of bank deposits increased more than loans during the first few months of 1993, a great deal of capital from banks flowed into the real estate and securities sectors in the form of call money. Hence, a lopsided "direct financing craze" appeared. Direct financing usually adopts high interest rates to absorb funds, and hence the market interest rate continues to climb. Even though the state has set a low legal interest rate, large numbers of enterprises still find it quite difficult to obtain low interest loans, with many being forced to pay high interest rates simply to obtain funds. Even though the low interest rate policy is designed to protect enterprises, actual implementation has been contrary to the wishes of the state. In fact, the capital costs of enterprises have risen steadily, a fact which defies economic law. Therefore, we must firmly grasp the crucial problem of economic swelling. The only way to achieve desirable effects is to remedy the causes.

It is imperative to regulate the macrocontrol policy to a certain degree. This can be accomplished in two ways: Firstly, maintaining the traditional operating mechanism of state-owned enterprises as the centre. Various auxiliary macrocontrol measures should be adopted, with financial and materials supply, and related policies focusing on operating mechanism. Secondly, maintaining the total balance and structural coordination in the macroeconomy as the central aspect. Various auxiliary macrocontrol measures should be adopted, with the focus being placed on financial and materials supply and related policies. At present, we favor the first choice. The goal is to maintain the operating mechanism of state-owned enterprises, with the supply of financing and materials being guaranteed by the state. Should the actual effect be less than desirable, more limits should be placed on the state, thereby forcing the state to bear an increasingly heavy financial burden. The existing policy resulted in an excessive drain on the state, and has provided no benefits to enhancing socialist economic strength. Proceeding under the conditions of socialist market economy, we must allow state-owned enterprises to engage in market competition, and resolutely close or force the bankruptcy of enterprises which produce inferior products and are incapable of reversing their loss-making predicament. By doing so we can effectively optimize the industrial complex, improve the macroenvironment and improve the national economy.

3. Views on the Current Inflation

Current inflation is one of the most hotly debated topics in China. Economists have different theories on how best to judge and deal with current inflation.

(1) How best to define inflation?

What in fact is inflation? This question has long been discussed by both Western and Marxist economists. Various arguments have emerged due to the different theoretical and ideological systems, partially from the varied origins of inflation. Nonetheless, arguments on inflation most often come to the same end. No matter how approached, inflation is bad. Who should bear the responsibility of inflation? In a highly summarized and concise definition, the answer is difficult to express in exact comprehensive terms. However, there is a consensus that inflation refers to a phenomenon arising in a national economy, i.e., the general price level (as expressed by the price indices of retail sales, indices for living expenditures and the GNP's reduction) which exhibits sustained increases in a relatively high margin of more than 2 percent over a relatively long period of three or more years.

Theoretically, inflation is formed by the following four factors:

Demand pull, or what is sometimes referred to as "buyers'

inflation." In accordance with the GNP calculating method used in the Western countries, total demand is divided into four items —consumption (C), investment (I), government expenditures (G) and exports (X). Therefore, price rises stem from either one, several or all of the items which surpass total supply.

Cost push, or what is called "sellers' inflation." In terms of national products or national revenues equalling 100 percent, enterprise costs, including wages, interest and land costs, equal 80 percent of the total, with profits accounting for 20 percent. Wages are in fact the major component of enterprise costs. Therefore, cost push inflation refers to price rise for products stemming from cost increases filtering down from product suppliers. The process is also referred to as wage-push inflation. In addition, price rises may come from the owners of monopolized sectors, who attempt to raise the share of profits. This then can be called profit-push inflation.

Whether initial inflation is sparked by demand pull or cost pull, rising prices will lead workers to ask for wage increases when negotiating new contracts. The scope of increase includes not only the existing inflation rate, but also the estimated inflation rate in the future. In this way, a cycle of price rises to wages rise followed by more price rises is formed. Prices and wages essentially push each other forward in a spiralling cycle, and hence the inflation rate increases at a rapid rate. For example, the inflation rate in the first year will stand at 4 percent, rising to 7 percent in the second year, and to 10 percent in the third year....

No matter what type, rising inflation will lead to a dramatic increase in currency in circulation (currency supply × the currency circulation rate). The following two situations provide clarification:

First, in terms of the theoretical mold, the currency supply serves as an external variable (M. Friedman's Mold). This simply means that the financial departments should be responsible for the increase in the money supply, which must effectively meet the needs of consumers, investors and the governments, a process resulting in demand-pull inflation. In reality, the money supply can also serve as an internal variable, meaning that growth in the money supply is the result of the increased expenditures of main consumers. Simply stated, this refers to the result of adaptive increases in the money supply.

Second, responsible financial departments face two choices in terms of cost-push inflation: (a) In cases where the adaptive increase in the money supply is designed to avoid unemployment, the employment rate may remain stable, but prices will rise correspondingly. The normal result is that wages and prices rise spirally. Under such circumstances, the only way to check inflation is to control rises in wages and prices. For example, the "New Economic Policies" introduced by the Nixon administration on August 15, 1971 were designed to freeze and control wages and prices. Yet another example is the former West German government, which often participated in drafting agreements between laborers and owners in order to ensure that the wage growth rate did not exceed the growth rate of labor productivity. The inflation rate was effectively limited within 5 percent. (b) A government must freeze (or reduce) the money supply in cases where the inflation rate is excessively high. The principle for setting prices on monopolized markets in the Western countries is cost-plus profit. When cost increases, owners of monopoly factories raise prices accordingly. The fact that the total money demand fails to increase correspondingly results in the rising unemployment and sluggish production. Between 1974 and 1975, for the first time ever all Western countries, without exception, suffered from sluggish economies and inflation, i.e., inflation and economic depression existed simultaneously. Stagnation mainly resulted from rapid rises in the price of oil, a fact which also resulted from a drop in agricultural production in the United States, which in turn led to price hikes for agricultural products. Prior to economic depression, the unemployment rate in Britain, France and Germany hovered at around 2 percent, a figure which jumped dramatically to 10 percent in the late 1980s, and even higher in the United States. Quite simply, the aforementioned countries were forced to pay dear costs to control inflation.

(2) The representative view is that inflation is "public enemy number one," hence we cannot adopt policy-related inflation measures to promote economic development.

Some experts have noted that with reference to the latest data released by the State Statistical Bureau, the nationwide retail sales price index in May 1993 was 12 percent higher than in the previous year's period. The living expenditures index, which includes monthly transportation tickets, housing costs, water, electricity, gas, and labor services, increased by 14 percent over the 1992 period. Prices in 35 large and medium-sized cities were significantly higher than other areas, with the retail price index hitting 16.5 percent, the living expenditures index hovering at 19.5 percent and closing at 20 percent. Such figures warrant our great attention. According to internationally accepted standards, an annual 3 percent inflation rate is listed as low-level inflation; 6 percent as a medium-level rate, and double-digit inflation as evidence of serious inflation. When judged by these standards, there is no need for reticence concerning whether or not China has entered a stage of serious inflation. Some economists contend that the Chinese economy is just beginning to release its inflation pressure; and the situation is far from rigid. We nonetheless think the view is misguided because to a certain degree inflation is determined by international standards, just as a thermometer is used to measure the temperature of a human being. Analogous to inflation, a temperature of 38° centigrade indicates a person is suffering from a "low" fever, while 40° centigrade indicates a "high" fever. Standards cannot be revised and changed at will.

According to one popular point of view, although prices go up, the average income of the people also rises. Certain levels of inflation remain within the tolerance limit of the people. This view will not withstand repeated deliberations. For example, we offer the following accounts: In the midst of price hikes, the rate of increase in prices for agricultural produces continually lagged behind that of industrial products, with the so-called scissor-type price differences between industrial and agricultural products widening continuously. On the one hand, prices for means of agricultural production, such as chemical fertilizers, pesticides and plastic film rose significantly. On the other hand, prices for agricultural produces dropped or increased by only a small margin. As a result, farmers' actual income dropped, which has adversely affected farmers' enthusiasm for production. For example, one farmer in Fengyang County, Anhui Province, noted the price per *jin* (1 *jin* = 0.5 kilogramme) of rice was 0.42 yuan in 1990, and only 0.22 yuan in 1992. The per 100 *jin* price for phosphate was 12 yuan in 1990, with the figure rising to 15 yuan in 1992. At present, an additional input of over 10 yuan is required for every *mu* (1 *mu* = 1/15 hectare) of farmland. In 1990, average per capita income stood at 596 yuan, with the figure dropping to 370 yuan in 1992. Therefore, when deducting expenditures in various proportions and using income to repair ponds, a farmer netted only 250 yuan annually. The fall in the income level of farmers is thus quite obvious.

The past few years have witnessed rising income levels for various individual households and owners of private enterprises, as well as workers and staff in some township enterprises in coastal areas and areas in the Yangtze River Valley, in addition to workers and staff of foreign-funded enterprises. However, the total number of people involved is only in the few tens of millions. Some two-thirds of state-owned industrial enterprises suffer from losses resulting from poor management. Many enterprises have been unable to pay wages, with some paying as much as 80 percent of wages to employees, let alone bonuses. Other enterprises are in an even worse predicament, with many having halted operations, or operating at far less than capacity. Therefore, from an overall standpoint, incomes for a considerable segment of workers and staff have dropped.

Large numbers of office workers and intellectuals are paid low wages. While grain prices have been recently decontrolled and housing costs have risen, wages have failed to follow suit. In addition, state subsidies are subject to new limitations. Financial difficulties have delayed the introduction of public service system. Only a few people who have quit their jobs in state departments or schools to engage in business and trade have been successful.

The adverse influences of inflation have led to at least a certain level of decline in the purchasing power of some 900 million farmers, 100 million workers and staff, and 40 million office workers, with the drops having led to a decline in their quality of life. At the same time, the quality of life of retired workers and cadres is getting worse on a seemingly daily basis. Such circumstances are indicative of the fact we would be misguided to use the term "having bearing capacity" as a general term to cover all contradictions. While some say inflation and fast economic growth can coexist in China, others feel that such a view is harmful.

Serious inflation is bound to hamper smooth economic development, and accelerated inflation has in fact adversely affected economic growth. For example, various problems have emerged in the agricultural, industrial and foreign trade sectors.

In some places, the fact that diesel fuel has doubled has seriously dampened the enthusiasm of 80 percent of fishermen to engage in ocean fishing, which has been compounded by the lack of price hikes for fish. The losses of fishermen outweigh gains if they operate diesel powered boats.

Farmers in certain provinces continue to use hand sickles to harvest wheat, while combines sit idly by while the families of combine operators themselves gather wheat by hand. At present, harvesting one *mu* of wheat costs 25 yuan, but farmers lack the funds to use available machinery. How then could anyone imply that this situation has no adverse affects on agricultural production?

A case in point is that price hikes led to a substantial decline in bank savings deposits in one particular, while industrial loans dropped sharply by some 75 million yuan causing some 20-30 percent of factories to either halt or severely curtail production. Banks in some provinces were faced with a lack of funds needed to purchase summer grains from farmers. In many cases loans were even denied to enterprises earning a large volume of foreign exchange or enterprises with high economic returns. A shortage of circulating capital prevented some factories from expanding production. The phenomenon forcing even a partial curtailment in production is quite serious. It is evident that inflation has brought about adverse affects to industrial production.

In the terms of foreign trade, the favorable balance has turned into a trade deficit, with the prime example being rolled steel, a previously exported product which must now be imported. In fact, the rising domestic demand for rolled steel stimulated price hikes on the international market. Japan, the Republic of Korea (ROK), the United States and European countries are all more than happy to export rolled steel to China. In addition, China has witnessed declines in exports of copper, tin, cement, electrical products and machinery products. The reason being that expanded domestic capital construction has stimulated rising prices on the Chinese market. As a result, domestic markets offer a greater opportunity to earn profits than do foreign markets.

Available facts make it much less difficult for Chinese citizens to see that inflation has already affected the normal operations of the national economy and has hampered sustained economic growth. In the 1980s, the United States saw prices rise by as much as 10 percent. President Carter announced that inflation was "Public Enemy Number One," and called for measures to combat its expansion. A point well worth noting is that current inflation in China is also our number one enemy. We must earnestly deal with the situation, and must refrain from slackening our vigilance.

Some experts also pointed out that since the current inflation is public enemy number one, we should in no way adopt policy-related inflation measures to boost the economic growth. They based their opinion on the fact the inflation policies can only be carried out under certain conditions. For example, under conditions when a large number of workers are out of work, economic depression reaches the extremes and social effective demand is insufficient, adopting stimulatory financial policies related to expansion of the money supply to increase social demand will in fact have an incendiary effect on economic growth. Keyne's theory on the expansion of social demand is suitable to the aforementioned situation, but not to certain other conditions due to the fact that increasing the money supply to stimulate the economic growth is a stop-gap measure. Once the state fully utilized all material resources, increases in the money supply will lead to price hikes. Increasing the money supply on the one-time basis will have an adverse influence, while continual increases in the money supply will result in price hikes and in turn lead to inflation.

Theoretical studies show that inflation-related policy fails to promote economic growth. It is true for the following reasons: Firstly, an inflationary environment increases factors of uncertainty in economic operation. Many emerging opportunities to develop production go by the wayside. In 1987, an authoritative research institute conducted a survey of 2,000-odd enterprises operating under the contract system, some 72 percent of which were large and medium-sized enterprises, with 94 percent of the total being highly competitive. The enterprises were questioned about their greatest worries. Some 15.1 percent of the respondents said their greatest worries prior to the introduction of the contract system were "product marketing and prices," with 24.7 percent pointing to "the supply of raw materials and prices." Respective figures for the period following adoption of the contract system stood at 16.4 percent and 46.9 percent for 69.3 percent of the total number of respondents. The survey also reveals that the greatest worry of enterprises was uncertainty related to prices. When confronted with continuous price rises, entrepreneurs most often anticipate even higher prices. Hence, there is little doubt that enthusiasm of enterprises for production and management is greatly affected. This indicates that normal productive and managerial activities will be restrained, while a great deal of speculative activities will emerge. Such factors are quite harmful to economic growth.

Secondly, inflation has seriously distorted the price system under the prevailing circumstances resulting from the incomplete market system. Sustained price rises do not necessarily portend simultaneous proportional price rises for every product. Quite to the contrary, while some prices rise rapidly, others rise slowly, thereby distorting the originally reasonable price relationship and distorting the formal price relationship even more. During the process of reform, the phenomenon of prices returning to old rut is closely related to inflation. In China, prices for basic products, such as farm produces and minerals, have long been on the low side. Although the state has readjusted prices on several occasions, prices for major basic products remain under control of the state's plan, while prices for many less significant products which have long been on the high side have been subject to slack control, and some cases have been decontrolled completely. The process of reform also leads to substantial increases in the price level of already high-priced products, while the level for low-priced products rises slowly, and in some cases remains at standstill. These factors have in fact negated the role of price readjustments, relegating the price relationship to the previous status, albeit at a higher level than before. The distorted price relationship has made readjustment of industrial complex even more difficult and has diminished the reserve strength of economic growth. Again, the fallacy that the economic depression prevalent between 1989 and 1991 had nothing to do with inflation is quite obvious.

Thirdly, inflation has led to insufficient compensation for enterprise assets. Due to China's low depreciation rate, in addition to the fact that the country has no so-called inflation accounting system, most enterprises, state-owned enterprises in particular, have been relegated to a status centering on living off past gains. Enterprises have no reserve strength for further development, and it is difficult to maintain long-term economic growth.

When viewed in terms of the basic conditions in the country, China is not suited to the implementation of inflation-related policies. Generally speaking, China faces a shortage of natural resources. At present, the major contradiction centers on demand exceeding supply, meaning that supply fails to effectively satisfy the increasing demands of economic construction and the daily needs of the people. The supply of energy, transportation, raw materials and other basic products falls far short of demand. Therefore, it is not realistic for China to attempt to use inflation related policies to stimulate the economic growth. Therefore, the prevention of inflation should be one of the basic macro policies that the Chinese government should adopt during the 1990s.

In short, some economists contend that rapid price rises have led to the emergence of inflation. We should attempt to gain a unified recognition of the current situation, resolutely clarify the fallacy that "inflation is harmless," and stabilize prices at the earliest possible date. This in turn will create social stability, which in turn will create a relaxed environment for supporting and deepening reform.

(3) Another point of view: the current economic situation is basically normal, with inflation remaining in check. In the process of economic growth and reform price levels will most likely maintain sustained growth.

Some experts say that while the concept of so-called inflation is likely to apply abroad, it is more complicated and more difficult to be explained in China. It seems that the more inflation is explained, the more confusing its meaning is. Therefore, it would be better use the term "price growth levels," which, unlike inflation, is a concept with a well defined meaning.

Why do price levels most likely rise in the process of economic growth and reform? Because price hikes will result from "combined effect," one force being the mechanism of speed and investment. A rapid rate is bound to result in the growth of investments, while rising investments exert force on the money supply and the quality of growth. Increases in the level of total demand lead to an imbalance between supply and demand, which in turn leads to a rise in the level of prices. A point well worth noting is that promoting this mechanism is the responsibility of various policy-making departments at the central level and various other levels, even including grass roots units. Chinese people place their hopes on promoting reform which will effectively change people's behavior patterns. In this way, the rapid rate increases are bound to be accompanied by inflated investment and the related chain reaction will most likely be broken. Reform is not only a process in itself, but also an objective necessity at present, which will not be decided by the good intentions of the people. During the transition from a planned economy to a market economy, this mechanism will inevitably exist for a period of time at least in China.

Another force revolves around the fact that reform promotes price hikes. This question seems to have been set aside due to the contradictions arising when making accusations that rising prices can in fact be attributed in part to reform. However, judgments of this nature are based on such a consideration that incomplete salaries, costs and prices are bound to be gradually replaced by complete salaries, costs and prices in the transfer from the planned to the market economic system. For example, there is widespread agreement that the housing system must be reformed. Then at least a portion of the housing burden will be added to salaries or other sources of income. A good example rests with the fact that if an apartment in large cities is sold at the price of 200,000 yuan, monthly rental costs should stand at around 2,000 yuan. Despite the fact that the average income in such cities is higher than the national average, the 400 yuan monthly income on average covers a mere one-fifth of rental fees. It is thus quite obvious that the salary must be increased considerably if the housing system is actually transferred to the track of the market economy. Health care is widely recognized as a global problem, with conditions in China calling for system reform. Chinese citizens will be required to shoulder the burden for a greater portion of medical expenses. However, a portion of such expenses must be subsidized by adding to an individual's salary or monetary income. Educational charges for children should be subject to the same conditions. One professor has raised the question of retirement insurance, with retirement funds also mentioned by some contract workers. However, not a single government functionary or staff member working in the science, education, culture and public health sectors has mentioned such an approach. If individuals are burdened with the responsibility to secure their own retirement funds, such funds must be added to salaries or other forms of monetary income. Such factors will force salaries to rise by a wide margin. Rising salaries will in turn lead to rising costs, as well as rising prices. Although not a direct ration, such factors are always relative. China's existing accounting system gives no consideration to inflation, and as a result fails to provide a true reflection of a factory's true production costs. Hence, it is quite obvious the existing system requires reform. In fact, costs must be increased in line with price rises. At the same time, the cost related to environmental protection is on the rise. Therefore, close scrutiny of the prevailing situation and increasing pressure requires that newly emerging expenses must be factored into costs. Comprehensive forces related to salaries, production related costs and other less obvious factors will lead to rising costs. Increasing costs will in turn lead to rising prices. These are in indeed the factors resulting in the spin-off of reform being price hikes. Factors such as these are bound to exist regardless of the monetary supply or market demand. Reform will inevitably lead to price hikes and increased costs.

The joint action of investment and reform mechanisms will ensure that the price level continues to rise, albeit that the rate of increase will fluctuate. Hence, the question arises as to what price levels are acceptable to ensure that the economy continues to grow at a rapid rate, and conversely, which levels are objectionable? On the other hand, what is society's psychological capacity to adapt to rising prices. Should that limit be exceeded there will be no way to carry out reform and no way to continue economic construction. Such limitations certainly seem to exist in accordance with the actual conditions in China. One argument maintains that price rises are of no consequence as long as actual living standards rise. However, such conditions do not exist in today's China. Nonetheless, it remains quite difficult to derive concrete figures in this regard. For example, in line with prevailing conditions in China, Chinese citizens might be unable to tolerate continuing double-digit price rises. The current 10 percent or so rise in urban living expenses is quite likely a good example, and the 15-odd percent price level in 35 major cities is most likely pressing the tolerable limit. It is quite likely a crisis will emerge if the tolerable limit is exceeded.

Some experts have pointed out that the Chinese economy has

maintained a steady trend of rapid growth since the early 1980s. The average annual growth rate of the gross domestic product since that time has been 8.9 percent, hitting 11.5 percent between 1984 and 1988. Rapid economic development has resulted in a trend to increases in the prices. In particular, high inflation in 1988 brought about by rapid economic development was the direct cause forcing the country to carry out improvement and rectification. High economic increase rate often follows on the heels of high inflation. Both have expressed the features of conjugate change and have been confirmed by economic practices both at home and abroad. The rapid rise in investments last year led to rapid economic development. All sectors of society have since paid greater attention to inflations. Theoreticians and actual working departments have pointed to the need for guarding against rebounding inflation. Fighting inflation has always been a major component of government macro-supervision and control. However, the economy has in fact developed rapidly under the conditions of low level inflation. What then are current views concerning problems related to prices and inflation? How will the relationship between economic growth and inflation be coordinated?

The current economic situation is still basically normal, with the trend towards active development. Total supply and demand are basically in balance, and the macro-economic environment remains relatively relaxed. This represents our basic analysis of the price situation. The present stage features the existence of both factors aggravating inflationary pressure and other factors controlling and alleviating inflation. At present, the latter is temporarily occupying the leading position, thereby facilitating rapid increases in the economy under the conditions of low inflation. When compared to inflation promoted by demand, inflations promoted by costs have had a greater influence on price stability. Hence, it is necessary for us to pay greater attention to the latter. While the price growth rate remains stable, the potential pressure of inflation will continue to increase. Effort to accelerate the pace of transference to the market economy has been dominated by recessive inflation in terms of promoting prices. Difficulties related to controlling excessively rapid price hikes surfaced in 1993, with the growth rate of prices for staple goods being greater than that in 1992. The 14-year market-oriented reform has witnessed great changes in China's economic environment and growth mechanisms. Relatively speaking, the formation mechanisms of inflation and form of expression exhibit certain differences when compared with the past. We should pay great attention to the aforementioned aspects when analyzing the current situation and predicting future trends. At present, various sources are igniting inflation, including rapid economic development, excessive rises in investments in fixed assets, the increasing volume of new loans, the issuance of currency that has considerably exceeded the economic growth rate, and the rising costs of production. At the same time, however, various factors have provided an avenue for controlling rapid price hikes. Actual price changes are simply the result of conflicts between the aforementioned factors. Notwithstanding, the latter has at least temporarily won an advantage under current conditions. These factors include:

Total supply and demand remain basically in balance, a factor considered the most important source of low level price rises. China's long-term shortage of supply accompanied by increasing demand has created a lingering tense situation in terms of the social economy. The economy grew rapidly between 1984 and 1988, and thus the contradictions between supply and demand were even more distinct. In 1984 alone, total demand of society outstripped total supply by 11.4 percent. In addition, demand outdistanced supply by 7.3 percent annually for three years running in 1986, 1987 and 1988. The decisive functions of market factors and the relationship between supply and demand to prices have increased steadily. Even though the limitations of price controls gradually reduced demand, total demand nonetheless surpassed the supply of economic resources by a considerable margin. Factors such as these were bound to ignite price rises. The imbalance between supply and demand was an essential catalyst for the large-scale growth in prices during the 1980s. However, extensive three-year improvement and rectification efforts controlled the trend towards excessive inflated demand. On the other hand, the continuing development of production effectively increased supply, thereby facilitating a relaxation in contradictions between supply and demand. In 1989, supply exceeded demand by 0.3 percent, with demand exceeding supply by 3.5 percent in 1990 and 4 percent in 1991. All were within the basically normal range of a 5 percent rate differential.

Industry has scored record production in consecutive years, with agriculture following suit with bumper harvests. The bumper harvests of the latter, in particular, have for many years running provided Chinese citizens with a good supply to ensure their livelihood. This fact represents a striking contrast to the fact that agriculture was in the state of stagnation between 1985 and 1988. Thereafter, however, bumper harvests provided abundant resources of materials fulfilling consumer demand. Food prices in particular have remained stable. In recent years, food costs have accounted for more than 50 percent of living expenses of Chinese citizens. Hence, changes in food prices are the major factor affecting retail sales prices. If food prices remain stable, retail sales prices will not change. In terms of conditions in the 1980s, the ratio of the average annual growth rate between food prices and the general index of prices for staple social goods stood at 1:0.84. Food prices in 1990 rose by some 0.3 percent, with the figure rising to 3.3 percent in 1991, and 7.7 percent in 1992. However, the 1988 growth rate for food prices hit a whopping 23 percent due to the overheated economy. Stability depends on the price and supply of cereals. There is currently an ample supply of food, with gradual changes in prices of various products. In previous years, low level economic development led to large stocks of consumer goods. Such factors enhance the consumption psychology of consumers and reduce expectations related to inflation. Last year, for example, the small-scale panic purchasing in some areas quickly subsided, and as a result failed to arouse significant market fluctuations.

Changing features in the income and expenses of Chinese citizens restricted increasing demand. Firstly, the growth rate in individual income slowed, thereby weakening the payment ability. Following the improvement and rectification effort, abnormal factors promoting the rapid rise in individual income slowly disappeared, and applied forces weakened. Statistics show that the growth rate in individual income slowed considerably after 1989, and in some cases recorded negative growth. Growth in the income level of farmers had remained minimal since 1989, with the income differences between urban and rural areas continuing to expand. When compared with the period between 1984 and 1988, the average annual increase rate in the living expenses as a proportion of the total income of urban residents fell by 2 percentage points between 1989 and 1991. At the same time, the growth rate in the average net income of rural residents dropped by 6.5 percent. However, when considering invisible income beyond salaries, the rate of decline in the growth of residential income was likely greater than before. The growth of income restricted increasing consumer demand.

A trend towards the continually widening gap in the income levels for various segments of society and regions exists in terms of the distribution of income of residents in inland areas. At the same time, however, there is a trend towards small income differences between departments and businesses. Generally speaking, however, the trend of the continually widening income gap exists in society as a whole. Income distribution is steadily moving to a high income structure which restricts the consumption patterns of members in the low income structure.

The lack of increased consumer demand resulted in the absence of pull-driven economic strength. However production picked up rapidly, with quick growth of supply. The number of enterprises producing mainly consumer goods in light industrial sector increased by some 20.1 percent in 1992, with the total value of retail sales of social commodities rising by only 15.7 percent when allowing for prices hikes, an actual increase of 9.2 percent. Supplies of most commodities either exceeded or were in basic balance with demand. In 1991, the Ministry of Internal Trade completed an analysis of supply and demand for major goods handled by commercial departments. For example, in terms of 539 major industrial products, some 5 percent of commodities were in short supply, there was a basic balance between supply and demand for 57.9 percent of the total, and supply exceeded demand for 37.1 percent. Perfectly adequate supplies were on hand for textiles, knit fabric, daily-use articles, chemicals, household electric appliances and electronic products. In terms of 101 major agricultural and sideline products, respective percentages for the aforementioned classifications of supply and demand stood at 15.8 percent, 51.5 percent and 32.7 percent. The rapidly increasing consumption of Chinese citizens during the 1980s was a vital factor sparking inflation. Consumer debt accruing before 1978 has been retired since the beginning of the 1990s. The living standards of the people are rising with the majority of the population having access to ample food and adequate clothing, and great changes have taken place in terms of consumption patterns. Ownership of durable consumer goods by urbanites has reached a high level characterized by continuing steady increases. By the end of 1991, each 100 households in cities had owned 68.4 color TV sets, 43.9 black and white TV sets, 80.6 washing machines, 48.7 refrigerators and 143.5 electric fans. At that same time, rural residents had lesser access to durable consumer goods and, by the end of 1991, each 100 rural households had owned 6.4 color TV sets, 47.5 black and white TV sets, 11 washing machines, 1.6 refrigerators and 53.5 electric fans.

Various areas were unable to significantly increase demand for durable goods due to restricted consumption conditions such as shortages of power and running water, and low-level income. The demand for durable consumption goods is difficult on the rise. General speaking, when compared with the "four hot consumer goods of the 1980s," i.e. TV sets, tape-recorders, washing machines and refrigerators, there is a noticeable shortage of new hot items with the capacity to arouse nationwide consumer demand. Production of some popular commodities, including newly designed household electric appliances, can easily meet demand due to low prices. On the other hand, ordinary families can hardly afford the excessively high prices for goods such as cars and commodity housing. Secondly, improvements in living standards have led to great changes in the consumption structure of Chinese citizens. The proportion of in-kind consumption has declined, while that of services is on the rise. Growth in the latter has relaxed the pressure of demand for consumer goods, thereby helping rationalize the structure of consumer expenditures. On the other hand, however, the growth rate in service prices has been noticeably higher than that of consumer goods in recent years. Therefore, it is incorrect to use the current retail price index as an indicator of inflation due to the fact that low estimates often cause problems. For example, living costs rose by 3.4 percent in 1991, while prices for consumer goods jumped by 2.9 percent and services costs by 8.7 percent. However, the proportion of services to the total expenditures of citizens remains low, thereby limiting the reliability of the low level estimate. Thirdly, various reform measures adopted in recent years have required Chinese citizens to assume at least a portion of expenses previously shouldered by the state. The "stock" and "real estate" crazes raised the proportion of the long-term expenditures and investments of individual citizens, altered the distribution of purchasing power and helped control rapid increases in current consumption. Various other reform measures, which are scheduled for adopting in the near future, including reform of the housing, public health and social security systems, will most likely increase expenses by a wide margin, but will also spur increased savings which in turn will lower current consumption.

The large volume of loans and issuance of currency, in addition to various rational factors such as accelerated economic development, the expanded scale of economic activities and the natural devaluation of the currency, have led to the emergence of inflation. The current situation has also been under the influence of a number of other factors. Firstly, judging by the issuance of currency, reforming the economic system, especially the reform of prices and the rationalization of the unreasonable price system, must be carried out by appropriately raising prices for products and services with very low prices. However, if high prices on products and services remain basically unchanged, the money supply must be increased. Secondly, the number of new companies and enterprises continues to grow. For example, in the first quarter of last year alone, well over 150,000 industrial and commercial enterprises were opened nationwide, with a corresponding increase in the grade and level of funding. Thirdly, purchases of stocks and real estate, as well as various raised funds combined to reduce the recovery volume of investments and led to increased cash expenditures. In terms of new loans, most were earmarked for overstocked products, with such funds failing to actually enter the circulation cycle. For example, in terms of the operations of less than 40,000 state-owned industrial enterprises at the end of October 1992, costs for finished products jumped dramatically by some 21.3 billion yuan over the beginning of the year, with earnings from such products standing at 134.37 billion yuan. In addition, a great part of new loans eventually found its way to saving accounts. On the other hand, the sluggish turnover rate for circulating funds increased the demand for loans. The turnover time for the circulating funds of independent industrial enterprises with in-house accounting systems averages 120 days in 1991, some 11 days less than during the Seventh Five-Year Plan period, with a 61.7 billion yuan increase in circulating funds.

The increasing production costs of enterprises are now being offset by raising marketing prices for products, a change which has led to the emergence of cost-driven inflation. But the consumption demand is not brisk. The supply of most consumer goods exceeds demand, or there is a balance between the supply and demand. The chance of shifting the price of newly increased costs has been obstructed, therefore the cost-driven inflation is short of external conditions for realization temporarily. Enterprises cannot obtain excess profits any longer as they did so before the improvement and rectification through unjustifiable price increase. A number of enterprises have difficulties even in making up costs. Some are settled in the internal enterprises and the other have to reduce profits and increase losses.

Modern economics features numerous theories on inflation. The famous Money Supply Theory promotes the concept that the level of ordinary prices is determined by the money supply which, according to the theory, has no influence on fluctuations in a substantive economy. Increases in the money supply under a market economy can result in rises in all costs, including salaries. However, inflation of this type has no effect on the activities of substantive economy. With one stroke of the pen, all prices will increase by 11 times if the government suddenly devalues the yuan by a ratio of 10:1. Nonetheless, such a move would have no effect on the activities of the substantive economy. Keynes and some similar schools of thought disagree with the aforementioned viewpoint, saying that increases in the money supply are likely to change the level of activity of a substantive economy. The macro-economics of New Classicism which emerged in the 1970s combined two viewpoints. According to the theory, if individual suppliers fail to anticipate a sudden increase in the money supply, suppliers mistakenly consider increased growth in sales. Therefore, the expansion of production stimulates activities related to the substantive economy. On the other hand, however, in cases when individual suppliers anticipate a certain inflation rate, and simultaneously understand that the increased sales can be less than beneficial due to rising costs, the activities of the substantive economy will not be influenced. The latter theory is known as the Lucas Rational Forecast Model.

In line with this theory, inflation has no influence or plays stimulatory role, and in fact is not a bad influence. In fact we have nothing to worry about if China's current inflation is simply a phenomenon resulting from increases in the money supply. Even though Hong Kong has recorded double-digit inflation in recent years, salary levels have increased more rapidly than prices, with the people in the area enjoying a rapidly rise of living standard resulting from actual salary increases. So long as investments earn desirable returns and productive forces increase, inflation is not necessarily a terrible thing under a perfect market economy.

Various other viewpoints center on that even though inflation is a fact of life, we cannot reach the conclusion that all inflation harms economic development. In the 1970s, both global economic deceleration and waves of inflation have simultaneously emerged. Should rapid economic development in the 1950s and 1960s be attributed solely to the control of inflation at that time?

Rapid economic development can in fact be explained by various other factors such as the rising tide of reconstruction and worldwide trade liberalization.

A number of countries with high inflation rates experienced lower or more rapid economic growth than those with low inflation rates. The conclusion is not as yet clear. The inflation rate in 20 developed industry countries in the West between 1955 and 1973 was under control. The growth rate of gross domestic product and inflation rate seemed to reach a point of equilibrium during the period. The per capita growth rate of the gross domestic product was greatest in countries with the highest inflation rate. The interactive function of the two is represented by Japan, a country with both the highest average inflation rate which hits 5.8 percent, and the highest growth rate in gross domestic product, a figure standing at 8.6 percent. With the exception of Japan, few links exist between the inflation rate and the growth rate of gross domestic product.

(4) The source of inflation is cost-driven and demand-pull.

Some experts have pointed out that even though the formation mechanisms of inflation in China are intricate and complex, the main reasons rest with cost-driven and demand-pull factors. An analysis of the mutual functions of the aforementioned factors constitute the basic analytical frame and policy-making concept.

Cost-driven factors serve as a practical catalyst for inflation. The main function of price changes comes from the main process of economic activities and non-economic links. A necessary aspect, however, is to reduce the degree of distortion of the price system and perfect economic relationships. A general survey revealed that increases in the fixed costs related to the production and operation of enterprises promote even more rises in production costs. In the end, pressures such as these will be shifted to prices.

Cost-driven factors are mainly manifested in the form of large-scale increases in costs for labor and materials, and lead to a steady decline in the input-output rate. Primary reform includes

a series of policies for increasing the purchase price of agricultural and sideline products, reducing the price of industrial goods,
increasing the income of urban and rural residents and expanding
the rights of enterprises to conduct their own affairs. As a result,
the process has led to a wide gap in terms of promoting increased
costs, i.e. a large-scale increase of the materials consumption rate.
In terms of a comprehensive survey, the rate of consumption for
China's five materials production departments has risen sharply
since the implementation of reform. For example, the figure was
56 percent in 1978, rising to 63.2 percent in 1991, still further to
64 percent in 1992, and even further to 65 percent in 1993. At the
same time, changes appeared in the pattern of distribution of
national income. As a result, the proportion of individual income
to national income rose considerably. The proportion of state
income in the gross domestic product declined from 31.6 percent
in 1978 to 14.2 percent in 1992. However, the proportion of
individual income to the gross national product (GNP) rose from
49.3 percent to 61.1 percent. When calculated in terms of current
prices, the 1992 GNP increased by 6.7-fold over the figure for
1978, while the disposable income of Chinese residents increased
by 8.1-fold. Changes in the pattern of income distribution included factors such as the repayment of personal income and consumer costs accruing to citizens. At the same time, the course of
reform has lacked effective mechanisms for balancing distribution. As a result, the distribution of income is the major concern
of individuals. Rapid increases in individual income led to an
annual declines in the total input-output level of society. The rate
of finished products available to society and the output of labor
services was calculated according to total costs for materials,
wages and government services. The figure was 60.5 percent in
1978, dropped to 48.5 percent in 1991, and stood at 48 percent in
1992. Due to the improvement of the organic structure of capital,
technological progress, and the low levels of management and
operations of enterprises the figure will continue to drop in 1993.

Direct harm resulting from cost-driven factors led to a large-
scale decline in returns on funds used, with a corresponding drop
in macro benefits. The rising costs of production and operations

were accompanied by a drop of returns for funds used. In the case of state-owned enterprises, profit and tax payments per 100 yuan stood at 18.3 yuan in 1978, a figure which dropped to 14 yuan in 1984. While the figure rose slightly to 15.1 yuan in 1988, the trend thereafter was for sharp decline with a fall of 8.4 yuan in 1990. The main economic target of industrial enterprises with independent accounting faced a similar situation, with profit and tax payments standing at 25.2 percent in 1980, a drop of 12 percent on 1992. The losses of loss-making enterprises increased from 3.881 billion yuan to 47 billion yuan, a 12.1-fold rise, or an average annual increase of 23.1 percent. The poor benefits accruing from the macroeconomy are indeed worrisome.

A direct cause of rising costs rested with large-scale increases in wages and the cost of products used by enterprises. Sharp rises in the cost of raw materials, fuel and energy also promoted increased costs for the products of enterprises. China's price system was distorted prior to the Third Plenary Session of the 11th Central Committee of the Communist Party of China. Costs related to the productions of mining and raw materials industries were on the low side, while costs for the industrial processing sector were quite high. Various unique factors and phenomena existed between prices for industrial products, a fact resulting from irrational price parity. Prices for many products failed to reflect both the value and relationship between supply and demand. As part of an effort to solve these problems, China has regulated prices for industrial and agricultural products. The effort includes the following aspects: 1) gradually increasing the purchase price for agricultural and sideline products, and reforming the related management system; 2) increasing prices for energy and a number of raw materials, and gradually relaxing price controls on the means of production; 3) gradually adjusting prices for transportation, communications, and posts and telecommunications; 4) regulating and decontrolling prices on some consumer goods; and 5) improving measures related to domestic pricing for imported goods and adopting the agency system for foreign trade. Along with implementation of the aforementioned policies and measures, producing enterprises and distributors earned profits from increased factory prices. On the other hand, however, the rise of purchase prices of investment products led to the increase of enterprises' expenditures. During the period of economic overheating experienced in 1988, the purchase prices for raw materials, fuel and energy rose by 20.2 percent on the previous year. For example, the purchase price of nonferrous metals rose by 30.7 percent, chemicals by 33.4 percent, and timber and paper pulp by 43.1 percent. Overall purchase prices rose by 26.4 percent in 1989, with the price of fuel and energy, ferrous and nonferrous metals, chemicals, building materials, non-metal products, agricultural and sideline products, and raw materials for textile rising by more than 20 percent. While the economy grew rapidly in 1992, costs accruing to enterprises jumped by 11 percent. For example, the purchase price of fuel rose by 16.4 percent, building materials by 18.8 percent, ferrous metals by 14.5 percent and rolled steel by 15.9 percent. In the end, rising purchase prices led to increased factory prices. Between 1985 and 1992, factory prices for all industries shot up dramatically by 96 percent, means of production by 107.8 percent, and consumer materials by 76.1 percent.

As mechanization level of agriculture improved, the volume of use of fertilizers and pesticide increased. The service systems of society in the countryside are unperfected, the distribution among specialized departments is undeveloped and the scale of production is small. All this is difficult for the mechanization of agriculture to give full play to the scale effect. As a result, it led to continuous rise of the cost of farm products. In order to guarantee the rise of farmers' net income, the country has to increase purchasing prices of agricultural products. At present, prices of a number of farm products of China have approached those of the international market. The consumption rate of materials of total agricultural output value increased from 30.2 percent in 1984 to 35.4 percent in 1991. The cost of net income of agriculture for every 100 yuan rose from 53.1 percent in 1982 to 134.2 percent in 1991. More than 50 percent of the income of China's residents' living expenses are used in foods, thus the rise of prices of agricultural products and foods brought in unfavorable influence in maintaining the stability of general level of market prices.

The essential factor of high cost is unreasonable structures of the supply. As a result, a great deal of production forces were idle and a large stock of products increased. In addition, there were both small and decentralized trends in investment. With divisions of interests, different regions and departments made blind and repeated constructions. The structure of increased amount of investment is unreasonable and the readjustment of the structure of storage amount is also difficult. The statistics indicate that the utilization rate of production forces of 45 varieties of industrial products is as follows: Products of more than 80 percent of utilization rate include raw coal, crude oil, steel, pig iron, ethylene, hydrochloric acid, synthetic rubber, fine carbinol, colorants, electric fans and beer. This figure accounted for 24 percent of main products, centering on metallurgical, chemical and foods industries. Those of 50-80 percent of utilization rate include sulphuric acid, concentrated sulphuric acid, caustic soda, chemical fertilizers for agriculture, nitrogenous fertilizers, phosphate fertilizers, agricultural chemicals, formaldehyde, paint, plastic, rubber products, finished steel products, fabrics, cement, plate grass, interior and outer covers of a tyre, automobiles and large and medium-sized tractors, films, radio cassette players, mechanical wristwatches, sewing machines, bicycles and white and black TV sets. The figure accounted for 62 percent of main products, centering on chemical, building materials and machinery and electric products undertakings. Those of less than 50 percent of utilization rate include household refrigerators, air-conditioners, washing machines for agriculture, dust catchers and color TV sets. This figure accounted for 14 percent of main products, centering on newly established businesses for daily-use household electric appliances. For example, the rate of utilization of household refrigerators and dust catchers accounted for 36.7 percent and 16.5 percent, a certain drop over the previous year. A small-scale production and low rate of utilization of production forces enabled the scale effect of modern production to be hardly realized. High fixed cost of products of unit will promote the rise of the cost of products in the end. The regulation of the structure of enterprises' products has not synchronized with the change of market demand over these years. Impeded marketing resulted in a large overstocking and the rise of circulating cost. The increase of circulating funds involved various factors such as low circulating rate of funds and influence of poor management and administration of enterprises. Forecast indicates that variable cost of the increase of enterprises' unreasonable and excess stocks comes to 50-80 billion yuan every year.

The pulling of the demand formed a stimulation of dominant inflation. Rapid increase of the demand and expanded gap between the supply and demand mainly came from the interim pulling function of investment, consumption and import and export.

The first factor from the expansion of the demand is the pulling of the expansion of investment. Since 1992 the trend of rapid increase has emerged in the investment of China's fixed assets. The volume of investment that year came to 758.2 billion yuan, an increase of 37.6 percent over the previous year. The rise of investment not only promoted rapid increase of economy but also enhanced the rise of market prices, increasing the pressure of inflation. Between 1984 and 1985, the investment in fixed assets in the whole society increased by 28.2 percent and 38.8 percent respectively. The Gross National Product (GNP) increased by 19.8 percent and 22.9 percent in the same period, with the index curtailment of the national economy rising by 10.9 percent. Obviously interrelated relations existed between the price index of investment products and investment of fixed assets, having a certain time-lag influence. Between 1985 and 1986, the price index of investment products rose at an average rate of 9.7 percent. Between 1988 and 1989, the price index of investment products hit 13 percent or so. The rise of the price index of investment products often undergoes 6-10 month time-lag, and then will be represented by the price of consumer goods. However, the first to be affected is the rise of the price index of residents' living expenses, including fees of housing, medical treatment, transportation and infrastructure facilities, as well as various services.

The second factor from the expansion of the demand is the influence of expansion of consumer demand. An obvious feature, which follows the price rise in China's consumer goods, is sharp changes between the consumption, supply and demand, the price rapidly rising. Before China implemented the reform policy, the country carried out a purchasing and marketing policy of products related to low salary, low price of goods, high subsidiary, and issuing coupons when goods were insufficient. Between 1953 and 1978, retail sales price of goods rose at an average rate of 0.7 percent annually, and actual level of residents' consumer goods went up at an average rate of 2.2 percent yearly. Between 1979 and 1991, the level of residents' consumer goods actually increased at an average annual rate of 6.5 percent. At the same time, the growth rate of retail sales prices hit 6 percent, with price index of workers' and staff's living expenses hitting 6.7 percent. Following the expansion of consumption demand, the price of goods rose month by month. In terms of the expansion of market price in 1992, the volume of retail sales of goods in the whole society reached 1,089.4 billion yuan, a rise of 15.7 percent over the previous year. The wage volume of workers and staff in the year amounted to 289 billion yuan, an increase of 17 percent. The income of living expenses of rural residents was 1,826 yuan, up 18.2 percent. Net income of rural residents per capita was 784 yuan, a rise of 10.6 percent. The price of retail goods went up by 5.4 percent in the year over the previous year. The price index of residents' living expenses rose by 6.4 percent, with an increase of 8.6 percent in cities (the figure hitting 10.9 percent in 35 large and medium-sized cities) and up 4.7 percent in rural areas. In 1993, the price of retail goods will rise by about 7 percent, and the price index of residents' living expenses, by 8 percent, with a rise of 9.5 percent in cities (the figure standing at 13 percent in 35 large and medium-sized ones).

The third sector from demand expansion is the transmission function of the international trade. The economy of a country can be divided into a number of partial and regional markets in light of different areas. The imbalance between the supply and demand can cause a rise or fall of the price of goods related areas. The transmission among regions is conducted through the channels of domestic trade. The international trade has many common grounds with domestic trade, but doesn't have so as well. For example, the limits of Customs duty and imports and exports exist in the international trade. Such limits cannot enable the economy of a country to become enclosed economy. Thus the transmission produced through the channels of trade still exist in the international economy.

The transmission moved to non-opening departments from opening ones, affecting the alternation between domestic industries and employments. Therefore, the change of domestic supply and demand is bound to be affected by the change of the world's market price. Since 1978, the proportion of the total volume of China's imports and exports analogous to the gross national product has risen year by year, with external debt balance being larger and larger, and the proportion analogous to the total volume of exports being higher and higher. In addition, the transmission produced through the regulation of exchange rate also affected the alternation of domestic prices. Taking the formal devaluation of exchange rate of free and official markets to the influence of prices of goods as an example. It is known to all, the exchange rate is one of the most important prices of the economy in a country, which links up international and domestic price system and decides relative prices between trade goods and labor, and between non-trade goods and labor. Between 1980 and 1990, official rate of exchange of Renminbi devaluated 223 percent, a drop of 10.6 percent in 1991 and 7 percent in 1992, being bound to bring a certain pound to domestic prices.

Although the expansion of the demand manifested themselves in investment, consumption and foreign departments, it centered on marking the increase of money supply by a big margin.

It is known to all, in China's economic life, the amount of the supply of money plays an important role in deciding the level of prices, total demand of the society and output. From the investigation of historical angle, the period when loans and money are issued is also the period when China's price of goods rises. With the time-lag influence of social demand when loans and money are issued, the expansion of the demand would certainly lead to the aggravation of the increase of prices of goods. For example, the trend of the overheating of economy emerged in the second half of 1984. Net money issued by banks amounted to 30.1 billion yuan. The circulating volume of money at the end of that year increased by 49.5 percent as compared with the figure over the beginning. At that time, the total demand of the society rose by 31.8 percent. The price index of workers' and staff's living expenses rose by 11.9 percent, with the total index of prices of retail goods up 8.8 percent, these figures greatly surpassing the previous growth rates of 2.7 percent and 2.8 percent. It was forced to implement policies which reduced finance and credit. In addition, the amount of the supply of money sharply increased to 68 billion yuan in 1988, with the growth rate of 46.7 percent, directly leading to a serious inflation. That year, the total index of prices of retail goods rose by 18.5 percent, with the total price index of workers' and staff's living costs increased by 20.7 percent. It was made to conduct improvement and rectification. In 1992, additional 100 billion yuan was supplied. Initial survey indicated that the issued money surpassed the development of economy between 1979 and 1992. Although part of money was obtained through the rise of prices of goods, the current circulating volume of cash still exceeds 75 billion yuan. Though the total index of prices of retail goods of the society was controlled at the planned growth rate of 6 percent in 1992, the price index of residents' living costs in cities including 35 large and medium-sized ones rose month by month. As compared with the same month of the previous year, the price index of residents' living expenses in 35 large and medium-sized cities rose from 8.2 percent in June to 13.4 percent in October. In addition, the price index of service projects increased from 16.4 percent to 27.6 percent, averaging the growth rate of 3 percentage points every month. In terms of the whole year, the price index of living costs and service projects rose by 10.9 percent and 21.3 percent respectively.

4. Measures Should Be Adopted to Solve Existing Economic Problems

Experts contend that present economic conditions are quite different from the previously overheated economic development. Therefore, they say China should refrain from adopting readjusted means of retrenchment, but should instead proceed on the basis of deepening economic structural reform to regulate the operations of the market economy, while at the same time giving due consideration to the relationship between development and reform. In addition, the government should pledge to develop the economy in a healthy manner, while simultaneously cooling overheated economic development.

(1) Different opinions on control.

Some people say China should adopt methods used in 1988 to quickly put the brakes on the present overheated economic development and prevent inflation from surpassing that in 1988. Other people, however, say that present economic problems are emerging as a result of development, particularly problems related to the transition from the old to new systems. Many say experiences gained from the readjustment of the original planned economy are far from suited to present demands, and new experiences are lacking. As a result, such problems cannot be explained in terms of either Western or original planned economics. For example, some professors have advanced the idea that present increases in materials are simply an aspect of the monetary phenomenon, and that prices should be raised under conditions of sufficient capital. However, in line with actual conditions of China, prices rise during periods of tight money. How can this be explained? Those holding the latter opinion insist that the introduction of immediate braking procedures are unfeasible, but instead advocate appropriate control measures. They point to the fact that the implementation of 1988 measures not only sparked a significant drop in the development speed, but led to a major reduction in economic efficiency. The resulting effects were a dear lesson indeed. Maintaining economic stability makes it worthwhile to slow the development rate by adopting control measures, but economic results should at the same time be raised. However, the results of the measures introduced in 1988 sacrificed both speed and efficiency, aspects warranting deep thought. Should China reintroduce such an approach, both speed and efficiency will once again be sacrificed, and the effort would fail to overcome economic difficulties. Quite to the contrary, the situation concerning national finance will become increasingly grave and the number of loss-making state-owned enterprises will increase. Prior to 1988, the number of loss-making state-owned enterprises accounted for less than 20 percent of the total, a number which expanded dramatically to over two-thirds of the total. In fact, analyses carried out under the new accounting system revealed that such enterprises actually accounted for about 80 percent of the total. The fact is the result of major reduction in efficiency resulting from the implementation of economic improvement and rectification carried out in recent years. Such dire costs are unwarranted. Yet another concept circulating through domestic economic circles over the past few years says that reduced efficiency is the price that must be paid for economic improvement, and that rectification inevitably involves costs. In our opinion, this is an absurd formulation. While the rate may be down, how can economic efficiency be down? In fact, if efficiency dropped, it would be extremely difficult to expand the economy. The heated debate on this issue continues. In terms of current conditions, the majority of people advocate urgent controls, while a minority favor freeing the system. In 1988, the number of people advocating freeing the system was even lower than at present. Practice proves that rectification should not be hurried or strict, and that the adoption of appropriate soft measures may be correct even though a low cost must eventually be paid.

Experts contend the government must play a part in correcting market dislocation. The money supply must be controlled by monetary policies. The best method is to ensure the growth rate in the money supply does not exceed three time of the economic growth rate in the same year. At the same time, the tax rate should be properly readjusted.

Current inflation on the mainland of China features rising land-use costs, with such costs being forced upwards by speculators. This same phenomenon occurred in Taiwan, Hong Kong and Japan. This problem is solvable provided that policies and regulations are implemented correctly. Another factor leading to inflation has been the sharp increase in construction, with cities throughout the nation buzzing with construction projects. Limited capital has created difficulty in terms of both investment in the manufacturing industry and in real estate.

Older and younger scholars hold differing views on how best to control inflation. For example, scholars under 50 years of age, who have been influenced by the Western theory, are in fact strong in terms of theory, but find it difficult to avoid idealized opinions. On the other hand, scholars over 50 base their views on study and long-term experiences. Some basic principles of Western theory, such as opportunity costs and paying commissions on profit, are of course valuable references. However, the actual benefits accruing to developing countries from the studies of the concepts of Western scholars are few. The method for solving problems in developing countries should rely on young scholars striving to develop innovative theories.

(2) Allowing government functions to play a role in preventing and controlling inflation, and using systematic operational means to check galloping inflation.

Chinese experts point out that changes have taken place in China's current economic operation, and that their influence on economic development should be fully considered.

Experts suggest that China should make further efforts to check inflation. Inflation emerges when the growth rates of commodities and labor services exceed the growth rate of total output. The emergence of this situation tends to lead to a decline in purchasing power. The method for measuring excessive demand involves estimating the balance between total social supply and demand. Cost-push weakens the ability to increase total social supply, while the expansion of total social demand is directly associated to the emergence of galloping inflation. In terms of long-run equilibrium, inflation can be anticipated when supply reaches its potential level, with economic policies remaining unchanged, and inflation and total social demand continuing to rise at a fixed rate. Under such circumstances, the rate of inflation is equal to the sum of cost-push and growth rate of nominal demand. The rate of increase for commodities and labor services equal the sum of the growth rate of costs and demand. Long-run equilibrium is difficult to achieve, but supply increases continuously on an unfixed potential level. Therefore, actual demand increases with growth of income, as does actual supply.

Inflation to a great extent sparks panic and uneasiness in society. On the other hand, however, it may help improve price distortions and imbalances in the allocation of resources, while at the same time raising competitive efficiency. These aspects require correct understanding, particularly in countries in transition from a planned to a market economy, and attempting to readjust the functions and goals of key policies, such as demand policy. Since the introduction of reform, management over demand has required indirect levers for regulating the activities of economic entities, with enterprises having been granted expanded decision-making power. Hence, demand policy has become a key means and the functions of macroeconomic management have gained increasing importance.

One approach involves striving to reduce the costs of production. China is currently confronted with the rising pressure of inflation. Increased costs are the basic characteristic of existing production carried out by society. Improvement in modern technologies and price rises for the raw and auxiliary materials used by enterprises has given rise to factory prices, and eventually influenced retail prices. The rise of tertiary industry has been the major reason leading to increasing prices for services, as well as for structural changes taking place in prices and basic policy for developing the tertiary sector itself. In addition, the rise of the sector has led to the emergence of competitive prices which have led to differences in the psychological outlook and actions of the people, created a long-term wide imbalance between supply and demand, and sparked the speculative psychology related to prices and the erosion of wages over profits. For example, the 1992 price index for living costs in 35 large and medium-sized cities rose by 13.3 percent, while the growth rate in prices for service items jumped by 32.9 percent.

Another aspect involves accelerating the steps involving price reform. The highly centralized and unified system of price management prior to reform relegated the Chinese economy to an inert position. The period featured a low rate of growth, rapid economic development and fairly large increases in income, all of which were determined by the low level of horizontal natural expansion characteristic of the 1950s. That particular period was characterized by a small-scale peasant economy and self-efficiency, and was a period when people were barely able to reach the subsistence level. However, in later years, standing on the side and viewing the environment of rapid development in neighboring countries failed to satisfy psychological outlook of the Chinese people, actions seemed inappropriate, and economic strength was far from in tune with the nation's image. The situation called for the injection of new vigor into economic development. The reasons behind the stagnation of resource allocations, employment and product circulation under the system of low prices were rooted in long-term price distortions. Although in some cases price controls maintain a transient balance in economic development, support social stability and spur low level production cycles, the government must also continuously liberate social economic operations by providing large price subsidies. Such actions are merely compulsory measures. They may push overt inflation to the track of cover inflation and satisfy the needs of national economic development. As a result, trial price reform, such as reform carried out in 1989, was confronted with pressure resulting from overt inflation and was fraught with failure from the very beginning.

Appropriate measures must be taken to control social demand. Low level inflation may in fact invigorate the economy, due to the fact that inflation is an inexorable reflection of economic and price distortions. However, galloping inflation offers no advantages to the economy, but the advantages of low-level price rises far outweigh disadvantages. In the final analysis, prices represent actual demand and lead to a balance between supply and demand. The history of social economics has witnessed certain periods of complete balance in economic activities, but most often people have experienced greater levels and longer term economic imbalances. Balance is determined by the general economic structure, favorable industrial structure and the balance between product purchases and marketing. In light of current conditions in China, an inflation rate ranging between 3 and 5 percent should add vigor to long-term, sustained and stable economic development. An inflation rate somewhat less than 10 percent might be acceptable under certain circumstances and appropriate economic conditions. Therefore, during the stage of rapid economic development, the practice of controlling price is far from the only starting point for economic activities. Excessive incentives and expansionary monetary policies will not be adopted under any circumstances since doing so might lead to subsidiary inflation. Efforts in 1990s should center on avoiding galloping inflation resulting from faulty policies and stable monetary policy. Therefore China should further emphasize policies on finance and monetary and more effectively adopt financial regulation.

Government functions should play a major role in preventing and controlling inflation. Galloping inflation may disrupt society and greatly harm the government image. Carrying out government functions and exercising administrative power are not the only way to halt runaway inflation, but are also a method for forecasting the form and occurrence of inflation. Such efforts depend on a set of operational norms to control and guide runaway inflation, with efforts drawing support from financial, credit and monetary guidance mechanisms, and in some cases policy interference.

The bearing capacity to withstand the effects of inflation should be strengthened. The incapacity to control inflation has led to people displaying differing psychological approaches and actions. People are most often frantic when confronted with medium-level and runaway inflation. While low to medium-level inflation may create certain losses in a large country such as China, it may nonetheless be advantageous to reducing economic distortions, rationalizing the relationship between the economy and prices, and avoiding the collapse of the economy. As a result of 14-odd years of reform, the government, enterprises and residents have all achieved gains resulting from radical economic changes, while light industry has developed rapidly and the social economy has been stable. Countless facts proved that a growth rate in prices of below 10 percent is well within the bearing capacity of the government, enterprises and citizens alike.

Experts contend that controlling the present overheated economy with macroeconomic control calls for accelerating structure reform of the economy, especially combining control measures with reform. The main goal is to avoid divorcing reform from development.

Various experts suggested drafting an interim anti-inflation policy based on the general goal of accomplishing the process gradually in order to ensure a soft landing. The implementation period from July 1993 to the end of 1994 focused on avoiding major fluctuations in economic adjustments.

Other steps included accelerating construction of a new socialist market economic system, reform of the monetary system in particular. It was determined that the Central Bank should advance first in reform, with stress on reorganizing the bank administration and strengthening its decision-making power, establishing money supply regulation mechanisms, extricating from the responsibility for credit business with nonfinancial organizations, accelerating the transfer special banks from state-own management into business administrations, rapidly separating policy-related banking from commercial banking, exercising a management system for assets and liabilities, and introducing standard management for non-banking organizations and strengthening examination and supervision of their registration and operations at the earliest possible date.

In addition, a controlled interest rate market must be adopted to strengthen the flexibility of bank rate mechanisms and the regulatory role of the supply and demand for currency. In terms of economic operations, the Central Bank should offer timely decision-making suggestions concerning rate adjustments, while various banks and financial organizations should adopt stipulations to determine floating rates based on the limits of reference rates published by the Central Bank. Moreover, the government should formulate a law prohibiting usury and adopt strict measures to ban organizations engaged in such activities.

Another aspect involves strictly managing money collection from the society and forbidding illegal call loans between monetary organizations. Initially, this should be carried out to eliminate the call rights of people's banks at the county and city level, as well as their rights to engage in the comprehensive settlement of interbank loans. A time limit should be instituted for the recall of illegal loans, and efforts should be made to license the management of trust and investment corporations and forbid banks from setting up such firms, while standard management should be introduced for joint ventures and rural foundations.

Efforts must also include strengthening the license administration of new projects and development areas, and real estate agencies and related business activities. The investment scale of fixed assets should be placed under control, and stress should be placed on control of the investment scale and readjusting the investment structure. Guarantees must be in place to ensure that collected capital meets the needs of agriculture, productive enterprises and key projects.

Tax collection and management must be strengthened. This initially involves strengthening tax collection in accordance with the law, strictly controlling the scale and amount of tax reduction, drafting a unified plan for the scale and amount of tax reduction and exemption, and strictly banning tax reduction and exemption exceeding the planned target. On the existing tax collection base, efforts should center on expanding the tax base and collection scale, opening new sources of tax collection and increasing tax revenue. While integrating reform with legislation, steps should also be accelerated in terms of real estate management, the administration and examination of drawback for export duties paid, and due attention should be paid to the supervision and examination of tax evasion practices by some foreign-funded enterprises.

The on-going process involves strengthening macro control and management on foreign exchange. Over the long-term, China will always face a shortage of foreign exchange. Therefore, the government must not take a laissez-faire attitude, but instead must strengthen macro control and management. The existing system of retaining foreign exchange should be reformed at the earliest possible date. A system for the certification of allocated exchange should be practiced during the transition period. Secondly, an exchange stabilization fund should be established as quickly as possible. The government should allocate a certain sum of foreign exchange and Renminbi, and in turn assign the related functional departments of the Central Bank to use the funds to control the exchange market. Thirdly, foreign exchange markets throughout the nation must conform to the new standards. A few foreign exchange centers should be established in large cities with large-scale circulation, and small foreign exchange markets linked with central markets in major cities may be established in some specified central cities. Other cities should not establish foreign exchange regulation markets.

The administration and organization of imports and exports must be strengthened. In 1993, we must strive to increase the growth rate of exports by 15 percent at least and expand channels for foreign trade. Efforts should focus on the guidance and management of imports and the creation of foreign exchange in order to maintain the balance between international income and consumption. Greater attention must immediately be paid to overseas investment in order to avoid an excessive outflow of foreign exchange.

Great attention must be paid to controlling the expansion of consumption funds. Measures are urgently needed to ensure the management of social institutional purchases in order to limit excessively rapid growth in such purchases. We must conscientiously carry out the effort to separate enterprises from administrative institution in order to prevent individuals from using their power for personal gain. In addition, we must alter the excessively tough methods for controlling investments in fixed assets, and soften methods for controlling inflationary factors affecting the consumption fund.

We must also simplify the administrative structure, lower staff levels and reduce the financial burden. Based on the principle of efficiency, government departments must reduce staff. Redundant staff should be retrained and assigned to departments as taxation, finance and social intermediary organizations which have an urgent need for staff. Remaining staff members will enjoy more benefits in line with the social services system.

Chapter VI
Develop the Market Economy
While Opening to the Outside World

1. The Position and Role in Development of China's Market Economy

(1) China's reform and open policies have gained universally acknowledged achievements. Practice has proved that localities fully open to the outside world have marched rapidly ahead in development of the market economy.

Various foreign economists have pointed out three basic characteristics involving China's reform and opening: a) Reform and opening have not depended on the support of foreign experts. b) The process has proceeded in accordance with the sixteen-character principle which calls for the prescribed order, gaining increased might from small beginnings, continuing readjustments, standing firm and engaging in the continuous struggle. c) China has paid a low price to maintain a high economic growth rate. In general, both Chinese and foreign economists hold that China has gained tremendous achievements in reform and opening. They say opening has given added impetus to reform of the structure of China's economic system and development of the market economy. Localities fully open to the outside world have kept pace with the rapid development of the market economy, a point documented by countless facts with regard to coastal special economic development zones.

In the wake of the Third Plenary Session of the 11th CPC Central Committee in 1978, China introduced experimental economic reform in rural areas. The new system, known as the household contract responsibility system was linked directly to remuneration based on output. The system was later expanded to urban industry and the entire social economy. Extensive efforts over the past 10-odd years have produced extraordinary economic development. Recent statistics revealed that the GNP between 1979-1991 increased at an average annual rate of 8.7 percent and the average annual increase in national income stood at 8.4 percent, with both figures being higher than those recorded in Europe, the United States and Japan during their most rapid periods of development and a great higher than those Asia's so-called "four small dragons" recorded during a period of rapid development lasting for over 10 years. A good example is coastal provinces such as Shandong, Jiangsu, Zhejiang, Fujian and Guangdong, where the economic growth rate was from one to two percentage points higher than that the "four small dragons" registered during their most rapid periods of development.

The 10-year reform effort was characterized by different sectors making vastly different contributions. Between 1979-1990, the gross industrial output value registered an average annual increase of 12 percent at constant price, with the figure for state-owned enterprises standing at 7.6 percent rise and that of collectives at 17.8 percent. The period also witnessed the rise of township enterprises as a new force achieving progress which became the focus of worldwide attention. For example, their total output value rose from 38.53 billion yuan in 1978 to 869.89 billion yuan in 1991, a rise from 9.1 percent to 30.8 percent of the country's total industrial output value for the respective years. Since 1978, some 34.7 percent of the increased industrial output value was created by township enterprises. The factors clearly indicate that the national economy could not have an average annual growth of 8.7 percent without the rapid development of non-state enterprises, particularly township enterprises.

Over the past 14-odd years of reform and opening, China has gained universally acknowledgement for its achievements in modernization and construction. The achievements were a direct result of social and political stability, rapid economic development, a flourishing market and continuing rises in comprehensive national strength.

(2) Market economic development in China demands foreign impetus to accelerate links with the international market, and the absence of same will result in slow development

1) Many people have long held that only countries with small domestic markets and inadequate resources need to develop an export-oriented economy, while it is quite unnecessary for countries like China with large domestic markets to do so.

The present trend for world economic development proves the view somewhat misguided. World economic development history indicates that a nation's economy may be developed quickly by stressing interdependence, cooperation and competition with foreign economies, while a complacent, conservative and closed nation is destined to have a backward economy. The only way a nation can experience rapid economic development is to rely on opening to the outside world, effectively use both domestic and overseas resources, open domestic and foreign markets, participating in economic, trade, and technological exchanges and cooperation with other countries and regions and positively participating in competition on both domestic and international markets. Therefore, in order to be classified as a major economic country, it must first be a major business power. For example, the United States is a vast country with a broad market and abundant resource. It is not only the major business power in the world, but also leads the world in terms of economic might. Another example comes from the fact that the annual turnover volume of seven highly developed Western countries accounts for some 50 percent of the worldwide total.

China's 14-odd years' experience in reform and opening to the outside world has proved that there are no contradictions between national economic development and the development of foreign trade, but instead that the two are mutually beneficial. The flourishing development of the export-oriented economy in coastal regions has led to rapid economic development. A prime example is Guangdong Province which has ranked first in the country in terms of its import and export volume and economic development speed.

Reform and opening carried out over the past 10-add years has closely integrated the Chinese and global economies.

At present, the export volume accounts for 20 percent of the gross national product (GNP). The degree of China's economic reliance of imports has jumped for only 6 percent prior to reform and opening to a level over 10 percent. The ratio of imports and exports to GNP stands at 33 percent, a figure considerably higher than in many developed countries. Another example rests with the fact that near one-half of Chinese textiles and 90 percent of silk are dependent on the international market.

Several millions of people in China's coastal regions are currently engaged in processing with supplied materials, processing and assembling parts and components supplied by investor or clients, conducting compensation trade. One-third of the industrial and farming products produced in Guangdong Province are consumed internally, one-third marketed in other provinces, and the remaining one-third exported abroad. The export-oriented economy in some coastal regions has in fact developed to a high level. All these indicate that international market has become increasingly important to the development of the Chinese economy.

Moreover, although China is a large country with ample resources, its per capita share of resources remains quite low. Consumption will continue to rise along with the development of production, thereby making imports an ever more important means of solving contradictions between supply and demand.

Although China remains an oil exporter, imports of crude and refined oil have continued to increase in recent years, rising to 11 million tons or a figure equal to 50 percent of exports in 1991. The very next year, exports of crude and refined oil totalled 26.9 million tons, with imports hitting 19.04 million tons. In fact, the majority of imports processed and exported, and the annual volume of oil imports will continue to rise if the current trend continues to develop, and in the future will relegate China to a position as a net oil importer.

China needs to import a large volume of means of production every year simply to meet the requirements of the agricultural production. China is currently the world's major importer of fertilizers, with the import volume of chemical fertilizers accounting for 25 percent of the worldwide total, and the proportion of imported agricultural chemicals, plastic film, cotton and grain accounting for a major share of international business.

Since the introduction of reform and opening, the large volume of advanced technology and equipment introduced from abroad has played a major role in the development of productive force and the rise in comprehensive national strength. Nonetheless, the country has a long way to go when compared to advanced world levels. Therefore, accelerating modernized construction will require the continued importation of large volumes of advanced foreign technology and equipment.

China's processing industry has developed rapidly in recent years. The imported materials for processing accounted for 40 percent of China's total import and the exported processed products 46 percent of China's total export in 1992.

The stable growth of export requires China to import a large volume of raw materials.

The aforementioned facts reveal the close relationship between China's economic development and foreign trade. China, which most definitely hopes to become one of the world's major economic powers, must first become a major global business power.

Some experts hold that China's late start makes it impossible for the country to accomplish reform by relying solely on the natural progression of development. They say the country must instead depend on the impetus of the international market to guide the domestic market economy.

The Chinese market has not as yet matured, a fact quite evident by the shortage of regulations, wide differences between domestic and international prices, the poor quality of commodities, weak management and the obsolete methods adopted for opening the market. Therefore, China must accelerate efforts to link up international market and introduce advanced international systems to upgrade domestic systems. Facts have proved that more internationalized regions have been more closely in turn with the market economy and that internationalization indeed has provided the impetus for reform of the market economy. For example, Wuxi City, Jiangsu Province, has carried out the reform and marched towards the market economy by opening to the outside world. Several factors have exerted great influence on the domestic market economy. They include: a) The unification of policies is not only designed to remove obstacles between China and foreign countries, but also to eliminate resistance between domestic regions; b) Great effort should be placed on developing modern markets, including the futures market; c) Domestic enterprises should directly participate in international activities in order to strengthen their ability to attract foreign investment and raise the competitive level of products. They also should establish joint ventures with foreign enterprises in order to raise their capacity to engage in transnational management. The fact that domestic price reform has witnessed achievements shows that the overseas factor has played a positive role. Low priced domestic products have contributed to increasing exports and strengthening the ability to compete with foreign goods.

Some experts point out that the use of foreign capital and rapid development of foreign economic and technological cooperation have played a positive role in accelerating the reform of China's national economy.

China's use of foreign investment represents a new aspect which has emerged since adoption of the opening policy. Between 1979-1991, China had approved 42,000 foreign-funded projects, attracting negotiated foreign investments of US$52.3 billion, and an actual utilization volume of US$23.3 billion. Eighty-five percent of 17,000-odd enterprises in operation are productive ones. More foreign investment absorbed in 1992. A total of 13,052 foreign-funded projects approved in the first six months of the year, with a negotiated investment of US$14.677 billion, a rise of 24.4 percent on the previous year's same period.

The introduction of foreign capital, advanced technology and management skills has helped to overcome the domestic shortage of funds, strengthened the construction of infrastructure of the energy, transportation, telecommunications, promoted the adjustment of industrial structure and product mix, and led to rapid progress in the technology for manufacturing of automobiles, elevators, computers, color televisions, audio and video equipment, food and drink, instruments and meters, and glass. The utilization of foreign investment has played a positive role in expanding exports, increasing national revenue, expanding employment and opening new job opportunities, strengthening economic cooperation between the mainland and Hong Kong, Macao and Taiwan, and promoted the peaceful reunification of the motherland. Moreover, the establishment of foreign-funded enterprises has many advantages for the development of the national economy, and has been serving as a complement to the socialist economy. Statistics for 1991 revealed that the output value of the country's joint-ventures, enterprises solely owned by foreign businessmen and cooperative enterprises reached 137 billion yuan, or about 5 percent of the country's total industrial output value.

2) In answer to the question of how to further expand the opening, some experts think that the most important is to define clearly the goal. We should directly participate in the international division of labour instead of producing the products which use to be imported. While doing so, close attention should be paid to the role of transnational corporations.

A number of experts stress that China should enter the international arena, implement a strategy of market diversification, open international markets, expand overseas investment, participate in international market competition, start internationalized management and establish a group of transnational corporations with Chinese characteristics. The most important aspect for accomplishing the goal is to expand the management practice of grouping enterprises, while strengthening industrialization and internationalization. While operating on the basis of accepting sole responsibility for profits and losses, domestic enterprises should gradually unite to establish a group of export-oriented economic groups with a solid strength and capacity to open international market. Great effort should also be made to consolidate and develop the achievements made in the reform of the foreign trade system in 1992. While deepening reform of the foreign trade system, stress must be placed on improving import and export management measures, encouraging diversification of the foreign trade market, granting decision-making power for foreign trade to qualified enterprises and, gradually establishing a number economic complexes involving trade on industry, technology and agriculture, and integrated domestic and foreign trade. In addition, efforts should be also made to expand contracts for foreign projects and exports of labour services and develop transnational management.

Enterprise groups based on specialized foreign trade corporations have their advantages to practise internationalized management because they are familiar with international economics, technology, business practices and changing laws on the international market. In addition, they have a large number of qualified foreign economic and trade personnel, but are hindered due to the absence of powerful production backing. However, major industrial and enterprise groups, as well as integrated groups have their own advantages for implementing international management. They have strong productive strength and technicians qualified in various fields and can produce goods highly competitive on the international market. Nonetheless, such entities are short of competitive experience and need a period of time to familiarize themselves with the international market.

Experts point out that limitations between regions, departments and trades must be abolished so as to integrate industrial, agricultural, technological and commercial trade on the basis of equality and mutual benefit. A batch of transnational corporations with the strength to compete with Western transnational corporations should be established as soon as possible. Some Western transnational corporations focus on production enterprises, while others engage in the import and export in order to promote foreign investment and develop diversified management (such as comprehensive business firms in Japan). So long as it is benificial advantages to internationalized management, China can use either forms and should not spend a great deal of time and effort to discuss the question of who is the "dragon's head." Industrial enterprise and foreign-trade enterprise each has its own advantages and shortcomings. Only the integration of these enterprises can they have the ability to complete with foreign firms on the international market.

3) Some experts say the present opening effort has been subject to excessive limitations. They stress that China should be more positive and bold in using foreign capital and opening new channels of foreign investment, particularly in terms of tertiary industry.

At present, the two most appealing aspects attracting foreign investment in China center on the country's vast potential market of over 1.1 billion people and low labour costs. While using low labor costs to attracting overseas business people to establish technology-intensive foreign-funded enterprises, export-oriented enterprises and small and medium scale enterprises. At the same time China should further open its market for the products of foreign-funded technology- and capital-intensive enterprises. The effort will attract more transnational corporations to establish large and medium scale high-tech enterprises in China. The overall efforts will prove favourable for promoting the competitiveness of China's national industries.

Fields for foreign investment should be expanded. Foreign capital introduced thus had mainly been earmarked for the processing and hotel sectors. Foreign investment policies should be softened and sectors open to investment should gradually be expanded from the production sector to the banking, trade, commerce, communications, tourism and tertiary industries.

4) Experts have a common understanding that expanding opening must include efforts to deepen reform of the foreign trade system.

Reform of the foreign trade management system must be expanded. Through legal, policy, economic and necessary administrative means, efforts should be focused on strengthening the macrocontrol management on imports and exports, reducing microcontrol management, and further reforming management mechanisms related to planning, licensing, quotas, foreign capital, loans and foreign aid so as to establish a scientific foreign trade management system suited to China's actual conditions and generally accepted by international practice.

Reform of foreign trade enterprise mechanisms must be deepened and the transformation of the operation mechanisms of enterprises must be accelerated. The goal of further separating the functions of administration from those of management is to carry out the effective administrative management of enterprises and avoid runaway. On the other hand, enterprises can give full play to their decision-making power. Efforts should be focused on implementation of the Regulations on Changing the Management Mechanisms of Industrial Enterprises Owned by the Whole People to promote the transformation of the management mechanisms of foreign trade enterprise. Examination and approval of the import-export operation rights granted to qualified productive enterprises and enterprise groups should be quickened. Prefectures and counties (cities) with a high purchasing volume should be approved to establish some comprehensive business corporations. Management right over foreign trade of commercial groups, import-export right to operate on a specified scale in designated markets of some enterprises that contract foreign projects should be approved. Foreign trade enterprises can make experiments on stock system to promote the combination of foreign trade enterprises and productive firms, and gradually form some industrial groups and export commodity production bases, which are led by foreign trade enterprises.

With regard to reform in the management of import-export commodities, all commodities should be subject to open management, excluding strategic goods related directly to the national economy and the livelihood of the people. The management scale of various foreign trade enterprises also should be widened. We should make efforts to promote the carrying out of the export agency system. China should also reform the import system in accordance with GATT requirements and international trade norms so as to further open the domestic market.

In order to ensure the unity and transparency of foreign trade policy, policies for foreign trade must be unified and the management system for foreign trade should be published by related foreign trade department.

In terms of perfecting the coordination mechanism of foreign trade, stress will be placed on strengthening the coordination and service functions of import and export associations, and perfecting transportation, banking and insurance services.

2. The Impact of China's Reentry into GATT on Economic Development

The General Agreement on Tariffs and Trade (GATT), the world's largest multilateral economic and trade organization, is becoming increasingly important to the further reform, opening and development of the Chinese economy. Therefore, China's return to GATT under certain principles and conditions is gaining increasing urgency. However, China's reentry into GATT in no way implies that the country will simply enjoys additional rights, but instead means that it must also undertake appropriate duties. Hence, we can say that reentry into GATT presents both opportunities and challenges. Experts contend that under such circumstances, the only possible way for China to grasp the opportunity for economic development and provide the impetus needed to ensure rapid economic development is for the country to adopt correct policies and measures.

(1) Historical background for China's return to GATT

While China was one of the 23 founding signatory states of GATT, its relationship with the organization was later suspended. In July 1986, the Chinese government formally applied to GATT for restoration of its signatory status, a major decision with a profound historical background.

Firstly, historical trends in the economic development of the modern world indicate that China must refrain from drifting away from the powerful current on-going international economic development. As relationships in the global economy become more interdependent, no country can exist independent of the world economic system. China, a large developing country, must courageously join in international world economic competition and the worldwide development system, and take advantage of and create opportunities and conditions for self-development as part of its effort to achieve established goals. Joining the global economic organization is thus an "admission ticket" for entering the world economic system. While China is currently a member state of the International Monetary Fund (IMF) and the World Bank, it is still not a member of GATT, one of the three pillars supporting world economic development. Therefore, China's application for restoration of its signatory statues in GATT is deemed highly significant and urgent to ensure the future success of reform, opening and development.

Secondly, GATT, one of the largest modern multilateral international and trade organizations, which operates in conjunction with IMF and the World Bank, is widely recognized as one of the three pillars which regulates the international economy. GATT, which plays a special and irreplaceable role in global economic and trade development, is often referred to as the "Economic United Nations." The number of GATT member states has climbed from the original 23 to 104 members, with the trade volume of contracting parties accounting for well over 90 percent of the total world volume. Following eight rounds of trade negotiations, GATT is assuming an ever expanding role in adjusting world economic problems, and has, in fact, evolved into a legal standard for global economic and trade activities. China is a potentially large trade country. Along with the accelerated pace of reform and opening and expanding economic ties with foreign countries, China is in urgent need of an international economic and trade organization necessary for adjusting economic and trade relations with various countries across the globe. Membership in such an organization is necessary to ensure that China establishes mutually beneficial and non-discriminatory multilateral economic and trade relations. Therefore, the restoration of China's status as a contracting party to GATT is the only viable choice.

Thirdly, winning and safeguarding China's voice and protecting its interests in the international economic arena is an urgent requirement for China's effort to open further to the outside world and develop foreign trade. Global trade protectionism has become increasingly fierce since the collapse of the Bretton Woods System in the 1970s. Developing countries, especially developing countries which are not members of GATT, have been subjected to even greater suffering, with China being no exception. GATT, which serves as an effective weapon for safeguarding global free trade and curbing trade protectionism, is playing an increasingly important role in defending regulation of the multilateral free trade system. However, China's interests in terms of the international economic arena are seriously affected due to the fact it is not a member of GATT. Acting under the pretext that China is not a member of GATT, some countries impose large-scale trade restriction and trade retaliation on China, an action which seriously violates even the most basic GATT principles. China's trade interests are thus impaired and, even more importantly, to some extent such actions retard China's process of reform, opening and economic development. Restoration of China's status as a contracting party to GATT will make it possible to halt discriminatory trade practices which are contrary to GATT regulations, while at the same time safeguarding China's trading interests, creating a favourable international environment for accelerating the pace of reform and opening and provide greater impetus for the country's economic growth.

Fourthly, domestic reform, opening and economic development require external motive forces. Restoration of China's membership status in GATT will provide powerful motive forces and create new opportunities for China's domestic economic reform and development. A basic precondition for participation in international economic and trade activities and joining the international division of labour and development system is that China's economic operations and trade measures must conform with modern international economic standards and common trade practices. Restoration of China's status as a GATT contracting party will not only make it possible to accelerate the pace of domestic economic reform and opening to the outside world, but more importantly will promote links between the domestic and international economies on that basis, while at the same time meeting the requirements of international standards for economic and trade development. This, in turn, will add great impetus and provide even more opportunities for deepening reform, expanding the opening effort and promoting economic growth.

China advanced the following three principles when applying for restoration of its signatory status in GATT:

The first principle stressed the restoration of China's status, and the fact that the country was not joining, nor rejoining GATT.

GATT provisions provide two forms for joining GATT: The first, in line with stipulations in Article 33 of the agreement involves gaining membership following the negotiation of terms between the applicant and contracting parties. The second, in accordance with stipulations of Article 26 of GATT, requires that a signatory state publish a statement authenticating that it has accepted the General Agreement on behalf of a specified independent tariff territory, with the latter being immediately regarded as a signatory state of GATT.

The Chinese government formally applied to GATT for restoration of its signatory status in GATT in July 1986, with the application being the first of its kind in the history of GATT to breach the "restoration" approach. China's use of the special approach resulted a number of unique circumstances. While China was a founding signatory state of GATT, in 1951, Kuomintang authorities, acting as the representative of the founding signatory state, declared their intention for China to withdraw from the organization. The move resulted in the suspension of China's relationship with GATT. Two points of this issue deserved special attention. Firstly, since the founding of the People's Republic of China in 1949, the government of the People's Republic has been the country's only legal government, and as such has never declared that it was terminating its relationship with GATT. Secondly, in accordance with the inheritance principle regarding an internationally recognized treaty state, government succession occurs under circumstances wherein agreements under international law continue to exist. Therefore, agreements of the old regime should be transferred to the new government, thereby entailing changes in international relationships. Given this fact, the Chinese government had the right to replace the Kuomintang regime as China's legal representative in GATT. The two points mentioned above clarify that the Chinese government's request for "restoration" of its status, rather than that it was rejoining GATT, was both legitimate and reasonable.

The Chinese government's reentry into GATT using the special form of "restoration" has particular legal implications. First, the Chinese government will reach a "restoration protocol" following substantive negotiations concerning tariff reductions and concession, and using said protocol as the legal basis, formal restoration of China's signatory status in GATT will occur on the effective date of the protocol. This implies there is no need for China to rejoin the organization in accordance with the new member admissions method outlined in Article 33 of GATT, thereby making it possible to greatly accelerate the process of restoring the country's status as a GATT member. Second, the restoration protocol outlines the rights China should enjoy and the obligations it should assume. Therefore, questions relating to stipulations of Article 35 are simply inapplicable. This fact implies that no member state of GATT should refuse to establish a mutually applicable relationship with another signatory state. Third, the restoration protocol contains no retroactive clause which means that all mutual rights between China and other signatory states resulting from the period of the suspension of activities of China's status as a signatory state are invalid, and all sides should refrain from taking action against each other. The implication then is that China can include a new "Grandfather Clause" in the restoration protocol, and that the second part of GATT should be temporarily applicable to China within a maximum time limit which is not in conflict with current legislation on the day of "restoration." This in turn will achieve the goal of protecting various types of domestic industries, a goal which would be difficult to attain using any other approach. At the same time, the absence of retroactivity implies that China should be exempt from all membership fees accruing during the period, and respect revisions and supplements to GATT text implemented during the period of suspension of its signatory state activities.

The second principle is that Chinese government prepares to reach a restoration protocol based on tariff reductions and concessions, rather than on negotiations for import promises, but that the two former items should be reasonably limited and adaptable to China.

The most crucial question during the process of restoring China's signatory status in GATT centers on just what obligations China should assume in return for rights it will enjoy as a member of GATT. This then leads to questions related to the fundamental differences between the so-called market economic structure and the planned economic system, and actual influences of implementation of the GATT principle of mutual benefit. Western countries insist that prices under the planned economic system fail to true production costs, and hence tariffs cannot reflect the extent of protection. Therefore, they say negotiations on tariff reductions and concessions are meaningless. As a result, it is impossible to effectively implement the principle of mutual benefit between the planned and market economic systems. In terms of previous practice, two different modes for socialist countries to join GATT. The first mode involved decentralizing the central economy and weakening the planned economy, introducing and strengthening market mechanisms, and transforming tariffs into protection mechanisms, after which a country could join GATT on the same terms of tariff reductions and concessions applicable to countries with market economic systems. Countries fitting this description included Yugoslavia and Hungary. The second mode was to retain the original centralized planned economic system, and solve questions related to mutual benefit by employing the method of promising certain increases in the import volume to countries practising a market economic system, as well as joining GATT on as a precondition for enhancing domestic economic growth. Furthermore, the costs for admission to the organization were enormous. The status and interests of countries which joined GATT using this method were quite often seriously influenced.

When applying for restoration of its signatory status in

GATT, China, a socialist country, gave full consideration to the impact of its political and economic interests if joining GATT in accordance with the two aforementioned methods. China proposed using negotiated tariff reductions and concessions as conditions for the restoration of its status. In 1979, China began implementing extensive measures including reforms of its ownership structure, as well as its planning, price and foreign trade systems which are regarded as important tools for protecting and promoting trade, and gaining membership in the Customs Cooperative Council. In recent years, in particular, while comprehensively deepening economic reforms, China has also recorded major success in reform of its foreign trade system. While lowering the exchange rate of the Renminbi, China has comprehensively abolished export subsidies and instituted a new foreign trade system characterized by independent management which assumes sole responsibility for its own profits and losses. In terms of the import management system, it has already implemented, or is preparing to implement, a number of new measures. These measures have greatly reduced differences between China's foreign trade system and the GATT system. China's use of tariff reductions and concessions as conditions for negotiating the restoration of its signatory status in GATT has now entered a substantive stage.

However, while using tariff reductions and concessions as a condition for restoring its signatory status in GATT, the Chinese government has continually stressed that negotiations concerning the items should give full consideration to China's concrete realities, especially the degree of domestic adaptability. This approach includes two main aspects: a) When deciding the range of tariff reductions and concessions, countries with similar levels of development should be used as a reference; b) Steps for tariff reductions and concessions should be based on the ability of domestic enterprises to adapt to resulting changes.

The third principle centers on restoring China's signatory status in its capacity as a developing country in GATT. Establishing China's status as a developing country in GATT is highly significant. GATT in fact should grant appropriate preferential treatment to developing countries, which is explicitly stipulated in many GATT agreements such as in Article 18 of "government development aid," and Part IV of "trade and development" of the GATT. These different preferential treatments are especially important to a large developing country like China. Therefore, during the process of restoring China's status as a signatory state in GATT, it is an important principle for Chinese government to clearly define the country's nature as a developing country.

In actual practice, GATT has historically adhered to two requirements to judge whether or not a country is a developing state. First, the country's per capita income at a low level, and second, the country's industry is in the initial stage of development. When judging China's situation, it is without a doubt a low-income country because its current per capita national income is only about US$ 210. China's 1989 industrial output value accounted for 44 percent of GNP. Though it surpassed the proportion of its agricultural output value, agricultural manpower for the period accounted for 60 percent of that for the nation's total labor force, with over 60 percent being in the form of manual labor. In addition, its rate of industrial equipment was about 15 percent to that of developed countries. On the whole, China's industrial development remains in the primary stage. It is thus quite obvious that China is really a developing country. In fact, as early as 1983, the Textile Council of GATT confirmed China's status as a developing country and somewhat later, in 1985, China became a member of the "International Textiles and Clothing Bureau" of developing countries. At present China is participating in the activities of the informal consultation group of developing countries of GATT. Therefore, China is in fact recognized by the international community as a developing country, and hence any attempt designed to deny China's nature as a developing country under any pretext is unfair.

The aforementioned three basic principles are not only reasonable and legitimate, but also directly concern the conditions, status and interests of China's reentry into GATT. Therefore, negotiations concerning the restoration of China's status as a signatory state of GATT can only be conducted on the basis of said principles. Any practice contrary to the aforesaid principles is unacceptable to China. Judging from the actual situation there are no insurmountable obstacles to the implementation of the "restoration" and "tariff reductions and concessions" principles. However, the final negotiations will remain arduous due to obstacles in the principle whereby China demands that it be granted status as a developing country.

The rights China will enjoy and the duties it will assume as a result of the restoration of its status as a signatory state of GATT include:

Politically, China's return to GATT will greatly increase the country's say and initiatives in international political affairs; bring its role as one of the five major permanent members of the Security Council of the United Nations into full play; and further establish China's position in the international political arena. China will thus be able to make even greater contributions to the maintenance of world peace and development.

From a diplomatic standpoint, China's reentry into GATT will further expand the power of developing countries in GATT, and will allow the country to unite with other developing countries to play their due role in the establishment of a new comprehensive and just international economic order. At the same time, China's reentry into GATT will exert a positive impact on the great cause of the reunification of the Chinese nation. Hong Kong and Macao have already been confirmed as signatory parties of GATT in line with stipulations in Article 26 of GATT through joint declarations published by China and Great Britain and China and Portugal. In the near future, if the sovereign state bearing responsibility for the diplomatic affairs of Hong Kong and Macao remains outside GATT, a situation would arise creating serious inconveniences in terms of both economic development, and economic and trade development between the two regions, i.e. Hong Kong and Macao, and the hinterland.

Economically, links between China's economic operational mechanisms and the worldwide economic development system will not only can consolidate and develop the achievements of economic reform and opening, but will also increase China's overall national strength. The reform and opening policies, and various measures implemented prior to the restoration of China's signatory status in GATT, will all be included in the GATT protocol, which itself has status as international law. Simply stated, this means the intensification of China's reform and opening policies which are irreversible and the affirmation of the results of the reform. At the same time, it will produce a sustained and stable appeal to foreign investors. When the Chinese economy joins the international division of labour system, the competition system and the system of international economic development China will definitely be enabled to make greater use of its advantages, or comparative advantages, strengthen itself through competition, and continually readjust strategies and policies in the course of development. So China will thus be able to more effectively enhance its international competitiveness and comprehensive national strength.

Of course, China's rights and interests after reentry of GATT will primarily be manifested on trade which include:

First, China will enjoy stable multilateral and unconditional most favoured nation (MFN) treatment. At present, China obtains MFN treatment basically through bilateral trade negotiations. Quite obviously, bilateral MFN status is not only extremely unstable, but most often strings are attached which result in conflicts between nations with regard to economic and sometimes political relations. Situations such as these seriously affect China's reform and opening efforts and economic development. This is particularly for the crucial period during which China is in transition from the strategy of import substitution to the strategy of balanced development. Therefore, the achievement of a multilateral, stable and unconditional MFN status is vitally important.

Second, enjoying general preferential treatment is more desirable than simply enjoying MFN treatment. In 1965, the long-term endeavours and arduous efforts of developing countries led to the inclusion of a special clause for handling issues concerning the trade and development of underdeveloped countries into Section IV of GATT. The clause explicitly stipulates: In the course of trade negotiations, developed nations signatory to the agreement may not expect reciprocity with lesser developed signatory nations regarding reduction tariffs and other trade barriers. Somewhat later, the "Tokyo Round" of negotiations led to the establishment of a long-term legal basis for GATT to grant preferential treatment to developing countries in accordance with an agreement reached in 1979. During the "Uruguay Round," developed countries also promised to provide developing countries with special preferential treatment in line with related regulations. As a developing country, the restoration of China's status as a signatory state of GATT should enjoy all preferential treatment granted to developing signatory nations. In this way, Chinese products, manufactured products in particular, exported to developed countries will enjoy preferential treatment much preferable to MFN treatment.

Third, that is advantageous to reasonable solution to trade disputes. The question as to whether or not trade disputes can be justly and reasonably solved directly influence the trade interests of countries involved. At present, when proceeding with trade relations with China, many developed industrial countries often implement highly discriminatory anti-dumping and anti-subsidization measures which cause serious harm to China's trade interests. Reentry into GATT will enable China to eliminate discriminatory trade actions and achieve just solutions in trade disputes in accordance with relevant GATT procedures and regulations for solving disputes. The rights and interests of signatory states in GATT in this regard are quite evident. For example, the United States has levied discriminatory tariffs on imported oil, and ignored protests lodged by Venezuela, which is a not as yet a member state of GATT. On the other hand, Mexico, a member of GATT submitted a complaint and eventually won a lawsuit filed with the organization.

(2) Obligations, opportunities and challenges China will face after restoration of its status as a signatory state in GATT.

China's return to GATT will enable it to enjoy certain rights, but will also shoulder appropriate obligations.

During discussions of China's foreign trade system memorandum, a number of signatory states have pointed out that said system is in many ways inconsistent with GATT regulations, and thus raises relevant demands regarding restoration of China's signatory status in GATT. The demands include: a) Unification of the nation's foreign trade policies and rules, and striving to ensuring same comply with the demands of the framework and structure of GATT. Major signatory states complained that China practised two differing sets of foreign trade policies and regulations at the central and local levels, and much of the content of said policies were contrary to GATT regulations. In response, the Chinese government has promised to accelerate foreign trade legislation, particularly the formulation and adoption of a foreign trade law at the earliest possible date, with the overall effort being carried out in line with GATT regulations and international standards. Doing so will enable China to effectively perform its obligations for implementing unified national foreign trade policies and regulations. b) Simplification of the import management system, with promises to substantially reduce and concede tariffs. In accordance with GATT principles, various contracting parties must limit the use of tariffs to only a principal means of protection, and the rate of duty must be limited to a certain level. Major signatory states conducted an examination of China's foreign trade system claiming that the country's tariffs failed to play a key role in its foreign trade system, and its tariffs were too high. The Chinese government responded by promising to deepen reform of the country's import management system, and in turn ensure the principal regulatory role of tariffs in import and export trade. China also promised that it would proceed within sustainable economic limits, and would join in negotiations with signatory states on matters regarding tariff reductions and concessions, while at the same time gradually reducing its general tariff level to the appropriate level which GATT demands on developing countries. In fact, mandatory planning has already been reduced to a level of only 33 percent of China's total import value, and the country will cancel import examination lists for machinery and electronics products. With regard to tariff reductions and concessions, China earlier announced a unilateral reduction of import duty rates for 50 products, and recently announced another round of reductions covering import tax rates for 225 products. c) Based on the premise of substantial increases in exports, China will guarantee an appropriate proportion of imports, and at the same time rationalize nontariff measures. Admission to the Chinese Market represents a question of great concern of major signatory states. The Chinese government has answered by declaring it will further expand the scale of imports on the existing base, especially the importation of large turn-key projects. China has also promised to gradually abolish a number of nontariff measures, and has already abolished import licensing controls on 16 of 53 types of commodities. Within the next two to three years, China will strive to reduce the number by yet another 33 percent and will guarantee that it will refrain from using irrational technical barriers and other nontariff measures to restrict the importation of foreign commodities. At the same time, the Chinese government is also prepared to conduct substantive negotiations with signatory states concerning a series of nontariff barrier rules, and will undertake necessary obligations appropriate to the developmental level of its economy and trade. d) China has promised to adopt a timetable for price reform and to eliminate the distorted situation related to its foreign trade prices. China will accept selected guaranteed clauses long before completing reform of its pricing system. In this regard, the Chinese government has promised to accelerate reform of the pricing system, and substantially reduce the scope of state-set prices, to ensure that commodity prices will be automatically regulated mainly by the market forces involved in the relationship between supply and demand. e) Increasing the transparency of foreign trade policies and regulations. Major signatory states particularly complain that China is lack of transparency in its foreign trade system. The Chinese government has thus promised to review internal documents concerning foreign trade management. Documents requiring implementation will be issued exclusively by the Ministry of Foreign Trade and Economic Cooperation, and documents considered inappropriate for implementation will be annulled. Future rules and regulations concerning foreign trade management will be promulgated by the Ministry of Foreign Trade and Economic Cooperation prior to going into effect. Such steps are expected to fulfill the obligation of transparency. f) Gradually opening the domestic market within the bearable scope. While promising to gradually open its domestic goods market, China is also actively considering and in some cases implementing the opening of the domestic service market. At present, China has permitted certain foreign service trades to establish agencies in China, and will gradually expand the opening scope, while at the same time relaxing opening requirements.

Opportunities and challenges China faces as a result of the restoration of its signatory status in GATT. Reentry into GATT implies the acquisition of a legal and preferential "admission ticket" for entering the world market system. The opportunities accruing to a large developing country like China are manifested as follows:

Firstly, GATT membership allows a country to take advantage of the favorable environment of the world economy to accelerate the introduction of advanced technology, promote the upgrade of industry and speed up the process of industrialization. The current world economic structure is sloping gradually away from the manufacturing industry to the service trades, and the growth rate of the world services sector is much higher than that of goods trading, with the former maintaining strong development momentum. A bleak and depressed economic situation has generally emerged in major developed industrial countries and, according to predictions, a fundamental change in the situation will not reach fruition for quite some time. On the other hand, following a three year effort to improve its economic environment and rectify its economic order, China has adopted various new measures for reform and opening, with the effort resulting in rapid increase in economic vigor, accompanied by wide-ranging strong domestic and foreign demand which has appealed greatly to foreign investors. China's return to GATT will to a great extent enable the country to rid itself of import discrimination imposed on it as a non-member state. China can make full use of excellent opportunities offered by the changing world industrial structure and the low overall demand to accelerate the introduction of advanced technology and equipment from developed Western countries, promote technological innovation, upgrade domestic industries and accelerate the process of industrialization.

Secondly, by using reentry into GATT as a turning point, China will be able to rapidly establish and improve domestic market mechanisms, particularly market competition mechanisms, further standardize economic activities, and fundamentally tackle and swiftly solve long-standing problems regarding low economic returns. Factors affecting China's economic efficiency are mainly the lack of sound and effective operational market mechanisms, and universal non-standard economic activities. Reentry into GATT will make it possible to form an external shock wave against China's existing economic operational and circulatory system, and will thereby become a strong external force for solving the aforementioned chronic problems. Since reentry into GATT will compel China's economy to operate in line with GATT regulations and force China to standardize all its economic activities, which will effectively raise the efficiency of economic operations. At the same time, China's reentry into GATT is predicated on the condition of tariff reductions and concessions, and not on import pledges. This fact compels China to quickly establish and improve its market system in accordance with GATT regulations, bring the main regulatory role of market mechanisms into full play and weaken the government's function of economic administration. Doing so will enable Chinese enterprises to achieve a rational allocation of resources, accelerate technical renovations, learn from and draw on new management expertise and raise overall competitiveness. This in turn will make it possible for China to gradually solve the problem of the low efficiency of economic development.

Third, reentry into GATT can effectively apply pressure on and spark motive forces for China to deepen its reform and expand its opening. China's reentry into GATT will further establish the irreversible nature of its reform and opening, and will not only compel China to take bold strides in reform and opening, but also to a certain extent to clearly set goals for reform and opening such as establishing and maintaining an economic operational system characterized by rapid growth and high efficiency in accordance with common international practices. It will also ensure that the domestic economic operational system gradually conforms with the stipulated GATT system and will enable China's economic development to merge with the world market system, and thereby genuinely become an organic component of the world economy.

Fourthly, making use of the multilateral free trade system of GATT and all rights entitled to signatory states in the organization, China will strive to expand the scale of export which can improve China's situation of income and expenses and give full play to the so-called "engine" role of foreign trade in bringing about comprehensive economic growth. Reentry into GATT can help China open foreign markets previously closed, or partially closed, to China's export commodities and remove various discriminatory obstacles and open the door ever wider to China's export commodities, thereby allowing for the smooth implementation of the strategy for market diversification. While striving to expand its scale of exports, China can also improve the quality of export commodities through the international market competition. In this way, the situation regarding China's international balance of payment will without a doubt improve greatly, and its international payments capacity will be raised further. At the same time, China can use large amounts of foreign exchange reserves to increase the import volume of advanced technology and equipment needed for domestic economic construction. Such actions will effectively expedite the comprehensive growth of export-oriented industries and the national economy as a whole.

Fifthly, reentry into GATT can provide an excellent opportunity for the development of China's service trade industry. At present, international service trade has been developing rapidly, and it is becoming a leading industry in many national economy in many countries. China's service industry remains in its initial stages compared with the development of worldwide service trades. Therefore it is an urgent task for China to vigorously develop its service trade.

Reentry into GATT will also make Chinese economy confronting with severe challenges, including:

Firstly, within a short period of time, development of the domestic economy will unavoidably be subjected to the strong impact of the international market. Although China has recorded remarkable achievements in its reform and opening, the level of domestic economic development, the country's economic management system and the existing form of economic operations are out of line with the world economy. Along with reentry into GATT, the domestic economy will be immediately exposed to the international economy and its development will unavoidably be subjected to the strong impact of the world market.

Secondly, from a long-term standpoint, development of the domestic economy will be subjected to even greater influence resulting from the periodical fluctuation of the world economy. Under conditions wherein the domestic economy is separate from the world economy, fluctuations in the domestic economy are mainly dependent on the influence of domestic factors. However, once the domestic economy is incorporated into the world system, fluctuations in the domestic economy will mainly be affected by changing international factors, such as the world economic cycle, and major or sudden political, economic or military events in the world arena. These aspects will make it difficult for the country to single-handedly halt or eliminate such fluctuations.

Thirdly, the promise of market admission will cause the domestic economy to lose its previous sufficient protection for its development, and many domestic industries will face increasingly strong pressure from international competition. In terms of tariffs, after the previous seven rounds of negotiation, the average import tax rate of the developed Western countries has dropped from 40 percent to 4 percent, even that of the developing nations has also fallen to 13 percent. China's current tariff level, however, is the highest even among the developing countries. China's present average customs import duty rate ranks third after that of India and Bangladesh. While its customs import duty rate for consumer goods ranks first. A promise of tax reduction and concession inevitably requires a drastic lowering of import tax. As a result, the industries originally under state tariff protection will inevitably face fierce international market competition. Take the auto industry for example, the Shanghai Santana sedan cars are sold at 170,000 yuan each at home, while the same kind of product is sold at only US$10,000 at the international market price, the main reason for such a large price difference is automobiles belong to the industry under strict state protection, the import tax rate for cars has all along remained at about 200 percent. In terms of nontariff measures, China originally instituted a trade control system. In addition to tariff measures, there is a variety of nontariff measures. These measures have effectively protected the development of domestic industries. During the "resumption" of negotiation, the Chinese government has promised to gradually abolish various nontariff measures, such as import license, the quota system as well as technical inspection standard. The development of domestic industries has thus lost a layer of important protective screen, resulting in still larger competition pressure.

3. Tactics for Reentering GATT

Experts point out that the restoration of China's signatory status in GATT will enable China to advance into the world economic arena at a more rapid rate, thereby accelerating the country's economic construction, promoting the development of productive forces, enhancing its economic strength and raising the material and cultural levels of the people. Therefore, China should seize the opportunity and transform the challenge into a motive force suited to the needs of reentry of GATT.

China must first change existing ideas to meet the challenge. The Chinese economy has long operated and developed under the dual protection of the state in terms of limited quantities of imports and import tariff restrictions. Facts have proved that such stringent protection has led to low efficiency in terms of economic operations and development, and an ever widening gap between China and developed countries in terms of the level of economic development. Today's world is characterized by a period of peaceful development and competition. Countries desiring successful economic development must join the system of international economic development and competition. Therefore, the primitive concept of economic development based solely on state protection must be cast aside in order to meet the challenge of international competition, and must be replaced by a new concept based on striving for subsistence and development in terms of international economic development and a competitive environment.

Secondly, the socialist market economic system must be established and continually improved. GATT operates on the basis of the market economy and requires signatory states operate likewise. The history of mankind reveals that capitalism, which realized the value of social production and the market economy, eventually formed a solid material and technological foundation which triumphed over feudalism. Consequently, capitalism expanded and more closely linked production, circulation, distribution and consumption, as well as the rational allocation of resources, which gave rise to economic efficiency. The 14th Congress of the Communist Party of China (CPC) clearly advanced the proposal for establishing socialist market economy which would link Chinese economic operations more closely with the global market economy, thereby removing obstacles hindering China's reentry into GATT. Practice has proved that not one of the 104 signatory states has collapsed because they joined GATT, adopted market economies and advocated fair competition. Quite to the contrary, after joining GATT many realized an economic upsurge because of the expansion of international trade. On the other hand, however, there have been a number of cases when governments fell from power as a result of a failure to joining GATT, exhibiting an unwillingness to reform economic structures, or failing to adopt a market economy. Therefore, priority task at present is to strengthen reform of the economic structure and actively establish and perfect the market economic system.

Resolute measures must be adopted to guide medium and large scale enterprises to the market and to establish and improve the enterprise operations system, granting enterprises operational autonomy and making them responsible for their own profits and losses. Once China reenters GATT, the domestic market will gradually blend with the international market, and enterprises will inevitably participate in competition on the market. However, Chinese enterprises have long relied on the so-called "umbilical cord" of the state. Analogous to human beings stricken with "osteomalacia," enterprises lack life and vitality, with most characterized by low efficiency, huge losses and in some cases insolvency. Therefore, enterprises must learn to operate independently in the virtual ocean of the commercial economy and in turn strengthen their competitiveness, flexibility and ability to increase foreign exchange earnings from exports. In this way these enterprises will ensure their continued existence once domestic security is removed as a result of China's reentry into GATT. Opening the country's door completely will result in enterprises losing the protection of existing tariff barriers. Hence, simply to compete with foreign goods, enterprises must start at a high level and operate in line with generally accepted standards on the international market. Otherwise, consumers will reject their products because of prices much higher than those for foreign goods, as well as obsolete styles and inferior quality. On the other hand, in terms of competition, opening the country's door enables Chinese enterprises and to directly acquire advanced foreign technology and managerial expertise to develop industries that have the best chance of succeeding in the market. Various reports indicated that for an extended period Taiwan's beverage market was occupied by Nestle, Maxwell House and Coca-Cola, while a kind of indigenous beverage was in the throes of serious losses. Somewhat later, however, advanced equipment was introduced and marketing methods was improved so that production costs were lowered for this beverage. After five to six year's struggle, eventually the company gained prominence as the major beverage producer in Taiwan. A short time later its products were ranked as one of the world's five major beverage varieties, and the company has since moved into a position as Asia's major producer of powedered beverages. Facts have proved that enterprises faced with the pressure of market competition will be forced to learn and master advanced science and technology in order to gain victory in the highly competitive environment. Meanwhile, China's reentry into GATT will lead to the cancellation of subsidies for foreign trade enterprises, and will in turn enable such enterprises to operate independently, maintain separate accounts, assume sole responsibility for profits and losses, and bear total operational risk. By so doing, the enterprises will enhance their competitiveness and ardently strive for development. Speaking in specific terms, enterprises can adopt the following measures:

Enterprises should boldly introduce market mechanisms and employ management personnel familiar with the market economy. Medium and large scale enterprises should establish departments specializing in information collection, analysis and processing. They should conduct surveys and studies centering on the international market and adopt appropriate strategies.

They should conscientiously explore methods for establishing horizontal economic ties in order to realize large-scale production efficiency. The natural merging process has gradually led to the concentration of enterprises in capitalist countries, thereby forming an economic power for controlling the market. Once acquiring control, they effectively eliminated excessive state interference. Chinese enterprises are scattered and it is quite evident that business low-level capital can hardly compete with larger monopolistic enterprises. For example, while there are over 100 enterprises in the country's automobile industry, none have the capability of mass production or improving their technological level. Therefore, they lack the large-scale production efficiency and are unable to garner enough economic might to bargain with foreign manufacturers. This undesirable situation has led to an extraordinary waste of resources. Since there is no unified national market, localities proceed in terms of departmental interests and emphasize the necessity for the existence of inefficient enterprises. When considering the country as a whole, mergers should be encouraged and neither protection, nor support, should be granted to inefficient enterprises. This in turn would eliminate disputes concerning departmental interests, and lead to the natural formation of various enterprise groups capable of controlling the market and competing with foreign enterprises.

Accelerating technical renovations to keep abreast of the latest product trends on world market. Companies manufacturing products which have gained a niche in the foreign market should accelerate technical renovations and consolidate their market standing. For example, while Chinese textiles and garments account for a substantial proportion of European and American markets, problems exist regarding quality, patterns, varieties and guaranteed delivery dates. The Uruguay Round of negotiations may result in the gradual cancellation of quota limits on developed countries over the next 10 years. Nonetheless, the Chinese textile industry is highly concerned that Chinese products may be elbowed out of the market following the lifting of quota limits. Therefore, from this point forward textile mills across the country should accelerate technical renovations in order to safeguard the market standing of their products.

Using joint investments to integrate foreign marketing channels. Marketing channels in major developed countries are controlled by monopolistic enterprises which offer a relatively easy avenue for integrating foreign marketing channels. Joint investments with foreign enterprises, as well as sharing benefits with them, provide an excellent method for entering their marketing channels. At present, the enormous potential of the Chinese market holds great appeal for foreign enterprises. Deng Xiaoping's speeches during his south China tour stirred a strong response abroad, and sparked a strong desire in many enterprises for entry into the Chinese market. A move considered to be a valuable asset for enterprises. In addition, joint investment can directly help Chinese enterprises obtain timely information concerning the international market, and in turn help them to follow the latest trends for products.

Realizing transindustrial joint investment domestically to ensure the coordination of departmental interests. Full consideration should be given to the fact that China is a major consuming nation. However, we have failed to play this trump card due to divergent departmental interests. For example, the purchase of civil aviation aircraft usually involve contracts well into the billions of US dollars. Technology transfers could be demanded from the seller to promote the development of China's civil aviation manufacturing industry. The fact is that there is no direct benefits to the aircraft importing department but it creates burden to it. However, the establishment of a joint venture between the manufacturer and user of civil aviation aircraft would result in their sharing common interests, and would in turn promote the development of China's civil aviation aircraft manufacture industry. Similar situations exist in numerous other industries and trades.

In short, facing new circumstances regarding further reform and opening, and the continuing endeavour to reenter GATT, enterprises should explore new methods for seeking development opportunities by taking full advantage of both domestic and foreign markets. The most important factor is for enterprises to adopt active rather than passive business strategies.

Thirdly, the foreign trade structure is directly related to GATT. Market reform has provided basic guarantee ensuring the increased economic strength of Chinese enterprise, as well as for linking and coordinating the domestic system with GATT. Notwithstanding, specific details regarding the system during the process of restoring China's signatory status in GATT must be solved through the reform and improvement of the foreign trade structure. The structural reform of China's foreign trade involves three main aspects—the management system of foreign trade, the mechanisms of foreign trade enterprises, and the foreign trade regulation system.

Complete autonomy should be granted for management of the foreign trade enterprises. Whether or not China can take full advantage of the international division of labour and the changing international situation, and promote economic development following its reentry into GATT depends mainly on the international trade competitiveness of enterprises. The key factor for enhancing the competitive capabilities of enterprises depends on the foreign trade management system. Following China's reentry into GATT, the "overlapping density" of domestic and international markets will continue to increase and enterprises will inevitably participate in wide-ranging international competition. Only enhancing the international market competitiveness of enterprises and strengthening their ability to increase foreign exchange earnings can China undertake GATT obligations, such as tariff concessions, national treatment on imports, the single exchange rate system, the lack on limits on quantities and elimination of export subsidies. So China's economy won't be harmed even the protective screen shielding domestic enterprises is removed. Therefore, the traditional planned management system featuring centralization, unification, rigidity and restriction must be completely reformed. It must be replaced by a completely comprehensive multi-layered independent foreign trade management system offering decentralized competition. The nature of the foreign trade management system should be determined by the nature of the economic system, and the market economic model provide the basis for the establishment of a completely independent foreign trade system. However, the foreign trade independent management system can not be established after the formation of market economic trade. They should be established simultaneously during the process of marketization.

In terms of the current system, establishment of the new foreign trade system requires the reformation of the import and export planning and management system. The state should exercise planned control on only a small number of staple and sensitive goods and commodities made from natural resources, and should regulate import and export trade according to the market. With regard to the management system, a limited number of goods should be subject to state-controlled unified operations, with a selected number of goods subject to decentralized operations under certain conditions, and most goods subject to completely open operations. Assuming the existence of basic conditions for free operations, the import and export agency system will gradually be established to promote combined and integrated development of industry and trade. On the one hand, efforts should be made to integrate various production enterprises with foreign trade enterprises. Such an approach would effectively integrate industry (agriculture and technology) with trade. On the other hand, management autonomy to engage in direct foreign trade will be granted to qualified production enterprises.

Mechanisms must be established to enable foreign trade enterprises to maintain separate accounts and assume sole responsibility for their own profits and losses. Foreign trade enterprises willing to reap the benefits of profits, but unwilling to accept responsibility for losses, instead depending on what they see as inexhaustible public finance, remain a major problem in China's foreign trade arena. The government has simply approached the problem from the standpoint of the financial structure of foreign trade, with successive specific measures adopted over 10-plus years of reform having failed to solve problems regarding foreign trade losses and subsidies. In fact, the problems involve the enterprise system and thus cannot be solved simply by reforming the financial structure. In principle, GATT forbids signatory states to employ subsidiary means, a fact which requires enterprises engaged in import and export to maintain separate accounts and assume sole responsibility for profits and losses. The overall process of economic structural reform is impeded by the fact that state ownership of enterprises essentially prohibits the establishment of mechanisms to assign state-owned enterprises responsibility for their own profits and losses. The only way to establish such mechanisms is to transform the state enterprise system and proceed with the transition to the market economy. In fact, said mechanisms should be established simultaneously with the formation of the market economic mode. When considering the current system, the key point is to transform government functions and delegate operational autonomy to lower levels.

Firstly, the relationship of administrative subordination between competent administrative departments and foreign trade companies should be changed. Secondly, the relationship of administrative subordination between foreign trade companies and local governments or other administrative departments should be realigned and the latter can specialize in administration, while foreign trade enterprises will become independent and be responsible for their own profits and losses. On the other hand, foreign trade enterprises should raise the quality of their staff, and enhance their concept and knowledge of the market economy; establish a system of collecting, transfering and processing informations; adopt a scientific decision-making system; strengthen their consciousness of competition and establish competitive mechanisms; and perfect their internal management and financial management systems.

A rational scientific regulatory system for foreign trade should be established based mainly on indirect means of regulation. The application of foreign trade regulatory means and the establishment of a regulatory system are directly and closely related to the GATT. The major policy means of the foreign trade regulatory system include exchange rates, prices, the collection and drawback of import-export tax, the retention of a share of foreign exchange, and import and export credits, licenses and quotas. Reform in these areas should adhere to the following principles:

Full consideration should be given to implementing the international practices of GATT and adopting internationally accepted norms to avoid trade retaliation; the effort should be conducive to establishing a foreign trade management system with full autonomy, as well as mechanisms making foreign trade enterprises responsible for their profits and losses; the effort should be devoted to promote domestic economic development and the rationalize of the industrial setup, improve the export structure, increase export efficiency and strive for equilibrium in terms of international payments; and various policy tools should be applied in a supplementary manner.

Reform of the foreign trade regulation system has experienced relatively rapid progress in recent years. The application of various policy tools are gradually coordinated and moving closer to international norms. All these have promoted China's foreign trade development. However, a massive effort will be required to restore China's status in GATT.

Firstly, China must further open its foreign trade policies, legislate related laws at the earliest possible date, and manage foreign trade in strict accordance with law. In accordance with related GATT provisions, China submitted a Memorandum of China's Foreign Trade to the GATT in February 1987, with said memorandum containing additional remarks on specific issues raised by signatory states. In recent months, the Ministry of Foreign Trade and Economic Cooperation promulgated 31 documents governing the internal management of economy and trade. The actions truly demonstrate China's sincere desire to restore its status in the GATT. However, China has not as yet formed a complete set of foreign trade laws, such as an anti-dumping law or a law of foreign trade. Therefore, it lacks a legal basis for appropriately addressing trade behavior which violates GATT regulations. Hence, the drafting and promulgation of laws related to foreign trade must be accelerated to provide a legal basis for the import and export trade, and for solving international disputes.

Secondly, exchange rates, tariffs, import taxes and duty reductions are important tools needed to regulate imports and exports. The exchange rate must be determined according to a reasonable and scientific formula. To this end, the fixed exchange rate system must be transformed into a well-managed floating exchange rate system. Since China has not as yet realigned its pricing system, so it can first adjust Renminbi exchange rates according to the average swap costs of export commodities, the actual use value of import commodities and the supply and demand of foreign exchange. Then it can adopt the so-called "crawling peg system," i.e. making irregular adjustments in the exchange rate within a narrow range according to fluctuations in the US dollar, or Special Drawing Rights (SDRs) on the international market. At the same time, full consideration must be given to both domestic and international inflation, as well as the actual needs of national economic policies. Finally, a managed floating exchange rate system must be established in line with progress made in reforming the domestic pricing system, and the establishment and improvement of the financial market.

Thirdly, an important rule of GATT is to negotiate reduced

import tariffs to promote trade liberalization. On the premise of price being more and more reasonable, we should use exchange rates and import taxation, mainly in the form of tariffs, to regulate the import and gradually reduce the import tariff to the level GATT required for developing countries. Since 1992, China has reduced tariffs of 225 varieties of goods, and at the same time the regulatory tax on 14 kinds of import commodities was cancelled. Nonetheless, China's present import tariffs are still higher than the level for other developing countries. According to the General Administration of Customs, the weighted average tax rate of China's import commodities is 22.5 percent, while the average tax rate of the other developing countries is 15 percent. In order to meet GATT requirements concerning tariff concessions, China can gradually undertake obligations in this regard according to its economic development and industrial policies.

Fourthly, employ every means possible to avoid the use of quantitative limitations on imports and exports. The first clause in Article 11 of the GATT stipulates that no quotas, import and export licenses or other measures should be adopted or maintained to limit or forbid the influx of products from other signatory states, or the export or sales of products on the territories of other signatory states. In order to promote the implementation of trade liberalization, we should gradually remove all quantitative limitations on imports and exports. As a matter of fact, however, quotas and licenses are effective tools often used in international trade. The fact that China was long accustomed to the direct management method made them the chief means for regulating imports and exports. The Chinese government recently announced its decision to cancel the import licenses for 16 commodities in the near future, and reduce the number of similarly managed commodities by some two-thirds over the next few years. Notwithstanding, if necessary China can appropriately use innovative methods of quotas and license while making every effort to act in line with the GATT rules.

Fifthly, export subsidies will be cancelled. Exchange rates and export rebates are used mainly to regulate foreign trade and exports. The second and third clauses in Article 16 of GATT stipulate that signatory states granting subsidies to certain export products may adversely affect other importing or exporting signatory states and in turn create inappropriate interference to its normal trade and hinder the implementation of the goals of GATT. Therefore, all signatory states should avoid granting subsidies to exports of primary products. The article also stipulates that refunds of tariffs or internal taxes equivalent to the amount paid cannot be regarded as a type of subsidy. In 1991, China implemented a program to cancel subsidies, replacing same with export rebates. However, China practices a tax system based on mainly the circulation tax, and thus work related to export rebates is both extensive and tedious, with the entire effort being carried out in the absence of unified standards. Therefore, current export rebates which adopt various accommodations similar to subsidies not only discourage exports and lower foreign exchange earnings, but are also easy to lead to disputes. China must accelerate tax system reform, and in the wake of establishing a new tax system based mainly on the value-added tax must introduce simplified tax refund methods in line with generally accepted international practices.

The legal framework of GATT is based on a number of regulations and related exceptions. The exceptions allow signatory states to disregard certain GATT articles under special circumstances. When applying various regulatory tools for foreign trade, we should fully use exceptions applicable to specific regulations in order to protect domestic industries and enhance the position of our export sector.

In recent years, customs barriers have increased with great rapidity despite GATT stipulations requiring signatory states to keep tariffs at a relatively low level. Discriminatory trade policies and practices, or so-called "gray areas," have appeared on the fringes or out of GATT's legal principles. They include subsidy, anti-subsidy and anti-dumping measures, technological trade barriers, guarantee clauses, government manipulating foreign trade, and unilateral export quotas and import quotas used as a means of limiting the quantity of imports. The aforementioned "gray areas" lack definition in appropriate clauses in the GATT, and the terms of their legal status remains unclear. All signatory states use those they find most favourable. China should earnestly study related issues and apply nontariff measures and "grey areas," as well as regulatory foreign trade mechanisms. In all cases, concrete implementation should be conducted in an appropriate manner, and at the most opportune degree, in order to avoid conflict with and retaliation from signatory states.

At the same time, China must pay close attention to the implementation of other measures, such as introducing advanced foreign technology, equipment and management expertise through joint ventures and cooperative business operations. Trade unions should be established and trade groups should make full use of their unique role in safeguarding the interests of domestic industries. Personnel training should be accelerated, especially for personnel in the trade, legal and management sectors, to suit for the needs of the new situation resulting from participation in international competition. There should be more commercial agencies established abroad, with each playing its unique role in terms of data collection, the dissemination of information and the creation of trade opportunities, as well as handling trade disputes.

Experts point out that China has long used tariff and licensing barriers as a means of protecting the domestic market. Generally speaking, the approach has prevented the Chinese market from being overwhelmed by foreign commodities. While it is impossible for a country's economic interests to exist based on the establishment of various barriers, a fact that must never be ignored is that dramatic reductions in tariffs and elimination of the licensing systems will result in a developing country like China being subjected to the sometimes fatal intricacies of the international economy. Therefore, in order to mollify the consequences, China must consider how best to protect its domestic market and support domestic production using methods other than tariffs, licensing and trade barriers. Perhaps the most effective method rests in enhancing its people's consciousness of domestic goods.

A major consequence of reentry into GATT rests with the

fact that foreign goods will have the same opportunity as domestic goods to enter the Chinese market. Therefore, in the wake of China's reentry into GATT, we must pay close attention to changes in the market share ratio involving competition between foreign and domestic goods. Foreign goods will rely on the timing of China's reentry and quality to gain market share. Domestic goods must protect their share of the consumer market by depending on favourable geographical conditions and the support of the people. This represents the only way national industry can continue to develop in the highly competitive market for foreign and domestic goods.

Historically, the struggle between foreign and domestic goods for dominance of the Chinese market following the 1840 Opium War, which marked the British invasion of China, centered on foreign goods maintaining their market by relying on quality and timeliness involving imperialist powers forcefully opening China's doors and signing a series of unequal treaties. On the other hand, domestic products countered by depending on favourable geographical position and the support of the people. The two aforementioned factors—geographical position and the support of the people in particular—enabled domestic products to retain their due share of the market. At the same time, it provided a respite for national industry and enabled the country to form a new national industrial system.

The primary purpose for enhancing "people's consciousness for domestic goods" centers on the fact that quality and variety of most domestic products are unable to match those of foreign goods in a short time and China's industrial setup has not as yet been perfected. Any attempt to use tariff barriers to protect the market will inevitably incur severe retaliation from other countries. In the initial stages, following reentry into GATT, we will not be able to properly apply various articles and regulation, and hence a "price" must be paid. In the event foreign goods gain a high market share, the "price" will indeed be dear. In order to gain additional time to improve product quality and adjust our industrial structure with the least amount of external pressure, we must learn to properly apply related GATT articles and regulations. So this is the only possible way to grasp new opportunities.

In short, the goal of our reentry into GATT is to narrow the gap between China and developed countries, gaining equality with some and surpassing others. The most effective way to achieve this goal is to open the domestic market to the outside world, while at the same time ensuring that China enters the international market. Therefore, it is absolutely necessary to protect and promote the development of national industry.

4. New Strategies for Opening SEZs to the Outside World and Spurring Economic Development

A decade of practice has enabled special economic zones (SEZs) to initially form the basic framework of the socialist market economy. The zones have created a miracle by taking a giant step forward as a result of rapid economic growth. The 14th Party Congress adopted the strategic decision to establish and develop the socialist market economy nationwide, and to introduce a new multi-level concept for comprehensively opening the entire country to the outside world. Under the new circumstances, how can SEZs take full advantage of their superiority, continue at the forefront of the country's reform and opening drive, explore the socialist market economy model at a higher level, and develop their economies rapidly to accomplish yet another new leap forward? This, indeed, is the strategic choice for further developing the SEZ market economy.

(1) Formation of SEZ socialist market economy

China's special economic zones were introduced a short 13 years ago. The essential objective of the developmental orbit of the SEZs over the past 13 years has been persist in market-oriented policies and firmly adhere to the road of socialist market economy under the macroregulation and control of the government.

In accordance with Deng Xiaoping's concept of SEZs, and the spirit of relevant documents of the CPC Central Committee, SEZs have from the very beginning adopted market-oriented reforms and pursued efforts to establish a new economic system based mainly on market regulation. From the very start, SEZs like Shenzhen acted in line with the envisaged new system of a planned commodity economy and considered the requirements of the export-oriented economy. They proposed the establishment of economic operation modes which were based mainly on market regulations, and operated in accordance with generally accepted international practices under the guidance of the state plan. The initial goal of the Hainan SEZ, a zone established much later than most, was to establish a socialist market economy. According to requirements outlined in documents from the CPC Central Committee, reform in Hainan Province was to be more flexible, and the framework of the new system was to be based mainly on market regulation. Strategies for economic development for Hainan, which were compiled by the Chinese Academy of Social Sciences, clearly stipulated that in terms of the economic system to be employed, Hainan Province will adopt a socialist market economy. While somewhat different from the capitalist market economy, the new system will nonetheless absorb and merge all beneficial practices and experiences. This particular innovative approach is more advanced than the concept "based mainly on market regulation" introduced in other SEZs.

According to requirements for the development of an export-oriented economy and the establishment of the new economic system based mainly on market regulation, SEZs have carried out a series of reforms in line with government macromanagement, centring on the enterprise, market and social security systems.

Reform has enabled SEZs to initially form an open socialist market economy system which has manifested itself in the following aspects:

Firstly, a mode of indirect government regulation and control has initially formed in the SEZs. Reforming the organizational structure, streamlining administration and delegating more power to lower levels have basically separated the functions of government from those of enterprises, simultaneously transforming of the functions of the government itself. Administrative departments in SEZs have taken steps to transform direct economic management into indirect management, microinterference into a combination of macroregulation and control, planned regulation into market regulation, and primary administration into economic and legal regulation. The governments have extended effort to foster the market to guide enterprises. Price reform has dramatically reduced the variety of goods subject to direct government management. Generally speaking, prices for the means of production and means of livelihood are now basically regulated by the market. The establishment and improvement of various production elements markets have created an environment for equal market competition. The fostering of the main part of the market, especially accelerating the transformation of the operational mechanisms of enterprises by introducing the share-holding system, has led to the establishment of a system under which the government regulates and controls the market while the market in turn guides enterprises. In addition, government macromanagement in the traditional sense is expanding greatly.

Secondly, growth of the SEZ market system has been a catalyst in rationalizing the allocation of resources. Reforms have accelerated the growth of the SEZ market system and expanded links with both domestic and foreign markets, thereby representing a giant step in establishing a unified and open market system. a) Mechanisms for allowing the market to determine prices has initially been established. Controls over prices for grain and the means of livelihood have been relaxed in the SEZs, which have instead adopted market regulation. The majority of means of production are also subject to market regulation. Controls over the cost of labour, foreign exchange regulations and real estate prices have also been basically softened. b) The commodities market and various types of production elements markets in the SEZs have witnessed healthy growth and are full of vitality. Over the past 13 years, Shenzhen has opened numerous meat and vegetable markets, daily-use industrial goods markets and markets for the means of livelihood. In addition, Shenzhen has taken the lead nationwide to establish a free trade zone, bonded means of production market, movables and estate auction houses and exchange firms, as well as financial, science and technology, information, personnel, futures, real estate and production elements markets. A multi-functional, multi-dimensional and multi-tiered market system has taken shape. c) Continued growth has enabled the market to give play to its fundamental role in the allocation of resources. Rationalization of the allocation of resources has led to the initial formation of the "survival of the fittest" mechanism in the enterprise sector.

Thirdly, the status of enterprises as independent manufacturers of commodities and managers is being established along with the formation of a modern enterprise system. While converting the operational mechanisms of enterprises, the SEZs have gradually adopted a modern enterprise system which includes the share-holding system, and limited liability and group companies which are ideally suited to the development of the Chinese enterprise system. The introduction of mechanisms related to competition, risk and "survival of the fittest" have effectively penetrated the traditional rigid system and brought the vitality to enterprises. By the end of 1991, Shenzhen had 108 share-issuing enterprises, including 17 listed companies. Hainan is currently home to 98 standard share-holding enterprises, including 5 listed in Shenzhen. Generally speaking, the share-holding enterprises have obtained relatively good economic returns. Meanwhile, the status of enterprises in the SEZs as relatively independent manufacturers of commodities and managers is being established. Reform of the government macromanagement system has given enterprises expanded decision-making power. Today, production and management activities of enterprises are basically directed by the market. Together with reform of various aspects of the labour and wage systems and the executive employment system, enterprises in the SEZs have gained considerable decision-making power regarding production, supply, sales and marketing, finance and materials.

Fourthly, the social and policy environment for equal competition among enterprises has gradually formed. a) Reform has greatly improved the policy environment for equal competition amongst enterprises. For example, the Hainan SEZ has continually improved policies ensuring equal competition amongst enterprises. All enterprises in Hainan, regardless of type of ownership, are allowed to develop free of restrictions in terms of proportion. All enterprises, again regardless of type of ownership, are subject to an income tax rate of 15 percent. Enterprises registered in Hainan can either focus on one sector, or develop a diversified economy, and thus have a relatively wide-ranging business scope. Enterprises and their staff can participate in social security affairs at the same standard. With the exception of certain special enterprises, all other enterprises can create appropriate conditions and adopt the share-holding system. In line with international practices, a registration, examination and approval system has been established to allow foreign-funded enterprises to participate in all projects. So the development of enterprises has been greatly promoted. b) Reform of the social security system has created a favourable social environment for the development of the market economy in the SEZs. All staff members and workers in Hainan Province, both permanent and temporary workers and disregarding type of ownership, can participate in social security affairs at the same standard. At present, over 67 percent of the in-service staff is participating in endowment insurance, while another 270,000 are participating in some form of unemployment insurance, and 100,000 are covered by industrial injury insurance. So all these have created social conditions ensuring the rational flow of labour throughout society and equal competition amongst enterprises.

Fifthly, basic features of an open market economy have formed. Reform has promoted opening to the outside world and the development of the export-oriented economy in the SEZs, thereby enhancing the features of the open market economy. Administrative offices and enterprises in SEZs are proceeding in accordance with generally accepted international practices and are developing an export-oriented economy guided by the international market. In the short five years since becoming a province and an SEZ, Hainan has attracted over 4,000 foreign-funded enterprises from 45 countries and regions. The number includes 3,393 solely foreign-funded enterprises, 1,188 Sino-foreign joint ventures, and 327 cooperative enterprises. Allocated foreign investments have soared to US$ 1.255 billion. In addition, Hainan is home to more than 8,000 domestic enterprises, with allocated investments of over 6 billion yuan. In 1992, Hainan's total import and export value stood at US$ 1.8 billion, a 9-fold increase on 1987, prior to the founding of the province. While developing its export-oriented economy, Hainan has created a mode based on "unified planning, the introduction of foreign investment, development of tracts of land and comprehensive compensation," all of which are salient features of the open market economy in the SEZs.

Market-oriented reform has greatly promoted economic development in the SEZs, while in turn leading to a miracle of rapid economic growth. Since its founding, the Shenzhen SEZ has doubled its major economic indices every two to two and one-half years. Over the past 12 years, its GNP has increased at an average annual rate of 61.65 percent, with its total export value increasing at an average annual rate of 63.71 percent. The zone's total foreign exchange earnings from exports rank second amongst major cities in China, following closely on the heels of Shanghai. It leads the country in terms of per capita foreign exchange earnings. At present, Shenzhen's per capita income stands at 8,000 yuan, while its accumulated tax revenue directly or indirectly remitted to the state has soared to 20 billion yuan. Shenzhen also leads the country in terms of per capita total output value, per capita tax and profits remitted to the state, per capita income and consumption level. The zone has attained standards for a relatively comfortable life, and has thus realized the second-step goal of the overall development strategies of the national economy in advance. Over the past five years of construction, the Hainan SEZ has witnessed rapid economic development and has basically realized the goal of "reaching the national average economic level in three to five years." In 1992, the province's GDP increased by 74.8 percent over that in 1987, with the average annual growth rate standing at 11.8 percent, a rate which effectively surpassed the national average growth rate during the same period. That same year, the province's per capita GDP reached 2,113 yuan, a level which for the first time ever exceeded the national average level for the year. In 1992, the output value of tertiary industry increased by 4.3 billion yuan, and accounted for 30.7 percent of GDP. Its export trade volume reached US$ 880 million, a dramatic increase of 633 percent over the US$ 120 million in 1987. Dramatic changes have taken place to Hainan, an area previously known as a poverty-stricken backward locality.

Market economic development in the SEZs has laid a solid foundation for new omni-directional opening to the outside world at multiple levels. Valuable exploration has been conducted and many successful experiences have been accumulated for the establishment and development of the socialist market economy throughout the nation. Without the 10-plus years' practice with the market economy in SEZs, it would have been all but impossible for the 14th Party Congress to adopt the strategic decision to establish the socialist market economic system.

(2) Problems, challenges and opportunities in the market economic development of SEZs.

SEZs have recorded major breakthroughs in market-oriented reforms and in the establishment of the socialist market economy. However, SEZs are still in the initial stages of market economic development and thus face many problems. Continuing market economic development in SEZs faces severe challenges in many aspects. By way of analogy, a boat sailing against the current must forge ahead or will be driven back. Whether or not SEZs can properly solve existing problems, meet emerging challenges and withstand the test directly determines whether market economic will proceed smoothly and accomplish a new leap forward in the 1990s.

1) Major problems

a) Reform of the administrative system has not as yet been completed and the macroregulation and control system must be improved. A major problem revolves around how the government will exercise macromanagement once enterprises enter the market. The structure and functions of SEZ governments have not as yet completely eliminated the old framework of the planned system. Greater efforts should be made to reform the organizational structure and delegate more power to lower levels. Even though economic and legal means have been introduced to economic management, it is still quite common to use means of the planned economy to manage the market economy. While granting micromanagement power to enterprises, the government must clearly define the scope of its macromanagement. At this point, problems related to what the government should relinquish and what it should retain have not been completely resolved.

b) Market mechanism remains imperfect, and the unified and complete market system is in its infancy. SEZs still face problems resulting from the incomplete growth of the commodities, labour, financial, real estate, technology and information markets. They are still plagued with problems such as small scale, low level and the lack of standardization. Intermediary market organizations have not as yet developed. In addition, appropriate links between SEZ markets and the international market have not been established.

c) Reform of the enterprise organizational structure has proceeded slowly and the modern enterprise system has not assumed the dominant position. Reform of the enterprise organizational structure in the SEZs, especially the adoption of the modern enterprise system which includes the share-holding system, and limited liability and group companies, is still in the preliminary stages. The relatively slow pace of reform has failed to suit the needs of "grouping and internationalization" in terms of enterprise operations. State-owned enterprises have not completed mechanism transformations, and as a result continue to suffer from low efficiency. Trade organizations in SEZs have not developed and there is a lack of coordinated and unified mechanisms between similar and related industrial sectors and enterprises.

d) While SEZs have been the beneficiaries of preferential policies, they nonetheless lack depth in reform of their mechanisms and systems. The past development of SEZs was to a great extent supported by special policies of the central government. Along with the on-going nationwide opening and the granting of similar preferential policies to other areas, SEZs must face the urgent task of developing further by relying on their own strengths and operating under the mechanisms of the market economy.

e) Industrial structures are parallel and technological levels are low. A number of SEZs have launched similar industrial projects, i.e. projects related to the electronics, automobile manufacturing, sensitive materials, beverages and chemical materials. This approach has resulted in an obviously identical structure and low-level repetition. SEZs feature numerous small and medium-sized joint ventures, but have attracted little direct investment from major trans-national groups; many non-productive investments compared to a small proportion of productive investment; many light industrial products, with few high-tech products; and many projects requiring the use of foreign exchange, but few which earn foreign exchange. Therefore, enterprises in SEZs face the urgent task of undertaking industrial adjustments and upgrades.

f) It is still quite difficult to link economic policies with international practices and the economic legislation lags behind. At present, China's currency circulation, valuation and tariffs are basically unaffected by changes in exchange quotations on the international financial market. This traditional closed financial system fails to keep abreast of requirements for the internationalization and enterprise marketization in SEZs. Although a number of economic laws and regulations have been enacted, they have failed to form an adequate system and many regulations and measures are still issued in the form of central government documents.

2) Challenges and opportunities

a) Challenges posed by the new situation of nationwide opening to the outside world.

Along with newly emerging situation related to national reform and opening, the SEZs have lost their prominence and a reduction in their previous advantages, a fact quite obvious to all. In the 1980s, SEZs benefitted from the so-called "time difference" by relying on the reform and opening and the introduction of state preferential policies. Benefits in terms of the system enabled them to take the lead and give play to the advantages of market economy. These aspects provided the uniqueness of SEZs. The uniqueness was mainly manifested in the following aspects: Firstly, a multi-polar (state, collective and individual) ownership structure based mainly on foreign-funded enterprises allowed for equal competition and development of enterprises under all types of ownership. Secondly, the effort to establish an export-oriented economy enabled SEZs to open international markets through regional associations in combination with domestic enterprises, as well as to introduce foreign equipment, technology and capital. Thirdly, the state mainly introduced policies rather than funds to the SEZs, with capital sources for construction in the SEZs mainly coming through the introduction of foreign funds. Fourthly, the management system was characterized by giving full play to the market, operating under the guidance of state plans. In summary, the uniqueness and superiority of SEZs rested with the fact that they took the lead to open to the outside world, and in using preferential policies to carry out market-oriented reforms.

During the 1990s, and especially since Deng Xiaoping's tour of south China, the country's opening and economic construction entered a new period and the new layout of omni-directional opening has taken shape at multiple levels in border and coastal areas and areas along the Yangtze River. Along with the establishment of free trade zones, high-tech parks, development zones and opening cities which implement similar or additional preferential policies, the advantages of the uniqueness of SEZs have been substantially reduced or in some cases have even disappeared. In particular, the extended radiation of Shanghai's Pudong Area will result in the eastward shift of foreign investment and economic cooperation between the inland and coastal areas. In addition, since the 14th Party Congress clearly outlined the strategic decision to establish and develop the socialist market economy nationwide, all localities throughout the country are developing the market economy and calling on the successful experiences of SEZs in the 1980s as a reference point. Hence, SEZs no longer have the advantage with regard to the market economy. This in turn has led to the emergence of great pressure on the further development of the market economy in the SEZs. The only alternative is to deepen, expand and amplify the performance degree of reform and opening to the outside world.

b) Challenges involving the restoration of China's status as a signatory state in GATT.

China's reentry into GATT poses a severe test to the market economy in the SEZs. However, reentry into GATT also brings new challenge to SEZs, as well as new opportunities. On the one hand, reentry into GATT will alter the existing regional preferential and lopsided situation involving increased state support. This holds true because preferential policies applicable to SEZs fail to conform with the GATT spirit of equal competition and fair trade. SEZs will lose most of their preferential policies and will have to ensure their existence and development by relying on their own economic strengths in the international market. Meanwhile, the export-oriented economy of the SEZs will confront intense competition in both domestic and foreign terms. Reentry into GATT will force China to conduct overall reform of its foreign trade system. SEZs and other areas will be subject to equal import and export trade conditions; SEZs will be forced to expand exports by relying on their own sources of goods, and by balancing imports according to internal demand. With regard to the use of foreign capital, foreign businessmen will gradually transfer their investments to previously undeveloped areas and industrial sectors in order to create new sources of profits. Therefore, the changing situation involving foreign trade merchandise resources and foreign investment will continue to escalate. Faced with the loss of support from state policies, SEZ products will lose their pricing advantages abroad, and shortcomings such as poor quality and low technical content will be exposed. In addition, reentry into GATT will intensify difficulties and place even greater pressure on the structural reform of SEZs.

On the other hand, reentry into GATT will offer a new opportunity for development of market economy in the SEZs. In fact, reentry may become a strong catalyst for accelerating the maturity of the market economy in the SEZs. Reentry into GATT will spark SEZs governments and enterprises to act more conscientiously according to international practice, enable the domestic market to expand links with the international market, adjust the industrial structure and product mix in line with the demands and marketing operations of international market, and promote technical progress and industrial upgrades. In addition, reentry into GATT will further smooth the path for foreign trade and the introduction of foreign capital. China will in fact once and for all solve problems existing in foreign trade with more than 100 countries and regions, and will ensure the continuance of most favoured nation treatment. At the same time, it will promote the import effectiveness of SEZs and meet their demands for internationally advanced technologies and raw materials currently in short supply. Reentry will enable SEZs to expand the use of foreign capital, raise the investment level of foreign-funded projects and promote overseas investment. It will also promote the growth and improvement of the market system in SEZs, promote the modern enterprise system, deepen and amplify structural reform, and in turn accelerate the overall development of China's market economy.

c) Challenges from development of international economy.

In an effort to contend with the expected increasing demands of the international economy in the 21st century, developed countries are accelerating their development of high-tech industries. Developing countries also vying with each other to introduce more flexible policies and are devoting greater efforts to developing free trade zones. Various neighbouring countries and regions are competing intensely with China in terms of opening and introducing foreign capital and advanced technology. Ever larger amounts of international capital are entering the financial market of the Asia-Pacific Region, with increasing competition in terms of selecting suitable investment sites. This then offers new challenges, as well as opportunities for development of market economy in the SEZs. Therefore, China should introduce even more open policies, otherwise, China's SEZs will be relegated to an unfavourable position in terms of international economic competition, and will in turn lose a golden opportunity for development.

3) The position and role of SEZs in the future nationwide reform and opening, and market economic development.

Faced with challenges from all sides, whether SEZs can maintain and give play to their existing superiorities, continue to be the vanguard of the nation's reform and opening drive, and take the lead to establish a complete socialist market economic system remain a question. Under the new circumstances, the state has set even higher demands on SEZs, and people throughout the country place even greater hope on their development. As part of an effort to remain at the forefront of nation's reform and opening endeavor, SEZs should improve their export-oriented economy, explore the operational laws of the socialist market economy at a higher level, continuously introduce new concepts, new experiences and innovative approaches for the nation's reform and opening, and market economic development. They should also give more play to their role as the "four windows," and as experimental bases for reform and opening. Meanwhile, SEZs should accelerate their economic growth to achieve a giant step forward and become economic centers facing the world and radiating through the nation as a whole in order to make even greater contributions to the economic development of China.

(3) Goals, methods and tactics for further market economic development of SEZs

Great efforts must be made to further develop market economies in SEZs. The most important aspects are to expand opening, deepen the reform and determine the goals, methods and tactics suitable for such development.

1) Goal: Wide open market economy.

Over the past 10-plus years of practice, SEZs have initially established the framework of the open socialist market system. Under circumstances in which the entire nation accelerates reform and opening, and establishes and develops the new socialist market economic system, it is quite reasonable for SEZs to develop a wide open socialist market economy with extensive links to the international market and which act in accordance with generally accepted international practice. The new system offers the following basic features:

a) The introduction of a new macromanagement system based on "small government, large society." Under this system, the government replaces micro and direct management with macro and indirect management. The management method changes from primarily administrative management to mainly economic and legal means. A coordinated and unified macroregulation and control system should be established.

b) A modern enterprise system, under which enterprises are responsible for their own decisions concerning operations and expansion and are responsible for profits and losses, as well as an enterprise organizational structure with clearly defined property rights should be established. Enterprises, regardless of type of ownership, should truly become independent producers of commodities and managers able to enter a market featuring fair competitions.

c) A fully functional unified and improved modern market system should be established. The system should incorporate all aspects of the international market and operate in the line with generally accepted international practices. The market, which could be considered as an invisible hand, should give full play to its role in the optimal allocation of resources and should promote the timely and coordinated balance between supply and demand.

d) An export-oriented economic system, guided by the international market and primarily based on the use of foreign capital, should be formed. The opening policy should be implemented comprehensively at many layers using multiple channels in order to form a perfected system which guarantees the rights and interests of investors, while at the same time improving the economic and legal systems.

e) A relaxed social policy environment which meets the demands of a wide open market economic system should be fostered to form a developed, highly efficient and complete system related to distribution, services, supervision, social security and social welfare required by a modern society.

2) Method: Emulating Hong Kong to build socialist SEZs

Deng Xiaoping has on numerous occasions likened the construction of SEZs to building more Hong Kongs. He has pointed out, "I often said that we should build several Hong Kongs. Simply stated, we should continue to implement the opening policy. China should be more open. Otherwise, it can hardly develop." This strategically significant innovative concept points out the essential approach to further developing the socialist market economy in SEZs. Should SEZs fail to achieve breakthroughs in "building more Hong Kongs," they will accomplish little in the development of the market economy, and it will be quite difficult to regain their status as "special."

Hong Kong is the world's most successful free port. As part of their effort to build more Hong Kongs, SEZs should proceed according to the demands of wide open market economic system. They should further expand opening, deepen reform and use Hong Kong's successful experiences as a reference point. This in fact is the only way SEZs can become international cities like Hong Kong, as well as economic centers in south China, bridges linking domestic and foreign markets, pivotal centers organizing domestic and foreign commodity circulation and transit, evolve into transfer stations introducing advanced technology and management expertise. Only by doing so can they better play a role of key cities like Hong Kong and become multi-functional cities involved in international trade, communications, information processing and tourism.

3) Policy orientation: Implement of the basic policies of free ports.

In order to further develop a socialist market economy and build themselves into a city like Hong Kong, SEZs should introduce international practices, boldly borrow the successful experiences of Hong Kong, Taiwan, Singapore and Japan, and implement the basic policies of free ports. The following policies require deliberate consideration:

a) Free tariff policies. SEZs such as Shenzhen, Hainan and Xiamen should consider the adoption of the free tariff policies. With the exception of selected varieties of goods such as cigarettes and wine which are currently taxed at half the lowest tax rate, or are otherwise levied according to regulations, other products and daily-use life goods should be exempt from tariffs in order to allow SEZs to become major free trade zones.

b) Foreign trade policies. All limitations on foreign trade in SEZs should be eliminated, and a foreign trade policy featuring open operations should be adopted. In fact, trade liberalization is a basic requirement of GATT. Simplifying the import-export management system and decreasing the level of trade protectionism are a true mark of trade liberalization being carried out by a country or region. The development of Hong Kong, Taiwan and Japan demonstrates that rapid economic growth must be accompanied by trade policies which are adjusted in a timely manner to realize trade liberalization. SEZs are basically qualified for the adoption of trade liberalization. Essentially, they can remove import-export limitations on enterprises, cancel the import-export licensing and ration systems, and simplify customs entry, while at the same time taking the lead in meeting GATT requirements for foreign trade.

c) Financial policy. SEZs should adopt a financial and monetary policy focused on the free convertibility of currency. It is only a matter of time before the Renminbi becomes a freely convertible currency. SEZs should act promptly and extend great efforts to overcome shortcomings involving the inconvertibility which leads to over valuation. They should establish a financial policy system that conforms with the modern market economic system and the requirements of GATT to ensure the currency gains convertibility and funds flow freely. This will in turn promote the development of the open market economy in the areas.

d) Tax policy. The tax system should undergo further reforms on the basis of the current financial system. Firstly, contradictions in the current tax system such as the inconsistency between domestic and foreign trade and the unfair tax burden on enterprises with different types of ownerships should be solved. Secondly, the tax rate should be readjusted to realize an average tax rate and gradually meet the requirements for GATT signatory states. And finally, SEZs governments should be allowed to adopt tax policies, enact local tax laws, determine tax items and adjust tax bases.

e) Entry and exit policy. In line with Hong Kong policies regarding the free entry and exit of personnel, entry visa of foreigners and entry procedures for Hong Kong, Macao and Taiwan residents should be further simplified. Foreigners should be issued a landing visa. Limitations regarding exit visas for SEZs government functionaries and residents should be relaxed and related formalities should be simplified. Enterprises with import-export rights should be given the right to examine and approve personnel travelling abroad in line with their needs, with the government providing only necessary services. SEZs residents should carry ordinary passports for private matters, travel, visit relatives or otherwise conducting business abroad.

f) Industrial development policy. In this regard, Taiwan's industrial development policy which follows the orderly step by step advancement should be used as a reference. When considering the current weak points of SEZs, such as repetitive industrial structures and low technical level, active policies for industrial development should be adopted to help SEZs enterprises adjust their structure and undertake upgrades. Innovative encouraging measures should be adopted to protect and promote the development of high-tech industry in SEZs. At the same time, appropriate measures should be adopted to accelerate the development of tertiary industry to ensure a rational proportion between the primary, secondary and tertiary industries.

In addition, Hong Kong's policy of "active non-interference" should be used for reference. Simply stated, the market and legal regulations should control all economic activities. The government relationship with enterprises should be as follows: to levy taxes according to law, punish those violating the law and liquidate bankrupt enterprises. However, the government should not attempt to interfere in the production and operation of enterprises. Such a policy would be conducive to strengthening government macroregulation and control, as well as to ensuring the economy is managed according to law and without petty interference in economic activities.

4) Tactics: major reform and development measures.

In order to establish and perfect a wide open socialist market economy at the earliest possible date, SEZs must deepen reform, expand opening, and properly handle the relationships between the government and market, enterprises and the market, prices and the market, state-owned assets and the market, society and the market, and between the domestic and international markets. However, the top priority must center on improving the macro-management system for the administration of SEZs, while at the same time accelerating reform of the enterprise system, especially with regard to guiding state-owned assets into the market, further fostering the market system and promoting reform of the social security system.

a) Streamlining administration and delegating more power to lower levels, transforming government functions, and improving the government's macromanagement system.

—Once enterprises enter the market, the level of acceptable government interference must clarified. We should make use of the Singapore model under which the government guides the market and defines the government's position and role in economic activities.

—The government should participate in enterprise investment, either directly or indirectly, and should exerts due influence on the industrial structure by the management and value increase of state-owned assets and the share holding and control methods.

—The government adopts market policies and relies on intermediary organizations to standardize the operations of enterprises and improve the operational system of the market.

—Greater efforts should be dedicated to streamlining administration and delegating more autonomy to enterprises so they can truly become independent producers and operators.

b) Accelerating reform of enterprise organizational structure to form a modern enterprise system based on the share-holding system at the earliest possible date.

—Extensive effort should be devoted to promoting the share-holding system and giving full play to the merits of stock enterprise to ensure the share-holding system becomes the focus of the modern enterprise system.

—Enterprises which fail to adopt the share-holding system can be transformed into limited liability companies. Property right relationship should be adjusted so as to transform enterprises subordinated to municipalities or provinces, various incorporated domestic enterprises and state-owned enterprises into limited liability companies.

—Group companies should be formed and strengthened. The scale of operations advantages offered by groups should be recognized in order to enhance the competitiveness of enterprises on the international market.

—State-owned assets should be quickly guided to the market in order to completely transform the operational mechanisms of state-owned enterprises.

—The transfer or sale of company property rights and stock rights should be widely promoted as a means of realizing the optimal combination of the production elements structure.

—Administrative limitations on the business scope and operational mode of enterprises should be relaxed, with the simultaneous transformation of the franchise system into the criterion system.

—The management on companies should be strengthened, and systems relating to company bankruptcy compensation and cancellation have to be established.

c) Further improving the market system.

—Great efforts should be made to develop the initial configuration of the commodities market; improve the financial market related to stocks, bonds and futures; form markets for property rights, information and technology; and establish a modern market system linked with the international market at the earliest possible date.

—Intermediate market organizations should be established

and improved. Great efforts should be extended to developing intermediate organizations related to the supply and demand of elements such as financing, labour, technology and information, and notarial organizations. These factors cannot be ignored in standardizing the growth of enterprises.

—Construction of market system and legality of the economy should be strengthened. Barriers between higher and lower levels, or between different departments and regions, as well as blockades and monopolies should be eliminated in order to form a complete market legal system which conforms to the operational rules of the international market.

d) Comprehensive reform of the social security system should be carried out.